STATE GOVERNMENT

STATE GOVERNMENT

CQ's GUIDE TO CURRENT ISSUES AND ACTIVITIES 1997–98

edited by Thad L. Beyle

University of North Carolina
at Chapel Hill

Congressional Quarterly Inc.
Washington, D.C.

Editor: Thad L. Beyle
Contributing Editor: Tracy W. Villano
Cover: Paula Anderson
Index: Bernice Eisen

Congressional Quarterly

Congressional Quarterly Inc., an editorial research service and publishing company, serves clients in the fields of news, education, business, and government. It combines the specific coverage of Congress, government, and politics contained in the *Congressional Quarterly Weekly Report* with the more general subject range of an affiliated publication, the *CQ Researcher.*

CQ Books publishes college political science textbooks under the CQ Press imprint and public affairs paperbacks on developing issues and events as well as information directories and reference books on the federal government, national elections, and politics. These include *Guide to the Presidency, Guide to Congress, Guide to the U.S. Supreme Court, Guide to U.S. Elections,* and *Politics in America.* CQ Books has published a three-volume encyclopedia of American government, including *The Presidency A to Z, The Supreme Court A to Z,* and *Congress A to Z.* The *CQ Almanac,* a compendium of legislation for one session of Congress, is published each year. *Congress and the Nation,* a record of government for a presidential term, is published every four years.

CQ publishes the *Congressional Monitor,* a daily report on current and future activities of congressional committees.

An electronic online information system, Washington Alert, provides immediate access to CQ's databases of legislative action, votes, schedules, profiles, and analyses.

The Library of Congress cataloged the first edition of this title as follows:

Beyle, Thad L., 1934-
    State government.

    Bibliography: p.
    Includes index.
    1. State governments—Addresses, essays, lectures. I.–Congressional Quarterly Inc. II. Title.

JK2408.B49   1985   320.973   85–9657

ISBN 1-56802-097-X
ISSN 0888–8590

Contents

III. POLITICS: PARTIES, INTEREST GROUPS, AND PACS

IV. MEDIA AND THE STATES

V. STATE LEGISLATURES

VI. GOVERNORS AND THE EXECUTIVE BRANCH

VII. STATE BUREAUCRACIES AND ADMINISTRATION

VIII. STATE COURTS

IX. LOCAL GOVERNMENT

X. STATE ISSUES

Boxes, Tables, and Figures

BOXES

TABLES

FIGURE

Preface

The states have acquired considerable importance over the past three decades. Their growth—as measured by the reach of policies and programs, the size of budgets and bureaucracies, as well as states' overall responsibility to their citizens—is unprecedented. Their problems, too, are unprecedented, and the uncertainty in the federal system over the outcome of the current federal budget conflict threatens to compound the problems the states face.

This increased visibility and influence are tied to a major shift in how our federal system of government operates. In the late 1970s, the national government began cutting back in ever-increasing proportions its commitment to handle the domestic issues facing the country. State governments were asked to shoulder more of the domestic policy burden while the federal government tried to cope with the national debt and issues of national defense.

The states' response to the fiscal challenges of the 1980s became an issue of national as well as local importance. It fell mainly to state governments to take up the slack created by a federal government pulling back on support for domestic programs. The states were able to meet this challenge in an expanding economy where revenue estimates were always too low and extra funds were usually available.

Toward the end of the 1980s there were signs that this buildup of budgets and programs based on ever-increasing revenues was coming to an end. And end it did. The 1990s brought a tough twist for state leaders as the economy went into recession. Adding to the melee, the 1992 elections saw the national government refocus its attention on deficit reduction and large-scale cutbacks in the armed forces. Then came the major changes brought on by the 1994 elections, which gave control of Congress to the Republicans. State leaders became fearful that the federal budget would be balanced on the backs of the states, causing even more problems for the states. Then, as the 1996 elections grew closer, Congress passed, and the president signed into law, a major welfare reform bill that would have a significant impact on the states. The trials that state governors and legislators have been facing in the 1990s often verge on the impossible.

For several years this fiscal situation

meant that state leaders had to cut back on needed programs and at the same time raise taxes. This is the worst possible position in which political leaders can find themselves: having to raise the taxes of the voters while reducing what they get for those taxes. Citizen approval ratings reflected this situation, as public regard for governors and legislators plummeted in many states. Erstwhile heroes became political targets for retribution. State leaders fear this scenario could return with new demands for services and less help available from the federal government.

Despite all this bad news, many seeking political careers see the states as where the action is and where those seeking to have an impact on government and policymaking turn. The states are also important rungs on our national political career ladder, as three of the past four presidents have been governors.

According to Carl Van Horn of the Eagleton Institute of Politics at Rutgers University, over the past few decades state governments have undergone a quiet revolution. This revolution, in which "states reformed and strengthened their political and economic houses," now finds the states occupying "a more important role in American life" as they pioneer "solutions to some of the country's most difficult problems and demonstrate effective leadership."[1] But in the 1990s, "the stakes will be higher than ever before.... How well state political leaders handle these difficult challenges will determine how the nation is to be governed and how its citizens are to be served in the coming decades."[2]

State governments are no longer sleepy backwater operations located in far-off capitals where few people know or care what they are doing. In many ways, it might be better to look at state governments as big-time organizations comparable to some of the world's largest nations or our country's largest corporations. From this perspective, the roles of state leaders in governing the states could be compared with those who govern large nations or run large corporations. They are large, complex organizations with a range of operations and goals—and they warrant the attention of both national and international policymakers.

The 1997–98 edition of *State Government: CQ's Guide to Current Issues and Activities* includes recent articles that define and analyze these state issues and agendas. Short background essays introduce the articles and highlight developments.

The organization of this book parallels that of most state government texts. First is politics: the most recent election results and the roles of direct democracy, interest groups, political parties, and the media. Next are institutions: legislatures, governors, bureaucracies, and state courts. The final two sections focus on local governments and some issues of primary concern to both state and local governments.

There are many to thank for assistance in developing this book. Among them are David R. Tarr, executive editor of the Book Department at Congressional Quarterly, for his support, and Tracy Villano for her fine editorial hand. This is our thirteenth compilation of the *Guide,* and we are still learning. Any errors you find are mine. I hope you will send your comments and suggestions so that we might be able to improve the 1998–99 edition.

Notes

1. Carl Van Horn, "The Quiet Revolution," in *The State of the States,* 3d ed., ed. Carl Van Horn (Washington, D.C.: CQ Press, 1996), 1.
2. Ibid., 11.

I.   POLITICS IN THE 1990s

State officials continue to debate the timing of U.S. elections. Some argue that national, state, and local elections should be held at different times to keep separate the issues, candidates, and political concerns of each level. Following this argument, national elections for president, vice president, U.S. senators, and U.S. representatives would be held in even years, as they are now; exactly which year would depend on the length of the term—that is, representatives every two years, presidents every four years, and senators every six years. State-level elections for governor and other executive officials, state legislators, and state constitutional amendments and referendums would be held in "off-years" (nonpresidential election years) or possibly in odd-numbered years. And local elections would be at another time, preferably not in conjunction with either state or national elections.

Others advocate holding all elections at the same time to maximize voter interest and turnout and, not inconsequentially, to increase the importance of the political party as the main determinant of voters' decisions from the top of the ballot to the bottom. But there is not a single Republican party or a single Democratic party to influence voters' choices. At least fifty different Republican and Democratic state parties reflect the unique political culture, heritage, and positions of the fifty states. Add to that the increasing number of independents and other voters who split their tickets, and it is clear that this political party rationale for simultaneous elections will not hold up in the practical world of politics.

Neither side of the timing argument has predominated. During the 1996 presi-dential election year, forty-six states elected their legislatures and eleven elected their governors. Of these eleven states, New Hampshire and Vermont elect their governors to two-year terms, which means that their gubernatorial elections alternate between presidential and nonpresidential election years. Indeed, most states hold their gubernatorial elections in even, nonpresidential years, as in 1994, when thirty-six governors were elected, along with most legislatures; or in odd years, as in 1995, when Kentucky, Louisiana, and Mississippi held theirs, and in 1997, when New Jersey and Virginia are holding their state elections.

A major reason why some states have shifted their elections to nonpresidential years is because the personalities, issues, and concerns evident in presidential elections often spill over into state-level contests. While presidential elections are stirring events that bring the excitement of politics to the American populace and lead to higher turnout among voters, some state officials fear that the "coattail effect" of the national elections will change the results of their elections and, most importantly, obscure the state issues that voters should consider on election day. But there are other politics involved. For example, the Kentucky legislature recently drew up a proposed amendment to that state's constitution that would permit the governor to seek a second term and allow the governor and lieutenant governor to run as a team. It passed narrowly in 1992. However, legislative leaders killed a proposed provision that would have shifted the election timetable for governors to match that of legislators. The reason: "Because they feared that it would somehow weaken the power of the legislators if members ran the same time the governor did."[1]

Trends in Recent State Elections

Gender. During the 1980s and into the 1990s women have been increasingly successful as candidates for top-level state offices. These women can attribute their success to better fund raising, aid from other office holders who are women, more active financial support and counseling from female corporate executives, and more active support for top female candidates from men.[2]

To some observers, this set of victories by women represents the third wave of recruitment of women into state politics. The first wave, up to the early 1970s, consisted of women winning as widows, wives, or daughters of established male politicians. The second wave, through the 1970s, consisted of women active in civic affairs shifting their volunteer work and contacts into political affairs. The third wave now evident is of women who have moved up the political ladder by defeating other candidates while keeping their eyes on a higher political goal such as becoming a legislative leader, much as men have. In other words, the third wave consists of upwardly mobile politicians who happen to be women.[3]

Abortion. In July 1989, midway through the New Jersey and Virginia gubernatorial races, the U.S. Supreme Court announced a major decision on abortion.[4] In effect, the Court began the process of reversing the standard set in an earlier decision, *Roe v. Wade* (1973), which had provided women the right under the U.S. Constitution to choose an abortion within a certain time period. This earlier decision also had the effect of giving governors and "state legislators the opportunity not to choose sides in a wrenching political debate."[5]

The impact of the 1989 decision was almost immediate as candidates for office in the states were asked their positions on the issue: were they prolife or prochoice? In both New Jersey and Virginia the abortion issue hurt the Republican candidates for governor since they held prolife views, in contrast to the more prochoice views of the Democratic candidates. But as the Republicans began to feel the heat of the rapidly growing ranks of the prochoice activists—even from within their own party— and as they saw the numbers in their polls rising against them, they waffled on the issue, moving away from their previous prolife stand. That strategy seemed to hurt them even more.

Abortion politics continues to be a difficult problem for politicians. In the 1994 elections, exit polls found that between 8 and 18 percent of the voters indicated abortion was one of the two issues of greatest concern to them in voting.[6] Following the 1994 elections, twenty of the nation's governors were prochoice, and ten had a mixed record on the issue. In the 1995 state legislative sessions, at least thirteen states considered legislation calling for parental consent and notification and at least sixteen others considered mandating a waiting period.[7]

Independence. Voters in the states are becoming more independent in their voting choices. Increasingly, they are splitting their votes between party candidates. From the party politician's point of view, though, they are not becoming more independent, but rather more unreliable. Whether caused by splitting or unreliable voting, the impact of this type of voting can be significant. Some examples make the point.

A look at the way voters chose their candidates in the 1992 races points out how common ticket splitting is in the states. The fact that independent presidential candidate Ross Perot received 19 percent of the vote nationwide indicates that nearly one-fifth of the voters had to have split their ballots if they voted for anyone else in the election. In Indiana, incumbent governor Evan Bayh (D) won with 63 percent of the vote while incumbent U.S. senator Dan Coats (R) won with 58 percent of the vote—a swing of twenty-one points. In 1994 Vermont governor Howard Dean (D) won with 70 percent of the vote, U.S. senator Jim Jeffords (R) won with 50 percent, and at-large congressman Bernard Sanders (I) won with 50 percent. In the 1996 elections in West Virginia, President Clinton won with 51 percent of the vote, Democratic incumbent U.S. senator Jay Rockefeller won with 77 percent, while new Republican governor Cecil Underwood won with 52 percent, a swing of twenty-six points.

The results of such split ticket voting are evident in the winners of statewide elections. There are few states in which all statewide elected officials are members of just a single party: in Hawaii and Maryland all statewide elected officials are Democrats, including the U.S. senators, and in Wyoming all statewide elected officials are Republicans.[8] In 1997, Democrats control both houses of twenty state legislatures while the Republicans control both houses of eighteen. Twelve other states have split partisan control.[9] Add to these twelve split partisan control states the thirteen Republican governors facing Democratic-controlled legislatures and the five Democratic governors facing Republican-controlled legislatures and you have thirty states with a "power-split" in state leadership. This "power-split" is defined by having the governor a member of one party and one or both houses of the legislature controlled by the other party.

In the 1990 gubernatorial elections, two states elected independent candidates: Walter J. Hickel in Alaska and Lowell P. Weicker, Jr., in Connecticut. Both were former Republican office holders, but this time they ran as independents, defeating not only Democratic candidates but Republican candidates as well. Like the 1992 Perot voters, enough voters in these two states turned aside the two major party candidates for a leader free of normal party ties. In 1994 Maine voters also rejected both major party candidates and elected independent Angus King as governor.

Race. Virginia's 1989 gubernatorial race was significant for more than how abortion affected that state's politics. The Commonwealth's voters elected the nation's first elected black governor, Lt. Governor L. Douglas Wilder (D). Even though Wilder won, public opinion polls—even polls taken as voters exited the voting booths—showed him winning by a much wider margin than was ultimately the case. This phenomenon of inflated public opinion strength skewing projections has occurred elsewhere when a minority candidate was running for a major office. This indicates that a new and subtle form of racism exists in which voters are reticent to admit that they will vote or just have voted against a minority candidate; hence the difference between how they say they vote and the actual vote totals.

Issues in State Politics

Issues in state campaigns varied considerably, not only from state to state but also among offices being contested. For example, campaigns for state legislative seats tend to focus on the individual candidate as he or she seeks to achieve name recognition among the voters. Some candidates shy away from taking a position on specific issues, preferring instead to endorse economic development, reduction of crime, better education, and other broad issues. Others use specific issues such as antiabortion, tax repeal, or growth limits to achieve the name recognition they need to win. On the whole, however, candidates prefer to take a position on broad issues rather than commit themselves to a specific issue that could alienate potential supporters. As *State Policy Reports* has pointed out,

Campaigns rarely reveal candidate positions on the difficult questions of state policy. The easy question is whether candidates are for lower state and local taxes, better educational quality, higher teacher pay, and protecting the environment while stimulating economic growth. The candidates generally share these objectives. The hard question is what to do when these objectives collide as they often do.[10]

As a result, the average voter has a hard time discerning where the candidates stand on specific issues, and attempts to survey state legislative candidates on specific issues usually are not successful. But some issues are just too controversial and intrude into everyone's radar scope at election time. Abortion, as has already been noted, is one of these issues.

The state of the economy and, especially, individual state economies became the focus of some recent state campaigns, as did the question of the need for increased taxes to cover budget shortfalls.

Another set of issues revolves around the question of representation: more precisely, the staying power of incumbents and the need to redraw many state legislative and congressional district lines following the 1990 census. The incumbency question has become an important issue in many states—a sort of "throw all the rascals out" perspective stemming from scandals and a

realization that incumbents usually win. This drive has seen the successful passage of term limit referenda limiting selective service in some of the states. Thus, constitutional provisions in these states now restrict an incumbent's stay in office if the voters won't. More efforts are planned in other states, even though the constitutionality of such added provisions is usually contested in the courts.

No issue is as intensely and personally political to state legislators as what many must do following each census—they must redraw district boundaries for themselves, as state legislators, and for U.S. representatives to achieve equal representation. The definition of equality is flexible and changing, however. And the issue is intensely personal because it has much to do with the legislators' chances of winning another election to the legislature, and intensely political because each party is trying to maximize its gains and minimize the gains of the opposition party. Add lawsuits and court decisions to the mix and this issue can have a longer and more unsettling life than it should.

This section provides articles that focus on several of the issues of political concern in the states. Lynn Brezosky, in *Empire State Report,* takes a critical view of public opinion in elections. Andrew Busch, in *State Legislatures,* discusses the impact of allowing early voting on the sense of political community. Finally, Alan Rosenthal, in *State Government News,* examines the argument that incumbents have too great an advantage in elections.

Notes

1. Malcolm Jewell, "Amendment Changes Elections," *Kentucky Journal* 5:1 (March 1993): 16.

2. Meg Armstrong, "WSEG Campaign News," *Women in State Government Newsletter,* May 1986, 4.

3. Comments of Celinda Lake, Candidate Services Director of the Women's Campaign Fund, at a National Conference of State Legislatures seminar as reported by David Broder, "Hard-Earned Credentials Give Female Candidates an Edge," (Raleigh) *News and Observer,* September 15, 1986, 13A.

4. *Webster v. Reproductive Health Services* (1989).

5. Wendy Kaminer, "From *Roe* to *Webster:* Court Hands Abortion to States," *State Govern-*ment *News* 32:11 (November 1989): 12.

6. "More Election Vignettes: Abortion," *The American Enterprise* 6:1 (January/February 1995): 110–111.

7. Abortion and Govs," *The Hotline* 8:121 (March 17, 1995): 10–11.

8. "Statewide Elected Officials: Dems Hold 53% of All Offices," *The Hotline* 8:84 (January 24, 1995): 10–15. Updated.

9. "Statehouse Control, Post–'96 Election," *State Government News* (December 1996): 24.

10. *State Policy Reports* 2:20 (October 31, 1984): 13.

A Matter of Opinion

by Lynn Brezosky

An unfortunate occurrence scuttled what was supposed to be a good thing for Mario Cuomo, Herb London, and Karen Burstein in 1994: Election Day.

Widely reported polls leading up to Nov. 8 had shown each of the candidates with leads over their respective opponents. Newspapers endorsing Cuomo two days before the election had him leaving George Pataki behind. London sported an 11 point lead over H. Carl McCall a week before the polls opened, and Burstein on Oct. 27 carried a 45 percent to 29 percent advantage over Dennis Vacco.

But Pataki bested Cuomo, 49 percent to 45 percent, McCall buried London by 5 percentage points, and Vacco turned away Burstein by 1.5 percentage points, leaving the trio and others wondering where the polls might have gone wrong and why, once again, the media and public had been drawn to them.

"You [have] got to know how to read these things," says Hank Morris, Burstein's campaign manager. While reluctant to talk in terms of a particular race, Morris says experience has shown him that "people lie."

Now, with the 1996 campaign in full swing, polls are getting more attention than ever. And, accurate or not, the biggest news often seems to be in the numbers themselves. "We don't have that Rodney Dangerfield problem," says Andrew Kohut of the Pew Center for the People and the Press. "We get plenty of respect. But we don't get all that much affection."

Though the attempt to gauge public opinion is as old as the American political process itself, today's proliferation of opinion polls—public or private; scientific or unscientific; high tech or basic—has garnered considerable concern. Opinion poll results appear in the headlines almost daily in the months prior to elections, along with accompanying stories high on horse-race analysis but low on issues coverage. Beyond presenting both a questionable portrait of the electorate and sometimes dubious numbers, scholars say poll results oftentimes have the unfortunate consequence of influencing undecided voters—the ones who ultimately may end up swaying a close election.

Pollster John Zogby argues that the surveys offer an "objective, nonpartisan sci-

Lynn Brezosky is a staff writer for *Empire State Report*. This article is reprinted from *Empire State Report* (October 1996): 9–10.

ence for identifying Americans' preference and operating a mass democracy." But many in academia, including Thomas Mann and Gary Orren of the Washington Institute, worry about the "bandwagon" or self-fulfilling prophecy effects that polls can have on election outcomes.

Why, the analysts ask, would anybody contribute money to someone who's 20, 30 or 40 points behind in the latest poll? Why would they stumble out into the rain to cast a vote for somebody who, in the latest poll, was trailing by a wide margin?

Academics worry too about the impact polling has on the politicians themselves, many of whom end up seeking to reinvent themselves in order to conform to the latest opinion poll results rather than leading by example.

Richard Nixon is said to have earmarked a $5 million "special account" for private polls that measured what moves and concerns "the average guy," information he used not only to get elected but to make the policy decisions that he hoped would keep him in office.

Ronald Reagan supposedly based strategic decisions regarding Central America on public opinion findings.

President Bill Clinton likewise has been accused of keeping an overly close eye on what the polls have to say.

"Polls corrupt the leader's instinct to govern from the guts," writes Robin Gerber, a senior fellow at the Center for Political Leadership at the University of Maryland, in a *Washington Post* op-ed piece.

Putting too much stock in what the polls say can be high risk. For example, roughly 75 percent of New Yorkers in separate surveys conducted by Sen. Caesar Trunzo, a Brentwood Republican, and the New York State School Boards Association said they favor abolishing teacher tenure

in favor of renewable contracts. A curiously similar percentage answered in another poll issued by Republican Assemblyman John Flanagan that teachers should not lose their "right to due process protection."

That proves how "confused the public is about the issue" of tenure, says Linda Rosenblatt, a spokeswoman for New York State United Teachers.

"We asked one side of the question, [Flanagan] asked the other," says Chris Molluso, Trunzo's chief of staff. "There's no doubt about it. Questions can [be] and are manipulated to get a specific response."

Criticism also centers on the supposedly skewed portrait of public opinion offered by a select group of individuals: Poll respondents tend to be affluent, a trademark of the economically conservative, writes Scott Althaus of Northwestern University in the *Journal of Political Communication*. "Respondents from higher income groups can act as 'informed minorities' that cause opinion marginals to overstate the magnitude of economically conservative opinion," Althaus says.

The volatility of polls themselves—on March 2, 1991, George Bush sported a 91 percent approval rating, largely due to his handling of the Gulf War, according to a *USA Today* poll, but by Dec. 1, 1991, the rating had fallen to 46 percent, according to a *Time*/CNN poll—also frustrates critics, who wonder why the media places so much stock in them, given their fleeting shelf life.

Poll results showing an upswing by presidential candidate Robert Dole around the time of the Republican National Convention in San Diego were as predictable as they were short-lived, critics say. When the numbers died down once Democrats got their turn to cheer Clinton a week later in Chicago, it was, they say, yet another example of polls fluctuating wildly around the events of the day and media publicity. "We know there's going to be a bounce, a rebound, that it's fleeting [and] temporary. Unfortunately, it's timely, it's close to a political event," says Marist College pollster Lee Miringoff.

"I do think we make too much out of the trial heats, a year ago they were asking Dole vs. Clinton, that's a little much," says Rex Smith, managing editor for the Albany *Times Union*. "I'm sure right after the November election there's going to be Gore vs. Kemp."

"You have to ... be real confident in the validity of your poll data," Smith says, adding that he doesn't want reporters writing about the polls without first having seen the instruments and interviewing the people that conducted them.

But Smith also defends polling, some of which his newspaper sponsors. A recent *Times Union* poll conducted by Zogby found that it's not important for a presidential candidate to have congressional or military experience, a sure blow to candidate Dole, whose campaign efforts attempt to flaunt both at Clinton's expense.

"It turns out that it's more important that a person be willing to compromise on issues," Smith says. "That's got to be useful information."

Despite criticism that other information the polls provide is questionable, or that it unduly may influence elections, pollsters say business is excellent. "I covered polls for years, and I was dubious. But I came to appreciate them," says Quinnipiac College pollster Maurice Carroll. Polls may be "part science, part art," he says, but "politicians know this [stuff] and we should too."

Early Voting: Convenient, But...?

by Andrew E. Busch

Look at the TV pictures of eager voters, patiently waiting in line after walking six miles in the rain to the polling place. One thing you can be sure of: They're not in the United States. If there's any inconvenience at all, many Americans just don't vote.

With voter turnout declining steadily from 63 percent in 1960 to 50 percent in 1988, states have sought ways to increase participation by making it easier to register and more convenient to vote. The federal "motor-voter" bill of 1993 has increased the number of registered voters across the country, and reforms in two dozen states have led to a variety of "early voting" systems, including:

• Unrestricted (or "no excuse") absentee voting—first used in California in 1978 and now used in a dozen states. Voters can apply for an absentee ballot for any reason and without notarization.

• Walk-in early voting—first used by Texas in 1988 presidential elections. Seven states now use some variety. Voters can vote in person at their county clerk's offices or a satellite office usually 20 to 40 days before Election Day.

• Mail-ballot elections, permitted at the county level in 17 states (usually for local nonpartisan elections). All registered voters are automatically mailed a ballot. Nevada, North Dakota and Oregon have begun using it for statewide elections.

Although early voting proponents have framed citizenship primarily in quantitative terms—that is, by rates of voter participation—there are other important issues. What effect does early voting have on the ability of citizens to cast informed, well-reasoned and judicious votes? If people vote too early, will they miss important information that could sway their choice? Will early voting—especially by mail—erode our sense of democratic community?

Voters Like It

The most obvious consideration of early voting is whether or not it succeeds in increasing the number of people who vote.

Andrew E. Busch is an assistant professor of political science at the University of Denver. This article is reprinted from *State Legislatures* (September 1996): 25–27.

By all reports, it has proved to be quite popular. In California, approximately one out of every five voters casts an absentee ballot in general elections. Texas elections in 1992 and 1994 saw about one-third of the votes cast early. Polls indicated that voters in mail-ballot counties in Washington state supported the innovation at a rate of 7 to 1.

Despite the popularity of early voting, the effects on overall turnout are mixed. It is not yet clear whether the added convenience encourages new voters or simply makes voting easier for people who would have cast a ballot anyway. Looking at the percentage of registered voters who have voted in each of these states over time seems to suggest that the effects on turnout are minimal.

California, with the oldest unrestricted absentee program, has shown a broad decline in overall voter turnout since 1980. In general elections, absentee and precinct voting are evidently substitutes for going to the polls. Most absentee voters would have voted anyway, though this is less the case among primary voters.

Texas has the most experience with early walk-in voting. Turnout remained stable in the first election using early voting, but then rose 6.7 percent from 1988 to 1992, approximately the same as the national increase. Midterm election turnout went up by about 3.5 percent from 1986 to 1990. Turnout in off-year local elections continues to hover around 10 percent to 20 percent, despite the option of early voting.

If there is a long-term effect on turnout, it is relatively modest and inconsistent. It will probably take several election cycles to thoroughly sort out this question. Many states have only recently adopted early voting, and many short-term increases have come at a time when turnout has been on the upswing nationally, even in states without early voting.

There does, however, seem to be a more substantial pattern of increased participation in traditionally low-turnout races when mail-ballot elections are used. A 1987 study of mail ballot elections in seven cities in California, Oregon and Washington indicated that mail-ballot elections produced increases of about 19 percent. In Washington's recent elections, officials in the secretary of state's office called mail-ballot elections "truly amazing." Turnout in the counties using mail ballots in the 1994 primary was 53 percent, compared with 38 percent in those same counties in 1990 and 33 percent in counties that did not use it. The two Washington counties that used mail-ballot voting in the 1994 general election saw turnout rise by 6 percent to 7 percent over 1990 (compared with a statewide increase of 1 percent). The few jurisdictions in Florida that have used mail-in ballots report high turnout. Collier County has seen unprecedented turnout of 65 percent to 80 percent for referenda elections since 1989.

In Colorado, mail-ballot voting has doubled or tripled turnout in local elections. A special school board vacancy election in Mesa County in early 1993 saw turnout rise from an average of 10 percent to an unheard-of 58 percent. Overall, the 29 Colorado counties that used mail ballots in 1993 had an overall turnout of 43.4 percent while only 27.6 percent of registered voters showed up at the polls in the other 34 counties.

Oregon election officials were pleased with the turnout in the nation's first all-mail state elections in December 1995 and January 1996. This special election and its primary were held to fill the U.S. Senate seat of Bob Packwood and saw turnout of

Absentee Ballots Create Delays in Tallies

… Absentee ballots require three to four times the labor to process, according to election officials.

Because absentee ballots are assumed to be ripe for fraud, election workers devote considerable time to assuring that they are legitimate. When the ballot is received, a worker usually checks the name on the envelope to verify that the person is a qualified absentee voter and that signatures match. The worker also must verify that the person has not already voted.

In many states, the ballot may then be entered into a computer that counts it, but by law that ballot cannot actually be tabulated until after the polls close on Election Day.

In contrast, ballots marked in the voting booth are presumed to be authentic and are counted either at the polling place or a central election station when the polls close.

Because many absentee voters mail in or drop off their ballots at the last moment, elections workers are already swamped with regular returns when the last batches of time-consuming absentee ballots come in. They are usually set aside, sometimes by law, to be dealt with the day after the election—or as long as it takes to verify they are not fraudulent.

In California, that process usually lasts a few days because of sheer volume. In other states, the process can take more than two weeks because election workers wait for all ballots postmarked on Election Day to arrive. In Washington state, for example, officials will count qualified absentee ballots received as much as 15 days after the election, if the ballot is postmarked on or before Election Day. California and Oregon will only count absentee ballots received before the polls close, at 8. p.m. on Election Day.…

Source: Lori Nitschke, "Absentee Ballots Create Delays in Tallies," *Congressional Quarterly Weekly Report,* November 2, 1996, 3168.

57 percent in the primary, the highest for a nonpresidential primary in Oregon history and far higher than the 43 percent recorded for the 1994 primary. Turnout for the special election was 66 percent, a bit lower than the 68 percent in the regularly scheduled 1994 general election, but much higher than in other special elections.

While most evidence indicates that mail-ballot voting positively affects turnout, there are exceptions. Clark County, Nev., reported a decline in turnout in its 1996 Republican presidential primary compared with 1976 and 1980.

Voting From Your Easy Chair

Aside from the uncertain turnout effects, early voting clearly has the potential to affect citizenship in a number of other important ways. These issues may be more difficult to assess than the sheer numbers of participation, but they are no less important and should be thoroughly considered by policymakers considering early voting. In the absence of clear turnout trends, other citizenship issues become that much more important. Two major arguments favor early voting from a citizenship standpoint, besides whatever statistical increase in turnout may be attributable to it.

Importance of local politics. Supporters of early voting can argue that it is particularly well-suited to enhancing participation at the local level. To whatever extent there are turnout effects, they seem to be greatest in local races. This is especially true of mail-ballot elections. When people participate at the local level, they can more easily gain hands-on experience in self-government. Even if early voting does not substantially increase turnout in national elections, it may have a positive effect by stimulating interest and participation in local elections.

Better-informed voting. Early voting proponents also argue that voters are likely to be better informed and to make electoral judgments more carefully. In this view, cited by election analyst Margaret Rosenfield, early voting "will force campaigns to get more information to voters earlier instead of waiting for a last-minute blitz." Voters using unrestricted absentee rules or participating in a mail-ballot election will also be able to review information about candidates and issues, and perhaps even discuss it with family members, immediately before voting at home.

Even in a walk-in setting, early voters have more time in the voting booth to consider their decisions. If a large percentage of the electorate uses the option, regular voters will have more time on Election Day because lines will be shorter. If early voting becomes common, last-minute campaign smears won't be as effective. Supporters hope that early voting will improve campaign discourse and information.

Questions of Citizenship

There are two major arguments against early voting from a standpoint of citizenship and judicious voting. Citizens may vote too soon, perhaps before important information is uncovered. And early, vote-at-home methods may separate citizens even more from the political community.

Premature voting. Constraints on late information flow lauded by early-vote proponents could be a mixed blessing. Just as early voting might discourage last-minute smears, it might also prevent voters from taking into account late-breaking developments that should play a legitimate part in their decisions. In Texas ... the *Dallas Morning News* reported that "in 1990, significant changes in voter sentiment occurred during the final week of the campaign" when Ann Richards overcame Clayton Williams in the race for governor. Republican officials in California complained in 1992 that hundreds of thousands of people had already voted before economic statistics were released in late October showing strong national economic growth.

These concerns seemed to be validated in the 1994 Colorado secretary of state's race. Both daily Denver newspapers—the *Denver Post* and the *Rocky Mountain News*—initially endorsed the Democratic candidate, Sherrie Wolff, over her Republican opponent, Vikki Buckley. As the result of campaign controversies that included her misleading the press over her husband's tax troubles, both papers withdrew their endorsements in late October, 16 days after early voting had begun.

This turn of events seemed to have a substantial effect on voters. In two of seven representative counties reviewed, Buckley lost the early votes, but won the precinct votes on Election Day; in all seven, she did better on Election Day than in early votes. In those seven counties, Buckley averaged 55.1 percent of early votes and 60.2 percent on Election Day. This is all the more significant given that Republicans statewide tended to do much better among early voters than on Election Day.

Absentee Voting in Presidential Elections in California, 1976–96

Year	Percentage of precinct voters	Percentage of absentee voters
1976	95.5	4.5
1980	93.7	6.3
1984	90.7	9.3
1988	85.9	14.1
1992	82.9	17.1
1996	78.8	20.2

Source: *Campaign Insider* (a publication of *Campaigns & Elections* magazine) 1:6 (March 1997): 6.

A *Denver Post* column two days before Election Day pointed to the Wolff-Buckley race as an example of the problems associated with early voting, pointing out that the withdrawn endorsement came "too late for thousands of early voters."

Reduced sense of community. Many observers also have criticized early voting for reducing the sense of political community. Standing in line with neighbors to cast a vote on Election Day is one of the few civic rituals remaining in American democracy. Early voting destroys that ritual and undermines "a feeling of political cohesion." This problem is particularly acute in the cases of unrestricted absentee voting and mail-ballot elections. One party official in California has called his state's absentee program "a violation of the sacrament of democracy, which is walking or driving to your polling place and seeing the faces of your fellow citizens."

Gary King, a voter residing in Olympia, Wash., complained that the 1994 mail-ballot primary meant that "there was absolutely no sense of community." To King, mail voting felt "like paying a bill." It can be argued that this is hardly the sort of active, citizenship-enhancing local participation that we should desire.

Traditional absentee voting programs have recently fallen victim to fraud in several localities, most notably Philadelphia, Penn., where the courts ordered a reversal of a 1994 state Senate race because of rampant absentee voting fraud. Critics fear that liberalized rules merely increase the danger of fraud, especially in mail-ballot elections and no-excuse absentee voting. Proponents of the reforms counter that election officials have devised elaborate safeguards against fraud and that documented instances of fraud in early-voting jurisdictions have been minimal. San Francisco Registrar Germaine Wong testified before Congress in 1994 that "we have never had more than three voters who voted more than one ballot in an election." Nevertheless, even the perception that fraud is a real possibility might undermine public confidence in the electoral process.

Is It Worth the Risks?

Policymakers must weigh the possible advantages of early voting against the risks of premature voting, fraud and an erosion of our sense of democratic community. Mail-ballot elections, which clearly have the greatest potential for increasing turnout, also carry the most serious questions. Elections conducted purely by mail are probably most subject to the potential of fraud and threaten to reduce the act of voting to one of little more significance than returning one's Family Publishers Sweepstakes entry. So far, many of these questions have barely been considered in the rush toward voter convenience.

Political Protocol:
A Level Playing Field

by Alan Rosenthal

A major thrust of reformist politics is to reduce the re-election odds of legislative incumbents. "Level the playing field" sounds good, but the case for leveling is not strong.

It cannot be based on the need to revive party competition. The parties are now competitive at the legislative level in almost three-fourths of the states. Nor can it be based on the need to bring fresh blood into the legislature. That is already accomplished. In many legislative houses today the majority of members have served four years or less.

The case rests essentially on the principle of equity. The problem as reformists see it is that incumbents win too often.

Why do they win? Incumbents' success rates mostly are attributable to partisan demography. People who generally vote Democratic tend to live in cities, while people who generally vote Republican tend to live in suburbs. Anywhere from one-third to two-thirds of the legislative districts in the 50 states are safe for one party or the other. Is the remedy a requirement that people relocate so as to disperse Democrats and Republicans?

Redistricting contributes to the in-cumbency advantage. Whether done by the legislature or by commission, most redistricting attempts to minimize harm to incumbents and assist them to the extent possible. In the redistricting process, both Democratic and Republican legislators usually are assured comfortable bases of electoral support. A possible remedy here would be to ignore the wishes of incumbents, including having their residence located in the district they represent. Redistricting could be done as it is in Iowa, by computer, with no favor expected and none given. Indeed, some might even require antipartisan gerrymandering, so that Democratic and Republican voters in each district reflect the partisan balance in the state as a whole. The resulting districts, however, would probably have stranger shapes than they do now.

Money is said to be the root of just about all evil in politics. There is no doubt that incumbents overall amass more in

Alan Rosenthal is a professor with the Eagleton Institute of Politics at Rutgers University. He is the author of *Drawing the Line: Legislative Ethics in the States,* University of Nebraska Press. This article is reprinted from *State Government News* (December 1996): 16.

campaign contributions than do challengers. One reason is that they are frontrunners, and interest groups and PACs place their bets on the horses with the best chances of winning. Another reason is that incumbents have records in office that attract contributions from groups that like their positions or those who want to curry favor. We should not be shocked by groups contributing to promote their interests. The suggested remedy of expenditure limits would do more harm to challengers than good. Challengers need to raise more funds than incumbents to make their races visible and themselves known.

Much of what incumbents do in office is intended at least in part to help them get reelected. This can also be called responsiveness. In about one-quarter of the states, legislators have district offices and/ or personal staff to render service and case work to constituents. Where they have fewer resources they still help out the voters back home. Few of us would be willing to throw out the incumbent advantage by prohibiting them from doing constituent service.

Incumbents also get pork for their constituents, bring home the bacon and otherwise nourish their districts. If they were barred from voting on anything affecting their districts (because it might benefit them as well), the advantages of incumbency could be reduced. But, then, so would the principle of democratic representation.

Finally, incumbents are said to be better known in their districts than challengers. Incumbents may or may not be well known, but what is known is their record. Their roll-call votes, which run into the hundreds, are grist for an opponent's campaign mill. They can be taken out of context, deconstructed, and distorted and made the focus of attack ads. The trips they take, the gifts they accept and the company they keep are all the subject of negative scrutiny. In today's climate incumbents are as easy to hit as ducks in a shooting gallery.

The playing field on which incumbents fend off challengers is not as unlevel as charged. It might be better to leave it alone than make changes that would result in more potholes than progress.

II.   POLITICS: DIRECT DEMOCRACY

Voters in some states do more than choose candidates for state offices; they also vote directly on particular issues. Rather than have their elected representatives make the policy decisions, the voters themselves decide. This is called *direct democracy*. The concept of direct democracy has had a long history in the Midwest and West and at the local level in New England communities, where citizens and leaders often assemble in town meetings to determine the town budget as well as other policy issues.

There are three specific vehicles for citizens to use in states with direct democracy: *initiative, referendum,* and *recall.* In over one-third of the states, citizens may stimulate change in state constitutions by initiating constitutional amendments to be voted on in a statewide referendum. In nearly two-fifths of the states, an initiative provision allows proposed laws to be placed directly on a state ballot by citizen petition; the proposal is then enacted or rejected by a statewide vote. Three-fourths of the states have a referendum provision in their constitutions that refers acts passed by the state legislature to the voters for their concurrence before they become law. Most amendments to state constitutions are referred to the voters for approval; only in Delaware can the legislature amend the constitution without referring the proposed change to the people. In sixteen states, a recall provision allows voters to remove a state elected official from office through a recall election.[1] The most recent state to adopt the recall was New Jersey in the 1993 election when the voters approved it by a 3-to-1 margin.[2]

The importance of the voters' right to recall an elected official was demonstrated in Arizona in the late 1980s. The words and actions of Governor Evan Mecham, elected in 1986, angered many Arizonans sufficiently so that a recall petition was circulated to remove him from office. This drive was successful and was part of the series of events that led to Mecham's removal from office in April 1988, after he had served only seventeen months.

Mecham had won a three-candidate race by gaining only 40 percent of the general election vote. This political situation led to voter approval of a 1988 constitutional amendment calling for a runoff election should no candidate receive a majority vote in the general election—that is, no more plurality vote governors. However, the 1988 Arizona legislature failed to adopt the so-called "Dracula clause" in that state's constitution that would have barred Mecham, as an impeached official, from ever seeking or holding office again. He did seek the governorship in 1990 and drew enough votes in a third place finish to force the top two contenders into a February 1991 runoff. This again proves reforms often have unintended consequences.

Immediate Effects

The effects of direct democracy can be far reaching, affecting not only the state that has the initiative, referendum, or recall provision, but also other states and the broader political milieu in which state government operates. Some examples illustrate this phenomenon.

When California voters adopted Proposition 13 in 1978, they sent a message to elected officials across the country. This successful initiative put the brakes on state and local governments in California by restricting their ability to fund governmental programs and services. The initiative reduced property taxes to 1 percent of property value (a 57 percent cut in property tax revenues); future assessments were limited to an annual increase of only 2 percent; and a two-thirds vote of the state legislature was required for the enactment of any new state taxes.

The voters' message to state and local governments was clear: "We have had enough! We want less government, fewer programs, and greatly reduced taxes." This message—from what had been considered the most progressive electorate and state government among the fifty—prompted a widespread reevaluation of the goals of state and local governments. To what extent should elected officials expect the taxpayers to pay to achieve these goals?

In the 1990s, the issue is term limits. Since 1990, twenty-three states have imposed term limits on some of their elected officials in response to a general feeling that incumbents have too much of an advantage in any political campaign. Since the power of incumbency seems to be insurmountable in many states, the way to beat incumbents is to allow them to serve only a set number of terms or years. Starting with successes in three states in 1990 (California, Colorado, and Oklahoma), the movement spread to Washington state, where in 1991 the proposal was defeated by a narrow margin. In 1992, while everyone's eyes were on the presidential race, term limits were adopted in fourteen states, including Washington State, where it had reappeared on the ballot a second time.[3] Since then, the term limit movement has had some successes and some setbacks.

The vehicles used for winning these term limit victories are the initiative, which gets the issue on the ballot, and the referendum, which allows the people, not the legislature, to vote on the issue. Waiting for a state legislature to propose limits on its members' terms would appear to be fruitless, so success has been achieved through direct democracy (except in Utah). However, when the term limit movement meets up with states that do not employ direct democracy, it may well be stopped in its tracks unless some other vehicle can be found, or unless the political mood for term limits is so strong that a legislature must act.

One of the most interesting aspects of the term limit effort has been the level of government at which they have been directed. There would seem to be a strong argument that citizens can vote to limit the terms of elected representatives in state and local government by amending their state's constitution, although nothing is ever certain in our political system. But there has been a real constitutional question as to whether they can limit the terms of their federal representatives to the U.S. Senate and House of Representatives. This question was settled in a 5–4 U.S. Supreme Court decision on May 22, 1995, which rejected state efforts to restrict federal officials' terms.[4] Any change in the term limits of federal officials requires amendment of the U.S. Constitution, which sets only age, U.S. citizenship, and residency requirements.[5] This is not an easy prospect, a fact to which the inability of the new Republican majorities in the U.S. Congress to get enough votes in support of this amendment since 1995 attests.

In 1996, the proponents of term limits took a new tack. Voters in fourteen states were asked to support a measure calling on any candidates for congressional office to seek to have such an amendment pass once they are elected. If they decline to do so, and win, this would be duly noted on the ballot the next time they ran. These measures succeeded in nine states, but were defeated in five others. However, an immediate challenge to this constitutional provision saw the Arkansas Supreme Court strike down this "scarlet letter" notation. In February 1997, the U.S. Supreme Court let that ruling stand without comment. So now it is back to the drawing board for term-limit supporters.

Some Trends

In the first eighty years of this century there were about 500 separate initiatives placed on state ballots, an average of about 6 a year. From 1981 through 1990, there were over 270 initiatives on ballots in twenty-four states, or about 25 per year. California was the leader with 58 initiatives (21 percent), followed by Oregon with 37 (14 percent).[6] In 1996, there were at least 90 citizen initiatives on the ballots of 20 states.[7]

The initiative and referenda processes are not only becoming more prevalent in the states but more complex and expensive as well. The amount spent to qualify, support, or oppose the thirteen 1992 California referenda measures was over $40 million, with the opponents of a measure to increase a business tax spending nearly $10 million—"the largest amount ever spent to support or oppose a single state measure."[8] In 1988, the cost of fighting for or against the twenty-nine referenda on the 1988 general election ballot in California was $100 million, or $4 per capita.[9] Initiative and referenda politics are big business.

There is often a conservative ideological basis to these initiatives and referenda. That was true in the tax reduction efforts of the late 1970s, and is certainly true in the cases of at least two types of initiatives that

have come before the voters in the last few years: term limits and minority rights, specifically the civil rights of homosexuals and lesbians. Money, coordination, petition circulators, and other needs associated with running a successful initiative campaign have been emanating from sources on the right side of the political spectrum.[10]

In this section, Herbert Alexander and Nina Weiler of the Citizens' Research Foundation examine how well campaign reform referenda have fared in the past three decades. George Peery of *State Legislatures* sets out a time line on the history of term limit restrictions. Finally, Lawrence Sych examines the recall process in the states.

Notes

1. *The Book of the States,* 1994–95 (Lexington, Ky.: Council of State Governments, 1994), 23, 294–308.
2. "Election Results: Full Reports, State by State," *USA Today,* November 4, 1993, 4A.
3. For an in-depth discussion of term limits, see Gerald Benjamin and Michael J. Malbin Jr., *Limiting Legislative Terms* (Washington, D.C.: CQ Press, 1992).
4. *U.S. Term Limits v. Thornton* (1995).
5. See Article I, Section 2, clause 2, and Section 3, clause 3, of the U.S. Constitution for these requirements.
6. Joan M. Ponessa and Dave Kehler, "Statewide Initiatives 1981–90," *Initiative and Referendum Analysis,* no. 2 (June 1992): 1–2.
7. Elaine Stuart, "Voters Make Laws," *State Government News* (December 1996): 31.
8. "Initiatives Can Be Expensive," *State Legislatures* 20:1 (January 1994): 9.
9. "The Long Ballot in California," *State Policy Reports* 6:15 (August 1988): 27–28.
10. Discussion with Dave Kehler, April 20, 1993. See also Stuart Rothenburg, "Transplanting Term Limits: Political Amobilization and Grass-Roots Politics" (pp. 97–113), and David J. Olson, "Term Limits in Washington: The 1991 Battleground" (pp. 65–96), in Benjamin and Malbin.

Campaign Reform on the Ballot: 1972–1996

by Herbert E. Alexander and Nina Weiler

Continuing an ongoing trend that has developed since 1972, on November 5, 1996, voters in seven states across the nation were asked to cast their ballots on a variety of campaign reform measures.[1] Voters in the states of Arkansas, California (two issues statewide and one in Los Angeles County), Colorado, Maine, Massachusetts, Montana and Nevada voted on initiatives sponsored by private organizations or put before the voters by either state or local legislators. Taking full advantage of the initiative/referenda systems available in these states, public interest groups were largely responsible for placing seven of the nine propositions appearing on the ballot.

Also following a trend that has developed since 1972, the vast majority of these initiatives was passed by the voters. Of the nine measures placed before the voters, seven were enacted, one initiative was passed as an advisory measure and one initiative failed. The only losing ballot issue was campaign reform measure Proposition 212 on the California ballot, which was defeated by a slim margin at the same time that Proposition 208 won a solid victory with California voters.

Including the tallies for the November 1996 ballot propositions, initiatives and referenda that focus on campaign reform continued their strong showing on statewide and local ballots. Historically, measures that are labeled reform tend to be successful at the ballot box. In the fifty-one instances where initiatives, referenda, constitutional and local charter amendments have addressed the issue of campaign reform since 1972, forty-one of the measures have garnered a majority of voter support. For all state and local ballot measures, 80.4 percent have met with voter approval. Among the thirty-one measures solely affecting statewide campaign reform laws and regulations (twenty-nine binding and two advisory) twenty-four have won and seven have lost, for an approval rating with voters of 77.4 percent.

Each of the measures enacted into law in 1996 addresses issues of concern to vot-

Herbert E. Alexander is director of the Citizens' Research Foundation at the University of Southern California. Nina Weiler is a research assistant at the Citizens' Research Foundation. This article is reprinted from *An Update to Campaign Reform on the Ballot: 1972–1994* (Los Angeles: Citizens' Research Foundation, University of Southern California, 1997).

ers regarding money in politics. Eight of the measures were binding and endorsed restrictions on campaign contributions, and in some instances limited or precluded contributions from lobbyists and corporations. The state of Montana extended the existing campaign reforms adopted in 1994 to prohibit corporate contributions supporting or opposing ballot measures and initiatives. Maine voters reversed their rejection of a system of contribution limits and partial public funding of gubernatorial races that had been on the ballot in 1989; in 1996, the voters of Maine approved a system of partial public financing of certain statewide elections and established contribution and expenditure limits. Only the Massachusetts measure was not binding. Voters in twenty-four state representative districts in Massachusetts endorsed a ballot measure that instructed legislators to take action to curtail the influence of money in politics and endorsed the future creation of a public funding scheme for all state elections.

Only two of the measures voted on in 1996 dealt with the issue of public financing of elections. Since the 1976 Supreme Court decision in *Buckley v. Valeo* that barred spending limits for political candidates unless tied to voluntary acceptance of public funds, eighteen measures dealing with public financing have been placed before the voters, fourteen of which have been successful (twelve binding; two advisory).[2] Generally such measures have greater success at the local and county level where seven of eight ballot issues have met with voter approval (no local public financing measures appeared on the ballot in 1996). At the state level, the approval rate is somewhat lower: seven of ten have been passed by voters.[3] In 1996, both Maine and Massachusetts endorsed propositions ap-

proving the public financing of elections; however, as noted, the Massachusetts proposition was merely advisory. It remains to be seen whether voters will approve a public financing program once the proposed details have been fleshed out or whether the legislature will act.

Although in recent years voters in California and Washington had voted to ban public financing of elections, voters in twenty-four of Massachusetts' 159 representative districts answered in the affirmative to a question placed on the ballot that asked if state representatives should be instructed to vote in favor of legislation that would limit spending on political campaigns, remove the influence of large donors, and provide the option of public financing to candidates who agree to spending limits.[4] Of the 431,971 Massachusetts citizens who voted on the measures, 326,256 voted in favor, 43,986 cast their ballots against the measure, and 61,729 left that portion of the ballot blank. Therefore, the question posed to the voters in these districts met with an approval rate of 75.5 percent.[5] However, the question was only posed in 15 percent of all state representative districts and may or may not be a reliable indicator of statewide support for such reform measures.

Voters in the state of Maine voiced their approval for the Maine Clean Elections Act, an election reform measure that includes a system of voluntary public financing and contribution limits—the only 1996 ballot that provided for public funding. Additionally, the measure also restricted how much candidates can contribute to their campaigns from their personal funds. The Maine Clean Elections Act aims to increase the political participation of small donors by requiring that gubernatorial, State Senate and State House candidates receive a certain number of $5 contribu-tions from individuals in order to be eligi-ble for matching funds from the Clean Elections Fund. Other than the money contributed in the qualifying stage, partici-pants in the program may not receive funds from any other sources in the prima-ry and general elections apart from the money received from the Clean Elections Fund. The amount available from the Fund is equal to 25 percent less than the average expenditures per candidate in pre-vious years. In addition, candidates not par-ticipating in the Clean Elections Option are limited to donations of $250 to $500 from individuals. As is often the case with such measures, the Clean Elections Act will be the subject of a lawsuit: in December 1996 the National Right to Life Committee filed a lawsuit against the initiative and it is expected that the Maine Civil Liberties Union will file a suit against the new law in early 1997.

Most of the campaign reform mea-sures on the 1996 ballots attempted to limit the amount that individuals and groups could contribute to any one campaign. The ballot measure that succeeded in Maine set contribution limits of $250 for legislative candidates and $500 for guber-natorial candidates. Meanwhile, the mea-sure that passed in Los Angeles County provides for variable contribution limits that depend on whether candidates have agreed to the voluntary spending limits. For those candidates who do not agree to the spending caps, individuals may not contribute more than $200 to any one cam-paign. However, if a candidate does agree to abide by the spending limits, then indi-vidual contributions are raised to $1,000 for each election campaign.

Two of the measures in 1996 contin-ued the recent trend limiting contribu-tions to as little as $100 for legislative and/or local offices. The ballot proposi-tion in Arkansas imposes a contribution limit of $100 to legislative and local candi-dates. Colorado's Measure 15 limits contri-butions to legislative candidates to $100. Proposition 208 in California imposes con-tribution limits of $100 to those candidates who do not agree to limit spending in races involving districts with fewer than 100,000 residents.

Experience shows that contribution limits as low as $100 are vulnerable to court challenge and overturn. The recently-passed measures in Arkansas, California and Colorado will probably face legal hur-dles as well. In 1994, Oregon, Montana and Missouri voters passed initiatives designed to severely restrict contributions to $100 per candidate at lower levels. The Missouri election reform law passed by voters in 1994 has been struck down by the Eighth Circuit Court as infringing on the First Amendment rights of contributors.[6] The $100 contribution limit of the Oregon measure is still under litigation in a U.S. District Court. Additionally, a 1992 initia-tive passed by the voters of Washington, DC, which established contribution limits of $100 for mayoral elections and $50 for City Council races, was struck down on sim-ilar grounds by a U.S. District Court.[7] It is expected that a number of the measures passed on Election Day in 1996 will face court challenges.

One week after the passage of Califor-nia's Proposition 208, the California Pro-life Council's Political Action Committee sued in federal court to have the measure declared unconstitutional on the grounds that it violates the rights of free speech and due process.[8] Also, it is anticipated that at least three other lawsuits will be brought against Proposition 208. Had Proposition

---

Colorado, 1996: Parental Rights

Perhaps the most interesting initiated [1996] measure [in Colorado], one which failed, was a proposal to amend the state constitutional bill of rights to add a "parental rights" provision. It would have added as a "natural, essential and inalienable" right, these words: "and of parents to direct and control the upbringing, education, values, and discipline of their children." The parental rights proposal had a lead of 2–1 in the polls early on. At election time the lead had shrunk, but the measure was still ahead. But, when the polls closed, it had lost 57 to 43 percent.

A coalition of some 140 groups, including teachers, doctors, social workers, some parents, and prosecutors, had formed to oppose the measure. Among other concerns, opponents feared the amendment's potential for disruptive parental interference with school curricula and activities, and its use as a defense in child abuse cases. Further, it was said to be imprecise and thus a "lawyers full-employment" act. Opponents also made an issue of the origin and support of the proposal. Its origin and virtually sole source of financial support was the Virginia-based religious right group, "Of The People." "Of The People" had picked Colorado to test market their parental rights product because of its simple majority requirement for constitutional amendment passage. They had hoped to establish a beachhead and some momentum in Colorado, and then take the measure to other states. Around $400,000, or 98 percent of the supporters' budget, came from Virginia. Opponents, by contrast, raised roughly 95 percent of their funds within Colorado. This "carpet-bag" approach was well-reported late in the campaign and undoubtedly helped to sink the measure.

An additional factor that may have hurt the chances for passage was the announced opposition of former U.S. Senator Bill Armstrong. Armstrong is a visible and vocal evangelical Christian, and his stance surprised parental rights supporters and opponents alike. Ironically, Armstrong's announcement came shortly after Bob Dole voiced his support as he blew through Denver on a brief campaign stop. At the very least, the Armstrong announcement raised the visibility of the proposal, along with the question as to whether the guts of the measure were as attractive as its title.

Source: Excerpted from John A. Straayer, "Colorado, 1996: Parental Rights and Other Election Results," *Comparative State Politics* 17:6 (December 1996): 1–6.

---

212 been successful at the ballot box, it would have been subject to litigation because three of its provisions have been previously challenged in court—contribution limits of $100 and $200; mandatory spending limits; and a requirement that 75 percent of contributions come from within the candidate's district.

The battle in California for the passage of competing Propositions 208 and 212 was both highly publicized and costly. Although the campaign for Proposition 212 raised and spent substantially more money than the backers of Proposition 208, Proposition 208 was victorious at the polls, winning by a margin of 61 percent to 39 percent at the same time that Proposition 212 went down to defeat by a margin of 50.9 percent to 48.3 percent.[9] The passage of Proposition 208 establishes contribution limits for all state and local elections. The contribution limits are variable and depend on whether a candidate agrees to the voluntary spending limits established under the law. The contribution limits range from $100 to $500 for candidates who do not agree to limit spending, and from $250 to $1,000 for those candidates who voluntarily agree to the spending cap, depending on the size of the electoral district and whether or not the election is local, legislative or statewide. Among local and legislative candidates in local or legislative districts with fewer than 100,000 residents, the contribution limit for those candidates who opt to abide by the voluntary spending limits increases from $100 to $250; contributions to legislative and local races in districts with greater than 100,000 residents is increased from $250 to $500; and for all statewide candidates the contribution limit is raised from $500 to $1,000 for those candidates who agree to the spending limits. The new law also limits contributions from candidate committees to political action committees (PACs) and political parties, establishes special provisions for small contributor committees, restricts off-year fund raising and stiffens rules regarding the disposal of surplus campaign funds.[10]

A number of the 1996 propositions sought to restrict who or what entities may contribute to a campaign. Seeking to limit the influence of big money on politics, the California, Colorado and Montana measures included provisions limiting or precluding lobbyists, PACs, unions and/or corporations from donating to election campaigns. California's Proposition 208 forbids lobbyists from contributing to the campaigns of those individuals they seek to influence. Colorado's Measure 15 bans corporate contributions to elections while

Montana's Initiative I-125 prohibits corporate contributions to state initiative campaigns. Nevada's recently approved Question No. 10 extends the contribution limits of $5,000 that previously applied to labor unions, PACs and political parties to all contributors, regardless of affiliation.

Judicial precedent regarding limitations on who can contribute to campaigns is limited, but may signal that such restrictions are legally vulnerable. In 1995, a U.S. District Court declared unconstitutional an Oregon state law that required that 90 percent of contributions must come from residents of the district.[11] The outcome of the propositions approved in Montana, Los Angeles County and Colorado that curtail the contributions of corporate entities to certain campaigns could face future legal hurdles.

As already noted, city- and county-level election reform initiatives historically have been successful. Twenty such measures have been placed on the ballot since 1981 and all but three have been enacted. Nineteen have been binding on the local governments that they have affected; only the 1990 advisory vote in the city of Sacramento contained provisions that were not binding but were later adopted.[12] The November 1996 elections featured only one county-level proposition. Los Angeles County's Measure B passed with an overwhelming 75 percent of the vote. Voters approved an election reform ordinance limiting campaign contributions and the influence of money in county politics. The ordinance affects the County of Los Angeles. This new measure establishes a system of campaign reform for county-wide elections that includes variable limits on contributions, voluntary limits on campaign spending, and limits on contributions from lobbyists, PACs, political parties, and other organizations. The measure also establishes time limits for the receipt of campaign contributions and the disposition of surplus campaign funds.

Although in past years a number of cities have placed various election reform measures before the voters, none were voted on in 1996. Proposed measures in Washington, DC and Austin, Texas did not make it onto the ballot. Local election reforms have usually been successful, as voters in such cities as Washington, DC, Chula Vista and Los Angeles in California have at one time or another adopted public financing and/or campaign reform measures.

The November 1996 elections once again demonstrated the continued strength of election reforms with the nation's voters as well as the public's willingness to use the initiative and/or referendum process to enact campaign reform legislation when legislators may be reluctant or unwilling to do so. These results are reflective of a Conference on Campaign Reform survey in 1994 that found that 67 percent of the 1,808 people surveyed supported spending limits for campaigns and 55 percent supported contribution limits to reduce the influence of wealthy donors in a campaign.[13] However, while there is a general agreement that election reform is desirable, there is little consensus on how to implement solutions. As in past years, at least two of the measures passed in 1996—in Maine and California—are already the subject of court challenges. Moreover, past studies have shown that there is little direct correlation between the availability of the initiative process and a legislature's willingness to enact the desired reforms into law.[14] Once again, we must await implementation and court decisions to judge whether such voter-led reforms are achieving the desired results.

Notes

1. See Herbert E. Alexander and Lori Cox NyBlom, *Campaign Reform on the Ballot: 1972–1994.* Los Angeles: Citizens' Research Foundation, University of Southern California, September 1996.

2. *Buckley v. Valeo,* 424 U.S. 1, 1976.

3. Alexander and NyBlom, *Campaign Reform on the Ballot,* 19–21.

4. California Proposition 73 passed in June 1988 and prohibited the public funding of elections at all levels of government. Proposition 134 in Washington passed in November 1992 and also prohibited public funding of elections at both the state and local levels. Public financing in Los Angeles has continued following a court decision permitting it since Los Angeles is a Charter City (*Johnson v. Bradley* 4 Cal. 4th 389; 14 Cal. Rptr. 2d 470; 841 P.2d 990 [1992]). Public financing in Seattle and King County, Washington was ended in compliance with the Washington Proposition 134.

5. Secretary of the Commonwealth, "Return of the Votes for Massachusetts State Election November 5, 1996." Compiled by the Secretary of the Commonwealth Elections Division, November 27, 1996.

6. *Carver v. Nixon* (1995), U.S. Court of Appeals, 8th Circuit for the Western District of Missouri (72 F. 3d 633). Declared Missouri's Proposition A, approved by voters in November 1994, as unconstitutional. In reversing an earlier judgment by the district court, the 8th Circuit Court ruled that contribution limits as low as $100 violate contributors' freedoms of speech and association under the First Amendment.

7. *National Black Police Association v. District of Columbia Board of Elections and Ethics* (1996), U.S. District Court for the District of Columbia (Civ. No. 94-1476). Enjoined Initiative 41, approved by voters in 1992, which set contribution limits of $100 per election cycle to candidates for city-wide office including mayor, $50 per election cycle to candidates for council seats or political party posts, and $600 from any contributor to all candidates in any election. The Court ruled that the contribution limits curtailed candidates' First Amendment rights to speak freely during a political campaign, and prevents them from conducting an effective campaign.

8. "Antiabortion Group Sues to Block Prop. 208." *Los Angeles Times,* November 14, 1996.

9. Carl Ingram, "Campaign Fight Nears Spending Record." *Los Angeles Times,* October 10, 1996.

10. California Fair Practices Commission. "Campaign Finance: California State Law as Changed by Proposition 208." Sacramento: Fair Political Practices Commission, 1996.

11. *Vannatta v. Keisling* (1995) 900 F. Supp. 488.

12. Alexander and NyBlom, *Campaign Reform on the Ballot,* 1.

13. Committee for the Study of the American Electorate, Conference on Campaign Reform survey of 1,808 citizens conducted July 1994 by Princeton Survey Research Associates.

14. Alexander and NyBlom, *Campaign Reform on the Ballot,* 2.

A Time Line of Term Limits

by George Peery

1781 Articles of Confederation limit representation to "three years in six."

1787 New constitution for federal Congress has no limitations set on representatives or senators.

1951 Twenty-second Amendment to Constitution limiting presidential terms to two four-year terms is approved.

1978 U.S. Senate Judiciary subcommittee holds hearings on congressional term limits. No action is taken.

1988 GOP platform includes plank advocating congressional term limits.

1990 Oklahoma, California, and Colorado pass term limits on state elected officials. Colorado's provisions also include federal lawmakers.

1991 Washington state fails to pass term limits.

1992 Ballot initiatives limiting state and/or federal officials pass in Arizona, Arkansas, California, Florida, Michigan, Missouri, Montana, Nebraska, North Dakota, Ohio, Oregon, South Dakota, Washington, and Wyoming.

1993 Maine passes limits on state officials and becomes the first state to make limits retroactive.

1994 (March) Arkansas Supreme Court rules that voters cannot restrict the eligibility of federal candidates, but upholds limits for state lawmakers. Utah legislature passes term limits on itself.

1994 (May) Nebraska Supreme Court overthrows 1992 term limits initiative.

1994 (October) U.S. Supreme Court agrees to hear appeal of Arkansas case (*U.S. Term Limits v. Thornton*).

1994 (November) Alaska, Idaho, Maine, Massachusetts, Nebraska, and Nevada voters approve term limit measures for state lawmakers. Colorado voters extend limits to local officials. Utah's ballot initiative extending limits to local officials does not pass.

1995 (May) U.S. Supreme Court rules on *Thornton*, arguing that individual

George Peery is professor of political science at Mars Hill College in North Carolina. In 1995–96 he spent a sabbatical year with the National Conference of State Legislatures. This article is adapted with updates from "Transcending Term Limits," *State Legislatures* (June 1996): 20–25.

states may not limit terms in Congress.

1995 (October) Louisiana voters pass referendum proposed by legislature that sets term limits on state lawmakers.

1995 (November) Mississippi fails to pass term limit initiative for state officeholders.

1996 (February) Nebraska Supreme Court utilizes *Thornton* to overthrow the limits approved in 1992 in that state.

1996 (November) In reaction to *Thornton,* voters in fourteen states vote on a coordinated measure that encourages legislators to work for congressional limits. Voters in nine states—Alaska, Arkansas, Colorado, Idaho, Maine, Missouri, Nebraska, Nevada, and South Dakota—approve these initiatives. In these states, incumbents seeking reelection as well as their challengers will have their support or opposition noted on the 1998 ballot. Voters in five states—Montana, North Dakota, Oregon, Washington, and Wyoming—rejected these initiatives.

1997 (January) The first three chambers to be entirely "termed out" by these limits—the California Assembly and the Maine House and Senate—convene for their annual sessions.

1997 (April) A federal judge in California rules that the lifetime term limits ban imposed under California Proposition 140 is unconstitutional. The judge argues that the lifetime restriction "imposes a severe burden on the ability of citizens to vote for representatives of their choice," particularly on voters who "value legislative experience." She suspends implementation of her ruling for the 1998 elections pending the results of an appeal.

State Recall Elections: What Explains Their Outcomes?

by Lawrence Sych

... Like the initiative and referendum, the recall is typically based on a single issue, and has been used more often in the past 25 years than at any time since its inception during the Progressive era. Its recent popularity coincides with a rise in political cynicism, or distrust of government institutions and their elected leaders. Citizens who express cynicism are more likely to embrace electoral reforms or engage in nontraditional behavior in order to change the status quo. But while heightened levels of cynicism may explain the incidence of recall elections, it does not necessarily explain their outcomes.

Two explanations are commonly provided for recall election outcomes: a lack of turnout by supporters and the conversion of previous supporters on some issue or event that contributes to voter cynicism or distrust of the elected official....

The Recall Experience

Oregon in 1908 was the first state to adopt recall for state officials. However, recall is primarily a local phenomenon. Los Angeles held the first recall election in November, 1904. A machine councilman was removed from office. The success of this [recall led] to its widespread popularity among progressives.

The recall became closely associated with the Progressive Movement. In these years, recall, and especially the recall of judges, was seen as "a burning issue of the times." States of the west and midwest, where the candidacy of Theodore Roosevelt was popular, most frequently adopted recall of state officials. Of the 15 states that now allow such recalls, 10 had adopted the procedure by 1914....

Most recalls occur in city governments and school districts and states normally do not collect this data. There are also relatively few state recall elections to study. Only 19 state officials in 7 of the 15 states have ever faced a recall election.

Recalling state officials is more difficult than recalling local officials. Efforts to meet petition requirements commonly flounder. It usually requires a larger organization to recruit petition circulators and finance the sometimes major costs of print-

Lawrence Sych is an assistant professor of political science at Central Michigan University. This article is reprinted from *Comparative States Politics* 17:5 (October 1996): 7–25. References have been omitted.

ing and distributing petitions. Perhaps the most significant reason for the difficulty in recalling state officials ... is that most state elections are partisan, unlike many local recalls. Signing a petition for recall is often more than repudiating a single state official—it is also a rejection of his or her party. Recallers may also expect that if the official still retains solid party support, the party organization will mount a defensive campaign. In 1994, a California assemblyman switched parties during the legislative session. The party organization to which he switched gave him significant support in a losing battle against a recall.

Recall elections have become more common at both the state and local level. Eight state officials faced recall elections between 1908 and 1922 when recall was a novelty. But of the other 11, 10 did so in the 25 years between 1971 and 1996....

The Wisconsin recall election, held in March 1990, provides a good illustration of the recall experience at the state level. A 1983 federal court decision allowed six Native American Chippewa bands within the state to retain the right to spearfish, hunt, cut timber, and gather food on off-reservation public lands under treaties that ceded northern Wisconsin to the United States government. In a district dominated by the sports fishing and tourism industries, recall organizers successfully petitioned to hold a recall election of a Democratic assemblyman charged with supporting Republican Gov. Tommy Thompson's negotiated plan to lease the treaty rights of the district's band for 10 years. This plan failed to help settle the escalating confrontations between tribal and nontribal factions. The four-term assemblyman received the support of 26 assembly members, including 10 Republicans. Governor Thompson indirectly offered the incumbent support by

saying that the general election is the best time to make such recall judgments. The legislator weathered the recall effort, which later targeted other elected officials before it completely collapsed. The incumbent won with 60.1 percent of the vote. A light turnout of 38.3 percent of eligible voters was 26.1 [points] below the previous general election turnout of 64.4 percent.

Two Explanations of Recall Election Outcomes

Fourteen of 19 state officials that faced recall elections have been recalled [73 percent].... Two explanations are commonly given for recall outcomes. The first explanation's focus is on the level of voter turnout.... The second centers on the conversion of previous supporters.

The turnout explanation assumes that because fewer people vote in recall elections, an intense minority of opposition partisans who are unrepresentative of district opinion can defeat the incumbent. Indeed, the overall turnout in every state recall election ... has been lower than the vote in the original election. However, in some cases individual counties or precincts show increased turnout.... Partisanship in recall elections, according to the turnout explanation, only works to activate opponents. Partisan supporters become complacent and stay at home, thereby insuring an incumbent's defeat.

Election observers and recalled incumbents may provide a competing explanation of recall results that can be called the conversion explanation.... [This] argument ... suggests that after the incumbent takes office, a major event alienates original supporters without winning over previous opponents. Some former supporters feel betrayed and join opposition partisans in recalling the incumbent. Without such an event, threatened recalls of officials elected on a partisan ballot would remain mere threats.

... The recall ballot is often designed to highlight an official's past actions, especially if it includes statements of charges and a defense against the recall. Decisions on recall, then, are like the ones voters make in other legislative elections that depend on an assessment of the incumbent's policy records.

Two key differences exist between recall and other candidate elections. First, recalls are single-issue elections and are condemned as such. More important, the rules governing most recall elections may contribute to defeating that incumbent elected initially on a partisan basis by making the expression of conversion a good deal easier than in a general election. The ballot procedures in these elections allow loyal partisans to join with the opposition party voters to make a new majority, without having to vote in the opposition's party column. All they need do is vote "yes" for recall, or vote for an opposing candidate. Coalitions can form, which in a regular election would require the crossing of party lines.

...

[Based on an analysis of election results and a survey of district residents in this] Wisconsin example, the recall outcome appears best explained by a conversion of some initial supporters in scattered townships of the district. The Democratic assemblyman encouraged a sense of betrayal among some constituents, primarily resort owners and sports fishermen, by supporting a compromise to settle conflict over Indian fishing rights. After a successful recall petition drive, voters turned out in large numbers for the recall election.

But the numbers of opponents and their converts were not large enough to successfully recall the incumbent. Turnout, itself, had little effect on the outcome because opponents failed to convert supporters on the recall issue.

Conclusion

The Wisconsin example leads us to a greater conclusion about the recall issue as a whole. Voter turnout, at least in partisan recall elections, alone, is unlikely to account for their outcomes. A recall, especially a successful one, is more than a replay of the past election with the incumbent's supporters missing because of general apathy.

To bring about a successful recall requires a split in the previous political majority, which is not offset by support in the former opposition. A group of former supporters generally feels strongly that the incumbent officeholder betrayed their trust. The crucial defectors appear to be previous supporters of either party, or independents, who abandon the party nominee.

Thus, conversion generally explains the outcome of recall elections. A single incident or issue may be pointed to as not only sparking the recall effort, but also acting as the campaign focal point. In this regard, the state recall elections reflect those held at the local level. These results show that voter approval or disapproval of the incumbent's performance on the recall issue is the most important determinant of the outcome. Constituents make retrospective votes on the basis of prior incumbent performance that is shaped by the recall election campaign. Consequently, this recall election was a candidate-based campaign with party organization and partisanship exerting only indirect influence on outcomes.

III. POLITICS: PARTIES, INTEREST GROUPS, AND PACS

Politics in the American states is changing. Political parties, once the backbone of the U.S. political system and the chief force in state government, are becoming less influential, or so say many observers. As Malcolm Jewell and David Olson point out, "It has become a truism that party organizations are declining in importance, and there is no reason to anticipate a reversal of that trend."[1] Whether they are in decline or have just assumed new roles, most observers agree political parties are an adaptable and durable force in the states, as they "remain the principal agencies for making nominations, contesting elections, recruiting leaders, and providing a link between citizens and their government."[2]

But what are political parties? This question must be addressed before the reasons for these different interpretations can be understood. Are they the organizations from precinct to national convention—*the party in organization?* Are they the individuals who run, win, and control government under a party label—*the party in office?* Or are they the voters themselves, who identify more with a particular party and vote accordingly—*the party in the electorate?* Political parties are all three, diverse in definition and ever-changing in their impact on state government.

Perhaps the clearest signal that parties sway voters less than they once did is the rise of split-ticket voting. In state and local elections in 1956, only 28 percent of the voters who identified themselves as either Democrats or Republicans did not vote the straight party line but split their tickets by voting for candidates of both parties; in 1980, 51 percent split their tickets.[3] In 1986, 20 percent of those identifying

themselves as Democrats and 17 percent of those identifying themselves as Republicans voted for the U.S. Senate candidate of the opposing party.[4] This divided party voting and its impact is discussed in further detail in the introduction to Part I.

What's Happened to the Parties?

Various explanations have been offered for the decline of political parties. Direct primaries—the means by which party voters can participate directly in the nomination process rather than have party leaders select candidates—certainly have curtailed the influence of party organizations. By 1920 most of the states had adopted the direct primary.[5] No longer could party organizations or party bosses rule the nominating process with an iron hand, dominate the election campaign, and distribute patronage positions and benefits at will. The ability to circumvent official party channels and appeal directly to the electorate greatly increased the power of individual candidates. A candidate's personality has taken on new importance as party affiliation has become less influential in determining voting behavior.

In the political environment of the 1990s, parties are challenged by the mass media, interest groups, independent political consultants, and political action committees—vehicles that perform many of the historic functions of the political party. Public opinion polls, rather than party ward and precinct organizations, survey the "faithful." Today,

... [P]olitical consultants, answerable only to their client candidates and independent of the political parties, have inflicted severe damage upon the party system and masterminded the modern triumph of personality cults over party politics in the United States.[6]

One analyst argues, however, that the rise of the political consultant has opened up the political process through the use of polls and other techniques. Now candidates can talk about the issues voters are concerned about without the "party communications filter."[7]

Candidates have also changed, and some of these changes do not help the parties. For example, we are seeing more independent candidates running for office. These independents are no less political than other candidates, but are simply independent of the two major parties. At the national level, the 1992 and 1996 presidential runs by Texas billionaire Ross Perot is an example of this phenomenon. At the state level, two governors elected in 1990, Walter Hickel of Alaska and Lowell Weicker of Connecticut, both ran and served as independents, as did Angus King of Maine, elected in 1994. There are and will be others.

More important is the rise of the self-starting candidate with both fiscal and political resources of his or her own. These candidates can afford to run for office on their own, needing the party only for its nomination to get on the ballot. Such "candidate-centered campaigns are becoming more prevalent at the state level," and as they do, "party-line voting is declining."[8] Alan Ehrenhalt argues that "political careers are open to ambition now in a way that has not been true in America in most of this century."[9] He believes these self-starting candidates are motivated by their personal ambition, which drives their entry into politics. Because they can "manipulate the instruments of the system—the fund raising, the personal campaigning, the op-

portunities to express themselves in public—[they] confront very few limits on their capacity to reach the top."[10]

The 1994 elections, across the states, present an interesting contrast to the trends mentioned above. The sweeping victories of Republicans at all levels of government suggested the possibility that parties are not quite as moribund as many think. This possibility seemed especially plausible because the Republicans banded together with a common set of positions on certain issues, making their candidacies more party based than individually based. The results of the 1996 elections reversed the 1994 results to some extent, as many candidates resumed more individually based campaign styles.

To most citizens, parties are important only during the election season. Our system is unlike that of most European countries, where there are rigid election schedules in which campaigning is limited to a specific time period. The American state and local government election season is generally thought to start around Labor Day in early September and run until election day in early November. Cynics believe that this is too long, and that in most voters' minds, the season really begins at the end of the World Series in late October. Of course, the candidates have been at work for months, even years, getting ready for this unofficial election season, but the impact of other events, such as the World Series, often conspires to distract the electorate. (Of course, in 1994, due to the professional baseball strike, there was no World Series, and it thus was not a factor. Some have suggested that the loss of the World Series also had an effect on the fans, who, unable to vent their emotions during the games, did the next best thing by venting their anger at politicians.)

Signs of Party Resurgence

Yet not everyone is ready to declare the parties moribund. As noted, the party process is still the means of selecting candidates for national, state, and, in some cases, local office.

Control of state legislatures is determined by which party has the majority, with the sole exception of Nebraska. Appointments to state government positions usually go to the party colleagues of state legislators or of the governor.

Although the party in organization and the party in the electorate are weaker than they once were, the party in office may be gaining strength, argues Alan Rosenthal of the Eagleton Institute of Politics at Rutgers University. Legislators are increasingly preoccupied with winning reelection. The "art of politicking" may be superseding the "art of legislating."[11] Party caucuses have begun to play an important role in selecting the legislative leadership, assigning committee and other responsibilities, and establishing positions on issues. In fact, the party in organization may not be as weak as many think. Since the 1960s, budgets and staffs have grown in size, staffs have become more professional, party services and activities have increased, and elected leaders may be even more involved in party affairs.[12] Now, in the 1990s, some feel that the money these state parties can raise and the campaign services they provide to their candidates and local affiliates have made them a strong force in state politics.[13]

Of course, party politics differ in each state. As Samuel C. Patterson writes, "In some places parties are strong and vigorous; in other places, they are sluggish; in yet others, moribund. But, on balance, the state parties appear remarkably vibrant."[14]

Interest Group Politics

Are interest groups an evil that must be endured or are they a necessary part of the governing process? Is their impact on state government primarily beneficial or harmful? Perhaps most importantly, do the interests that groups seek to advance or protect benefit the whole state or only the lobbies themselves? State officials, pressured by a myriad of interest groups, wrestle with these questions and reach different answers.

Interest groups' influence on the political process varies from state to state. Business groups are by far the most predominant; the influence of labor groups pales in comparison. Thus, the interest group structure of most states is business-oriented and conservative.

Lately, however, groups representing government employees, local government officials, and the public interest (for example, Common Cause and environmental protection groups) have increased their visibility and effectiveness in state politics.

An interest group's effectiveness depends on the representatives it sends to the state legislature and executive branch agencies—the so-called professional lobbyists. Who are these people? Usually they have served in government and are already known to those they seek to influence. Their ranks include former agency heads, legislators, and even governors in private law practice who have clients with special interests. Some of the most effective lobbyists represent several interests.

The relationship between political parties and interest groups in the states tends to follow a discernible pattern: the more competitive the party system, the weaker the interest group system. More specifically, "the weaker a party is, the more leeway is given to other elements of the political system to fill the power vacuum. Because of the close linkage between parties and interest groups, this vacuum is filled largely by the groups themselves."[15] This apparently symbiotic relationship between parties and interest groups largely determines who controls state government.

Theoretically, in a competitive, two-party state, the stakes are more likely to be out in the open as one party fights the other for control. Conversely, in the noncompetitive, one-party state, the stakes are less easy to see as interest groups do battle with each other to maintain or change the status quo. Again, in theory, the power of the party flows from the voters through their elected representatives; the power of interest groups is derived from their numbers, money, and lobbying skill. But in practice the relationship is not as clear as this explanation would suggest. In fact, once the parties organize state government, state politics usually become the special quarry of interest groups—except, of course, on distinctive, party-line issues (such as selecting the leadership), or when there are other institutions with political strength, such as the governor or the media.

The Role of State Governments

State governments have two main roles vis-à-vis the other actors in state politics: they set the "rules of the game" in which parties and interest groups operate, and then they regulate their financial activities. The rules govern the nomination and election processes and the ways in which interests are allowed to press their demands. However, the rules change at a glacial pace because those who know how to play the game fear that change will upset the balance of power—or at least their

spot in the power system. In fact, it often takes a lawsuit by someone outside that power system to change the rules or a scandal to tighten financial reporting requirements.

Recently, the states have adopted policies that increase their regulatory role regarding political parties. Public disclosure and campaign finance laws are more strict, and political action committees (PACs) are monitored with a more watchful eye due to their increased activity. Some of these regulations have been successfully challenged in the courts. For example, the Republican party of Connecticut won its fight to allow some nonparty members, that is, independents, to vote in their primary despite a contrary state law, and California found its ban on pre-primary party endorsements invalidated.[16]

Part III provides some insight into politics at the state level. Charles Mahtesian of *Governing* reports on how state correctional officers are becoming an effective interest group in state capitals. Alan Rosenthal, in *State Government News,* examines where the public interest is when special interests are at work. And Floyd Weintraub of *Empire State Report* argues in favor of a switch from closed to open primaries.

Notes

1. Malcolm Jewell and David Olson, *American State Political Parties and Elections* (Homewood, Ill.: Dorsey Press, 1982), 280.

2. John F. Bibby and Thomas M. Holbrook, "Parties and Elections," in *Politics in the American States,* 6th ed., ed. Virginia Gray and Herbert Jacob (Washington, D.C.: CQ Press, 1996), 118.

3. David E. Price, *Bringing Back the Parties* (Washington, D.C.: CQ Press, 1984), 15.

4. Survey by ABC News, November 4, 1986, reported in *Public Opinion* 9:4 (January–February 1987): 34.

5. Price, *Bringing Back the Parties,* 32.

6. Larry Sabato, *The Rise of Political Consultants: New Ways of Winning Elections* (New York: Basic Books, 1981), 3.

7. Walter DeVries, "American Campaign Consulting: Trends and Concerns," *PS: Political Science and Politics* 12:1 (March 1989): 24.

8. Stephen A. Salmore and Barbara G. Salmore, "The Transformation of State Electoral Politics," in *The State of the States,* 3d ed., ed. Carl Van Horn (Washington, D.C.: CQ Press, 1996), 51.

9. Alan Ehrenhalt, *The United States of Ambition* (New York: Times Books, 1992), 272.

10. Ibid., 273.

11. Alan Rosenthal, "If the Party's Over, Where's All That Noise Coming From?" *State Government* 57:2 (Summer 1984): 50, 54.

12. Timothy Conlan, Ann Martino, and Robert Dilger, "State Parties in the 1980s: Adaptation, Resurgence, and Continuing Constraints," *Intergovernmental Perspective* 20:4 (Fall 1984): 23.

13. Bibby and Holbrook, "Parties and Elections," 83.

14. Samuel C. Patterson, "The Persistence of State Parties," in *The State of the States,* 2d ed., ed. Carl Van Horn (Washington, D.C.: CQ Press, 1993), 169.

15. Clive S. Thomas and Ronald J. Hrebenar, "Interest Groups in the States," in *Politics in the American States,* 6th ed., ed. Gray and Jacob, 131.

16. Patterson, "The Persistence of State Parties," 197. The court cases were *Tashjian v. Connecticut* (1986) and *Secretary of State of California v. San Francisco Democratic Central Committee* (1989).

The Uprising
of the Prison Guards

by Charles Mahtesian

California Governor Pete Wilson is not known for any particular rapport with unions. But when the California Correctional Peace Officers Association speaks, the governor listens.

Of all the state employee unions, CCPOA is Wilson's favorite. The only union to endorse him for office, the correctional officers organization also sided with him in tough budget fights when the state was mired in recession and stiff pay cuts had to be made.

Today, the prison guards' access to the executive office is a privilege no other union in California can boast of.

But that's not the only means by which CCPOA has entered the realms of power in its home state. The legislature also sits up and takes notice when the union calls.

While the Senate and General Assembly were debating the nation's toughest "three-strikes" sentencing bill, for instance, the state correctional officers weren't just patrolling the cellblocks at the state's 29 prisons. They launched an intense statehouse lobbying effort to pass the means to lock up habitual offenders. They also donated more than $100,000 to the referendum campaign that proved to be a powerful push toward passage of the 1994 law.

This full-court press was their first direct foray into sentencing policy. The prison-guard union was not the only group telling the legislature how necessary—and politically popular—a three strikes law would be. But it was among the most convincing, especially to those who remembered that the union had not been shy about putting its money on favored candidates. In the preceding election cycle, CCPOA had contributed in excess of $1 million to campaigns. More than 60 legislators who would vote on the three-strikes bill had received a check from CCPOA at one time or another.

Today, California prison guards rank among Sacramento's most powerful interest groups. They have been able to expand their issues beyond the usual union menu of benefits, wages and work conditions. Their purview now includes prison construction, prison management and sentencing policy.

Charles Mahtesian is a staff writer for *Governing*. This article is reprinted from *Governing* (August 1996): 38–41.

The rise to prominence of this relatively new policy lobbying force is starting to occur in a growing number of other states. And it is a force that is not easily defined. Prison-guard groups break with organized labor on some issues and sympathize with Republicans rather than Democrats on others.

Much of the muscle behind their increasing strength is a matter of numbers. Prison building is a growth industry. Due partly to stiffer sentencing provisions and stricter attitudes toward parole and probation, the inmate population of state prisons across the country has tripled from approximately 300,000 in 1980 to more than 900,000 in 1994.

Most states have been reacting to the population surge by continuing to build new facilities. For instance, although Illinois has already constructed 16 new penitentiaries over the past 18 years, two more are on the way. New York Governor George E. Pataki's most recent budget includes plans to build three maximum-security prisons over the next four years. California's prison building binge has included the construction of 18 new penitentiaries in the past decade, with about 20 new ones to be in service by the year 2000. Altogether, in 1995 alone, states spent an estimated $2 billion to construct new correctional facilities.

But that's just the beginning of the escalation in costs and numbers. "As long as there are bad guys, you'll need corrections officers to watch over them," notes Bob Lawson, communications director for Council 82 of the American Federation of State County and Municipal Employees, which represents more than 21,500 New York State corrections employees. "If you are going to build prisons, you've got to have the manpower to supervise the inmates in them." In no fewer than 16 states, the number of prison guards has more than doubled over the past 10 years. In Michigan, where the Department of Corrections recently became the agency with the most employees, the number of guards has tripled.

The surge in the number of prison guards "flies against the reality of what's happening with other state employees," says Rick Kearney, a professor at the University of Connecticut who studies labor relations. Budget figures support Kearney's point. Between 1994 and 1995, state corrections spending increased by more than 15 percent—from $22.8 billion to $26.3 billion—and labor costs were a healthy piece of that tab.

Nationwide, some 75,000 correctional officers are represented by AFSCME, in state affiliates that range widely in their bargaining power and statehouse sway. At this point, their issues in most states tend to be limited to work conditions, pensions and benefits. But their interests in complementary policy questions are expanding as their influence increases.

No other state's prison guards right now can match the scope and breadth of the California union's clout, but others are beginning to demonstrate an ability to develop a serious level of activism, organization and political muscle. The one correctional-officer union that comes closest to the California model is Rhode Island's. A look at the very different ways in which prison-guard organizations have prospered in those states suggests what may lie ahead for other states.

As state employee unions go, the California Correctional Peace Officers Association is something of an oddity. Unlike teachers or other state civil servants, the correctional officers who comprise CCPOA are independent of any national union. They gladly break with the traditionally Democratic politics of the labor movement to support Republican candidates for office.

Never was the union's maverick nature more obvious than when the state was mired in its 1991 budget crisis, searching desperately to hold down costs. CCPOA pulled a truly unexpected stunt that year: It was the first and only union to agree to a 5 percent salary cut. The idea was savaged by other unions. Even CCPOA's own rank and file threatened to revolt. Eventually, the offer came to naught. And by the next year, all state employees were forced to accept a pay cut.

But the correctional officers had scored a point. When it came time to recoup wage reductions, CCPOA's dramatic gesture was repaid. Governor Wilson gave the guards their new raises six months before the rest of the state employees. The thank you was neither a surprise nor exclusively a repayment for the pay-cut gesture, just a confirmation of Wilson's fondness for the guards.

The feeling is mutual. CCPOA President Don Novey has been known to make the point that his union helped put Wilson over the top in his close race.

For CCPOA, the evolution to kingmaker came rather quickly. When Novey, a former corrections officer himself, was elected in 1980, he presided over a quiet, 2,000-member public employee union. Beginning only with the notion that the guards' image needed some polish and professionalization, Novey almost singlehandedly built CCPOA into a political behemoth. Since he took over, membership has swelled to more than 23,000. Guard salaries have doubled. Moreover, the union's savvy has grown along with membership and wages.

CCPOA's legislative lobbying staff alone boasts eight staffers—and that does not include the organization's two Washington, D.C.-based lobbyists. According to the union, its lobbying operation sponsored and pushed to passage 59 separate pieces of legislation since it began in 1982. "We've written our own ticket politically," says Jeff Thompson, CCPOA's chief of governmental relations. "We have been a good advocate for paying the price for public safety."

Much of their clout derives from the current tough-on-crime climate. At a time when it pays to play hardball on crime and punishment, CCPOA plays the hardest. Its agenda is nearly untouchable. It subsidizes California's burgeoning victims' rights movement, advocates tougher sentencing provisions, backs efforts to reduce inmate rights and privileges and boosts additional prison-building efforts. For the candidates it supports, its backing is like having the crime-fighting equivalent of the Good Housekeeping seal of approval. "In an industry as deadly as peace officer work," says Thompson, "we have to have a say in how management formulates its policies because it directly affects the safety of our officers."

Twenty-five years ago, Rhode Island's corrections officers organized on their own for much the same reason. At its inception, the Rhode Island Brotherhood of Correctional Officers was a ragtag outfit of just a little more than 100 poorly trained and underpaid civil servants working in a violent and unsafe atmosphere. The idea of expanding prisoners' rights was beginning to take hold among reform-minded corrections administrators, and the guards, who were then members of the state employees association, didn't like what was happening but felt powerless to do anything about it.

Change in Total Number of Correctional Officers, by State, 1985–94 (percent)

Increased			Decreased
100% or more	50–99.9%	0–49.9%	
ID (264.4)	SC (96.2)	LA (41.7)	OK (–0.4)
MI (196.3)	MO (94.3)	VT (40.8)	TN (–11.5)
NH (171.7)	ME (92.4)	NM (37.0)	
PA (168.6)	NC (90.1)	NV (35.8)	
CT (162.3)	MA (90.0)	AL (35.2)	
IL (139.2)	MS (84.9)	MN (32.8)	
CA (126.3)	NJ (83.6)	KY (30.0)	
RI (120.2)	AZ (83.3)	WY (26.3)	
UT (119.3)	IN (77.5)	VA (22.5)	
OH (110.5)	AR (75.4)	ND (19.4)	
GA (110.2)	HI (73.8)	IA (18.8)	
CO (104.7)	WI (65.7)	DE (15.4)	
KS (104.5)	NY (65.4)	WA (13.2)	
FL (102.6)	MD (60.0)	NE (11.6)	
OR (102.2)	SD (59.7)	WV (11.3)	
TX (100.5)		AK (6.1)	
		MT (5.1)	

Source: American Correctional Association.

Dissatisfied with their representation in the larger union, they jumped ship and created the Brotherhood. Using the threat of strikes, they discovered that they could get a hearing for their grievances. Once at the bargaining table, they cut a deal on their initial contract that was—and continues to be—more favorable to the union than to management. Over the next few years, subsequent incidents of prisoner violence frightened the state into further concessions so that now, with more than 1,200 members, no one would call the Brotherhood powerless.

They fairly swagger through the state capitol with a clout that belies their relatively small membership. This year, for instance, the union successfully lobbied for a bill requiring hepatitis and HIV testing of new inmates and legislation making it a misdemeanor to impersonate a correction-

al officer. The union also managed to win creation of a special legislative commission to study the mortality rate of retired correctional officers. "More than anything else, they have staying power," says Phil West, executive director of Rhode Island Common Cause. "They understand the nature of incremental changes in statutes, year in and year out. After five years, there are substantial alterations."

Like many other prison-guard unions, the Brotherhood continues to focus primarily on job security, benefits and working conditions. Elsewhere though, as the unions begin to grow in size and stature, so does their desire to do as the California guards have done—that is, significantly influence corrections policy. What the union members are recognizing is that it is not enough to negotiate for additional wages and benefits; most states are not flush enough to keep parceling out lucrative pay raises forever. Instead, following the successful model provided by interest groups like the teachers' unions, the guards are branching out beyond bread-and-butter issues and into other areas of corrections policy such as sentencing guidelines, prisoner rights, victims' rights, privatization and prison construction.

"A lot of what we do is defensive," says Mel Grieshaber, legislative director for the Michigan Corrections Organization, "but the corrections area is taking such a big bite out of budgets that it offers us an opportunity to have our say."

Not all the fights prison guards take to the legislatures are winners for them. The one area in which unions have had much to say but little success is in for-profit corrections management. In Illinois, organized labor managed to push through a bill prohibiting prison privatization in 1991, but that accomplishment stands alone among the states. Today, there are nearly 100 private correctional facilities either in operation or under construction. Most are in states where labor unions are weak, but even in states where labor is active and there is a strong prison-guard organization, the momentum of privatization is proving hard to stop. In Michigan this year, after years of defense, MCO failed to block a bill that paves the way for the state's first privatized facility.

One state where the privatization movement has been slow to take hold is California, in no small part due to the presence of CCPOA. "One thing you'll note of the union's muscle is their monopoly in the prison business," says Franklin Zimring, director of the Earl Warren Legal Institute at the University of California-Berkeley. "Nobody is talking about privatizing California prisons."

At least not yet. Charles Thomas, a professor of criminology at the University of Florida and an expert on prison privatization, thinks that even CCPOA may not be strong enough to stop privatization momentum. Although California has been willing to ante up a lot of money for its present prison system, that may not last forever. "Even a pretty solid dam can only hold back a finite amount of water," Thomas says. "In my judgment, the dam is about to break in California."

If so, there will be a lot of folks happy to see CCPOA eat crow—even some of those in the labor movement. Resentment against CCPOA's success runs deep in Sacramento, especially among those who feel the union has distorted the crime debate to further its own goals. More prisons, notes Vincent Schiraldi, executive director of the Center on Juvenile and Criminal Justice, means more CCPOA members. "CCPOA has forced the debate way out of the bounds of reasonable discourse. They've added a thug-like element where they will brook no dissent to their positions," in the view of Schiraldi. "It guarantees growth of their union."

Others, particularly in the education establishment, complain that the growth of the corrections complex has come at the expense of other budget areas. A frequent criticism is that correctional officers are better paid than teachers and other educators. "We've added 10,000 prison guards and reduced 10,000 higher education employees," says Assemblyman John Vasconcellos, former chairman of the Ways and Means Committee. "That's not a formula for a hopeful future."

Vasconcellos has some familiarity with CCPOA. A former CCPOA campaign contribution recipient, Vasconcellos felt the wrath of CCPOA in 1992 after he led the opposition to a move to provide more state bonds for prison construction. CCPOA plowed almost $90,000 into a campaign to oust him. Vasconcellos survived but, says Ruth Holton of California Common Cause, "it sent a message to the rest of the legislature about what happens if you cross them."

And right now, as crime fears hover at the top of voter concerns, legislators are listening very closely. In the short term, both in California and elsewhere, that likely

means continued corrections budget growth, tough sentencing measures and more prison guards.

Whether that pace is sustainable is another matter. Already, a judicial backlash against harsh sentencing guidelines is beginning to make its mark. And in June [1996], the California Supreme Court neutered one of CCPOA's crowning achievements—the state's "three strikes" law.

Political Protocol: Special Interests

by Alan Rosenthal

Nowadays, the only life forms in worse repute than state legislators and members of Congress are lobbyists and the special interests they represent. In the pages of the press and the minds of the public, special interests stand accused of the failure of American politics. That is not only a heavy burden to bear, but an unfair one.

Ordinary citizens feel excluded from a system in which they see no lobbyists championing their cause. The truth, however, is that we are not unrepresented by lobbyists. Someone is out there expressing our points of view and our interests.

Take health care groups and lobbyists—hospitals, doctors, insurance companies, business, labor, seniors, pharmaceuticals and the self-styled public-interest groups. Nearly everyone's point of view is represented by one or several of the health-care contestants.

On major policy—health, education, the environment, employment and taxes—the desires of the most ordinary citizens are taken in to account by a system that is prone to responsiveness. Not infrequently, however, people do not have feelings—or do not have strong feelings—about an issue, and many of those who have them divide along opposing lines. On major issues, mandates are few and far between: usually, we have to settle for pluralities, because even relatively stable majorities are elusive.

On less visible issues the process may be more problematic. Such issues often involve the economic stakes of businesses, professions and occupations. These economically interested groups cannot afford to be without professional representation at the statehouse. They employ or contract with lobbyists because the legislature can determine whether these groups are marginally advantaged or disadvantaged in the marketplace.

Tort reform, insurance and product liability find trial lawyers on one side and business, insurance and doctors on the other. Hertz and Avis gang up on Alamo in what has become known as "Car Wars." Optometrists challenge the diagnostic and prescriptive control of ophthalmologists in "Eye Wars." Dog groomers take on veteri-

Alan Rosenthal is a professor with the Eagleton Institute of Politics at Rutgers University. This article is reprinted from *State Government News* (August 1996): 37.

narians over the right to brush a dog's teeth in what surely ought to be dubbed "Canine Wars." In a struggle with orthopedic surgeons, podiatrists lay claim to the ankle. Whether they succeed or fail depends on the definition, established in law, of where the foot stops and the ankle begins. The legislature has to decide issues like these, along with the big ones.

Where is the public interest in all of this? Nearly every group will make the argument that its case serves the public interest and certainly does it no harm. Few members of the larger public care, and the public-interest merits of each side are at the same time plausible and disputable. On issues such as these, lobbying assumes greater prominence.

Given the multiplicity of groups that lobby the legislature, almost everyone is represented directly or indirectly on selected issues by one or another of them. An estimated 70 percent of Americans belong to at least one association and 25 percent belong to four or more associations. In New Jersey, the Business and Industry Association, the Chemical Industry Council, the Food Council, the Society of Certified Public Accountants, the AFL-CIO, the Association for Children, the American Psychological Association, Prudential, Public Service Electric and Gas, Johnson and Johnson, and many others advocate the special interests of employers, employees or the self-employed.

Members of the public do not see themselves, but do see others, as having special interests (just as waste in government is not a program that benefits us, but one that benefits someone else). Teachers, for example, think of their association as lobbying on behalf of the children, while other people may think of the education association as lobbying on behalf of its members. It does both.

I vividly recall asking a member of the Texas Senate, years ago, about the influence of interest groups. He responded, "They accuse me of being a tool of the special interests. Damned right, I'm a tool of the special interests. Every son-of-a-bitch in my district has a special interest." The public can go its merry way demonizing special interests. But at least we should acknowledge that if special interests are indeed the enemy, then the enemy is us.

Primary Changes

by Floyd Weintraub

There is something happening across the nation regarding the primary election process that New York's political party leaders probably would rather not discuss privately, much less publicly. A little more than two months ago, California voters overwhelmingly approved Proposition 198, which opens future primary elections to all voters, not just registered party members. In the future, California becomes what is called a "blanket" or "one-ballot" state, joining Alaska, Washington and Louisiana, which feature primaries that list all candidates on one ballot by party affiliation with the top vote-getters going on to fight it out in the general election. This new system will apply to elections of the president, congressmen and officials.

This is not just another crazy California trend. Add these four states to the other 26 that now have open primaries, and New York finds itself among a shrinking minority of states with a closed primary system. In open primary states, all independents can vote in a party on primary or election day. Some of these states even permit Democratic or Republican voters to cross over and cast their ballots in the other party's primary.

So what is the attraction for this kind of change? According to its proponents, open primaries would give recognition to independent voters. Across the country, independents are the fastest growing group of voters. Some experts predict that independent voters may outnumber registered party voters by the year 2000. Open primaries will involve these voters more directly in the selection of candidates and possibly end the voter lament regarding the choices they have. One knows that a primary usually brings out the party's most ardent and ideological die-hards. For both Democrats and Republicans, this often means nominating a candidate too extreme for the general electorate to vote for in November elections. Like a failed Broadway show, New York's general elections are littered with the bones of defeated candidates whose extreme positions played well with those who loved them in the primary shows, but flopped when opened to the general public. Their review or obituary, as the case may be, is always the same: "They

Floyd Weintraub is publisher emeritus of *Empire State Report*. This article is reprinted from *Empire State Report* (May 1996): 54.

Are Parties Necessary?

It has been a long time since the rest of the country thought of Maine as a bellwether for much of anything. And it has been a long time since Maine wanted to be one. In politics, as in culture, its residents have come to take pride in being stubbornly different. As Maine goes, they like to believe, so goes Maine.

And so it has. More than 20 years ago, in the midst of a national Democratic landslide, it chose a cranky millionaire insurance salesman for governor on an independent label. In 1992 it gave Ross Perot a bigger vote than any state in America—a bigger vote than it gave the incumbent president. And in 1994, as Republicans were sweeping to power virtually everywhere else, Maine jumped the track again, giving the governorship to Angus King, still another wealthy businessman who proclaimed that the two major parties had misbehaved and needed to be taught a lesson.

Registered independents make up 37 percent of the Maine electorate, the largest single bloc in the state. For years it has been said that Maine really has a three-party system, with independents equal in status to the major two. But that isn't true anymore: The independents are well ahead now, and continuing to pull away.

All of this is easily sufficient to qualify Maine as the national capital of anti-party insurgency. But it may turn out to be more than that. In the 1990s, as voters in most of America express frustration with the two parties and with partisan bickering in general, you have to wonder whether Maine is an ornery backwater or a small symbol of things to come.

Source: Excerpted from Alan Ehrenhalt, "The Man Without a Party," *Governing* (October 1996): 26.

ate their own dog food." Open primaries, proponents claim, probably will ensure the nomination of more moderate or centrist candidates.

Another reason put forth by supporters for open primaries centers on the matter of reapportionment and the irrelevance of general elections, particularly in many federal and state legislative races. One at least should be familiar with the concept of "yellow-dog district syndrome." In Texas, it is said that "this district is so Democrat that even if a yellow dog was the Democratic nominee, it would win." While no similar expression springs to mind for the Republicans, there must be one. New York is also a honeycomb of safe legislative districts in which once the party candidate is chosen, the general election becomes a coronation rather than a contest. So by opening up the primary to independent voters, in many districts the voters can cast their ballots in the election that means the most.

Finally, potentially the strongest argument against closed primaries such as we have in New York revolves around money. Quite simply asked, "Why should taxpayer money pay for exclusive partisan activities?" At a time when the public is questioning how every public dollar is spent, such an argument will not fall on deaf ears, especially among independent voters.

Arguments against open primaries center on party discipline and real choice.

In open primary states as well as the blanket ones, there is less likelihood that the voters will be offered a clear choice of candidates with contrasting views. And think how hard it is now for legislative leaders to keep their party members in line when it comes to passing bills. Any additional deterioration of party discipline in Congress or in the state legislature could paralyze completely a system that, in the eyes of many, is already frozen. The parties themselves, viewed as irrelevant in many elections, would be weakened further by opening up the primary process.

Even without the anti-tobacco lobby, it would be hard to return to the days of smoke-filled rooms. Eliminating primaries and developing more comprehensive party conventions complemented by active caucuses like those in Iowa could lay this issue to rest. But that is highly unlikely. Anything that smacks of exclusion would have a hard time being instituted when both major parties are fighting for the middle ground.

The change in California … may signal the end of political parties as they currently are organized. For the Democratic and Republican party leaders in the Golden State, it is the equivalent of the San Francisco earthquake of 1906.

The current New York party primary system leaves much to be desired. Republicans, publicly taken to task during their recent presidential primary, have promised to reform the process. Democrats set up a process and then ignore it, often enabling virtually anyone with an interest to get on their ballot. Whatever reforms do occur here in New York, it is probably safe to say that changing to an open primary system, much less to a Californian one-ballot solution, is highly unlikely at this time. Then again, in 1980, many political prognosticators picked Bess Meyerson and Jacob Javits, respectively, to win the U.S. Senate Democratic and Republican primaries in New York. [Elizabeth Holtzman and Aflonse D'Amato did, and D'Amato edged by Holtzman in the general election.]

IV.   MEDIA AND THE STATES

"The media" is a broad term that needs to be broken into its components for us to better understand how the media operate in the states. There are the print media, the daily and weekly newspapers we read; the television stations, which provide local and national news; the radio stations, which offer a large variety of formats; and the wire services, which provide the backbone of news stories to the other media.

In fact, it is the wire services and the daily newspapers that set the agenda for television and radio, although TV and radio stations pick and choose what they want to cover. Look at your state's or city's major morning paper and compare the main stories on the front page with what you hear on the early morning radio news. Go into any radio or television station and watch how closely they follow and use the information coming over the wire services. A recent study indicates that state elected officials find newspapers and the wire services the two most politically significant media in the states. This is in contrast to the general perception that newspapers and TV are the most important media at the national level.[1]

There are assets and liabilities to each medium. For example, newspapers can cover a broad range of items and concerns, making them attractive to many readers. In fact, some critics argue that newspapers may be covering too many types of stories and may be losing their focus and concern over larger public issues. Television is a "hot" medium because stories are expressed through pictures, which is an easier way for most people to absorb the news. However, TV is limited by its own technology since it depends on pictures to carry the message; how does one take a picture of taxes? A study conducted in the mid-1970s of forty-four newspapers and television stations in ten cities found that newspapers allocated more space to stories on state government than did television stations. Newspapers also gave stories on state government greater prominence (front page location) than did the television stations (lead story status).[2] But Bill Gormley, the study's author, argued that even with this newspaper coverage, "few give [state government] the kind of coverage it needs."[3]

Gormley cited the comments of others who had misgivings about the media's coverage of the states. Political scientist V. O. Key, Jr., argued in 1961 that the media "may dig to find the facts about individual acts of corruption but the grand problems of the political system by and large escape their critical attention."[4] Former North Carolina governor Terry Sanford (D, 1961–65) questioned, "Who, in some 40 states or more, can say he begins to understand state government by what he reads in the newspapers?"[5]

State Media Structures

There is great variety in the media structures across the states just as there is great variety in population size, population centers, and economic complexity. For example, New Jersey sits within two major media markets—the northern part of the state receives broadcasts from the New York City metropolitan area, and the southern part receives broadcasts from the greater Philadelphia metropolitan area. Radio, TV, and cable stations emanating from those major markets dominate what is seen or heard in New Jersey, and there are no strong New Jersey-based media outlets to combat this. News about New Jersey must fight for a spot in these media outlets.

West Virginia also faces this problem: much of the state is served by media markets in Cincinnati, Pittsburgh, and Washington, D.C. West Virginia lacks its own major media outlet because its terrain makes it impossible for any station to reach all parts of the state. In his 1980 reelection bid, Governor John D. "Jay" Rockefeller IV (D, 1977–85) spent a lot of money on outlets in these large cities in order to reach potential voters in remote areas of the state. There were stories of voters in Washington, D.C., going to the polls to vote for Rockefeller because they had seen his ads on TV so often.

Then there are states that have many media markets within their own boundaries. California clearly is the leader in media markets because there are so many large communities to be served in the state, ranging from San Francisco and Sacramento in the northern part of the state to Los Angeles and San Diego in the southern part. And there are many other markets in between. Texas also has many media markets, as do Florida, New York, and North Carolina.

At the other extreme are states with only one major media market that dominates the state. Examples are Colorado, with the Denver media market; Georgia, with Atlanta; and Massachusetts, with Boston. In fact, the Boston media market spreads well into Rhode Island, southern New Hampshire, and southwestern Maine, making it difficult for residents there to get a clear understanding of what is happening in their own states. One New Hampshire state legislator worried that "most citizens in the lower one-third of the state get their news from Boston TV, so we have a very distorted view by many citizens of what is hap-

pening in state government."[6] When one such market or major city dominates the state, there is little chance for those in the remainder of the state to voice their own particular interests. A rural-urban or rural-suburban rift in the state's media coverage is the rule.

The states also vary greatly in terms of the number of newspapers published and television and radio stations broadcasting. In 1993, there was an average of 31 newspapers per state, ranging from 104 in California to 3 in Delaware.[7] In 1990, there was an average of 28 television stations per state, ranging from 108 in Texas to 3 in Delaware.[8] In 1990, there was an average of 212 radio stations per state, ranging from 689 in California to 21 in Delaware.[9] Much of the variation noted here is tied to the size of the state in terms of land area and population. But some of the variation is related to population diversity, with some newspapers and radio stations targeting specific populations.

How the Media Work in the States

There are several patterns in the way the media cover state politics and state government. They are tied to state politics, to policy making and administration in the states, and to the legislature.

During political campaigns, when candidates are vying for nominations and election to office, the media are involved selectively. Being involved can mean several things. The media cover some of the campaigns on a day-to-day or week-to-week basis, especially those campaigns with the greatest appeal in terms of what the media feel will sell papers or draw listeners and viewers.

In the 1990s, there is a perceptible decline in the coverage given to politics and government in the newspapers. For example, the political reporters in one large southeastern city were directed to cover only the presidential, congressional, gubernatorial, state legislative, and maybe one or two other contests. This meant the readers in that newspaper's market did not read anything about the other contests they would be voting on unless there was a scandal or major news event attending one of those races. There weren't, so in making their decision, the voters had to fall back on party identification, knowledge of the incumbent's name, or skip voting in that race entirely.

The media are also the major vehicle for political messages—the paid fifteen- or thirty-second campaign ads that we see on TV and hear on the radio and the printed advertisements we see in newspapers. In fact, a major new approach in getting messages to the voters is use of drive time radio, when potential voters are trapped in their cars and have to listen to what is coming at them from the car radio.

Some of the media become part of campaigns when they conduct public opinion polls, which delineate the important issues in the race and show which candidate is ahead. The media also become part of campaigns when they sponsor debates between the candidates and endorse candidates through editorials. A new role some newspapers have adopted is that of a monitor or critic of political campaign ads, especially those shown on television. In monitoring the ads, the papers have a reporter present the text of the political ad (often negative in tone and style), then match that with the facts of the situation. Then there is an analysis of the differences, if any.

For their part, candidates and their campaign organizations develop ways to obtain "unpaid media"—getting candidates and their names on TV or in print to increase their name recognition. Knowing when the major TV stations must have their tapes "in the can" for the nightly news can determine when a candidate makes an appearance or holds a press conference. Of course, any candidate is fearful of the "free media" coverage that comes with scandal or with missteps on his or her part.

A recent trend in some states and communities is for the media to practice what is called "civic" or "public" journalism. Here the media become part of the process of politics rather than just a reporter or critic of the process. The media actively try to set the political agenda rather than let the candidates do so. This is a controversial step, and nowhere is the controversy more heated than within the journalism profession itself.[10]

The second pattern in media coverage of state government is having the media become a part of the calculus by which decisions are made and actions are taken in politics and government. The best example of this is the pervasive influence that the *Manchester Union Leader* has on New Hampshire government and politics. This newspaper has run very conservative editorials on the front page for all to see. An observer of the state wrote in the 1960s that "[m]any state officials said they feared personal and vindictive editorial reprisal on the front page if they took exception to one of the paper's policies."[11] These officials felt "the paper has created an emotionally charged, reactionary atmosphere where new ideas are frequently not only rejected but fail to appear in print for public discussion."[12] In the 1980s, a political scientist observed that this paper "still profoundly shaped politics in the state,"[13] and in the 1990s, one state legislator grumbled that "political bias [is] demonstrated consistently in [its] stories as well as editorials."[14] This may or may not be an exception to how most papers operate. Sometimes such an atmosphere or situation can be created in more subtle ways than front page editorial attacks but exist nonetheless.

Other media organizations have acted in a more responsible manner over the years. These organizations have worked with those in government and politics to help their readers understand what is happening. For years, the *Louisville Courier-Journal* did this for Kentucky and for parts of adjoining states.[15] As one newsman argued, "Publishers have a responsibility to the public to do more. Call it public service, if you will ... but the press has the responsibility to enlighten and serve."[16]

The third pattern to media coverage and activity in the states has to do with the timing of state legislative sessions. There is an adage that when the legislature is in town, no one is safe. More to the point, when the legislature is in town, so are the media of the state. Not only do the capital press and media corps regulars cover general legislative activity, but specific newspapers and TV stations send reporters to cover the representatives from their city or county. Also, if there is some legislation that will have an impact on a particular section of the state, there most certainly will be media from that section to monitor what is happening.

This leads to some interesting observations by those who have watched this "cover-the-legislature-at-all-costs" phenomenon. First, coverage of other state government activities, programs, and individuals often is neglected as a result. Why? "[I]t's a lot easier to cover the legislature.... Stories are easy to get. Legislators seek out reporters, doling out juicy quotes and swapping hot rumors." Plus, editors want their reporters to be there. "When reporters aren't there, editors want to know why not."[17]

There have been some changes in the nature of the capital press corps. There tend to be fewer gray beards and more younger reporters than in the past. The tradeoff seems to be youth, vigor, and inexperience versus age and experience; hence the coverage may not be as good as in the past even though there may be more media folk involved. For example, the capital press corps in one state capital once operated under the following set of rules for new reporters: "(1) Don't fall down; (2) Don't get sick; and (3) Don't *ever* look like you don't know what you are doing."[18] No one knows what the rules might be now.

A major factor influencing how state governments and politics are covered by the media is the location and size of the state capital. In some states, the capital city is not the largest city; instead, it seems to be a "compromise" city between two large urban centers. Examples of this include Springfield, Illinois, located about two-thirds of the way from Chicago toward St. Louis, Missouri; Jefferson City, Missouri, located midway between St. Louis and Kansas City; and Trenton, New Jersey, located closer to the Philadelphia metropolitan area than to the New York area.

Some state capitals are near the geographic center of the state, such as Little Rock, Arkansas; Des Moines, Iowa; Oklahoma City, Oklahoma; and Columbia, South Carolina. However, several capitals are in what seem to be out-of-the-way locations, including Sacramento, California; Annapolis, Maryland; Albany, New York; and Carson City, Nevada. Still other states put their capital in the largest city, where most of the action takes place. Some examples of such capitals are Denver, Colorado; Atlanta, Georgia; Boston, Massachusetts; and Providence, Rhode Island.

When the state capital is in an out-of-the-way location, the media may find it more difficult to cover events since the government may be the only game in town. When there is not much action—or when the legislature adjourns—many in the press return to their home cities, leaving state government uncovered. When the state capital is located in the state's largest and most active city, there may be better coverage of state government, but that may be drowned out by the coverage of all the other activities in the city.

The National Media and the States

How do the national media treat what goes on in the states? One quick answer is that the national media do not cover the states unless a disaster occurs. Media specialist Doris Graber calls the national media's coverage of state issues "flashlight coverage."[19] She argues that there are basically two types of news in the eyes of the national media: high priority news and low priority news. The former is news that "has been judged in the past as intrinsically interesting to the audience by the usual news criteria…. [It is news that is] exciting, current, close to home, about familiar people, and audiences are likely to deem it relevant to their life." On the other side of the coin is low priority news, which "has been judged intrinsically uninteresting although it may be important."[20]

Graber argues that state news traditionally has been in the low priority news category, with only an occasional "entertainment or convenience item" receiving "a brief spotlight" in the news. However, when state news can be tied to high priority

news, such as national elections, coverage increases.[21]

Graber also argues that media coverage of state and local government has more holes than substance, which means "state and local issues get … short shrift in journalism." The media seek to "serve 'markets' rather than the political entities into which the nation has been divided."[22] Her prognosis for change is not good, "given the deep historical roots of our current media system."[23]

Working with the Press

There is another side to the media-government relationship: how those who serve in state government react to the role of the media. All governors, some state agencies, and a growing number of legislatures have established press offices to work with—and even cater to—the media and its needs. This means each governor has a press secretary or communications director. Recently, state legislators have realized the need for a media liaison who works either for a party caucus or the party leadership. Most agencies in state government have offices that work with the press.

For press offices, working with the media on a daily basis usually entails distributing press releases and answering queries. But press offices are also responsible for making sure that their bosses handle themselves properly with the media corps. At a recent New Governors Seminar sponsored by the National Governors' Association, newly elected governors were given the following advice on dealing with the media:

• Good press relations cannot save a poor administration, but poor press relations can destroy a good one.
• Never screw up on a slow news day.

• If you don't correct an error immediately, in the future you'll be forced to live with it as fact.

• Never argue with a person who buys ink by the barrel.

• When you hold a press conference and are going to face the lions, have some red meat to throw them or they'll chew on you. It should be something of substance, as long as the governor isn't the Christian.

• Never make policy at press conferences.[24]

At the 1990 New Governors Seminar, incumbent governors advised the newly elected governors to select their press secretary/communications directors quickly, as the position is a critical one. And in selecting that individual, "the main objective is to have someone who has the respect of the media and knows what is happening, and does not lie or misrepresent the Governor."[25]

Part IV provides some perspectives on the media in the states. Garry Boulard of *State Legislatures* shows how one influential state policy maker is able to control (or "stonewall") the press. Christopher Conte of *Governing* takes a careful look at "civic journalism," which some media are using to cover politics and government. And B. J. Roche of the new Massachusetts magazine *CommonWealth* talks about the all-too-familiar phenomenon of the disappearing family-owned newspaper.

Notes

1. Thad L. Beyle and G. Patrick Lynch, "The Media and State Politics." Paper presented at the annual meeting of the Midwest Political Science Association, Chicago, April 1991.

2. William T. Gormley Jr., "Coverage of State Government in the Mass Media," *State Government* 52:2 (Spring 1979): 46–47.

3. Ibid., 47.

4. V. O. Key Jr., *Public Opinion and American Democracy* (New York: Alfred Knopf, 1961), 381.

5. Terry Sanford, *Storm over the States* (New York: McGraw-Hill, 1967), 51.

6. Response by a New Hampshire state legislator to a 1990 survey question sent by the author.

7. Bureau of the Census, *Statistical Abstract of the United States, 1995* (Washington, D.C.: Government Printing Office, 1995), 580.

8. Bureau of the Census, U.S. Department of Commerce, "Cable Television, Broadcasting Stations, and Newspapers," *State and Metropolitan Area Data Book, 1991*, 4th ed. (Washington, D.C.: Government Printing Office), 280.

9. Ibid.

10. See Christopher Conte's article "Angels in the Newsroom" on pages 65–72.

11. Sanford, 50.

12. Ibid.

13. Richard F. Winters, "The New Hampshire Gubernatorial Election and Transition," in *Gubernatorial Transitions: 1982 Election*, ed. Thad Beyle (Durham, N.C.: Duke University Press, 1985), 304.

14. Response by a New Hampshire state legislator to a 1990 survey question sent by the author.

15. Sanford, 51.

16. Quoted in ibid., 52.

17. Jack Betts, "When the Legislature's in Session, Does Other News Take a Back Seat?" *North Carolina Insight* 12:1 (December 1989): 63.

18. Jack Betts, "The Capital Press Corps: When Being There Isn't Enough," *North Carolina Insight* 9:2 (September 1986): 48.

19. Doris A. Graber, "Flashlight Coverage: State News on National Broadcasts," *American Politics Quarterly* 17:3 (July 1989): 278.

20. Ibid., 288.

21. Ibid., 288–289.

22. Doris Graber, "Swiss Cheese Journalism," *State Government News* 36:7 (July 1993): 19.

23. Ibid., 21.

24. Thad L. Beyle and Robert Huefner, "Quips and Quotes from Old Governors to New," *Public Administration Review* 43:3 (May/June 1983): 268.

25. Thad Beyle, "Organizing the Transition Team," *Management Note* (Washington, D.C.: Office of State Services, National Governors' Association, 1990), 15.

Sensibly Stonewalling the Press

by Garry Boulard

The marble corridor of the statehouse looks more like a parapet for the press as dozens of print and broadcast reporters, tape recorders and microphones in hand, lie in wait.

Where do you stand on the controversial gun law being voted on today? How about the budget bill? The abortion amendment? The charges levied against you by your opponent back home?

What do you do?

If you're William Bulger, whose relationship with his home city press has been somewhat incendiary, you don't have to answer. Or you could even mutter the unthinkable: "I'm sorry, but I don't have an answer for you now. I'm still trying to think it out."

Heresy? In the era of hypermedia coverage, Bulger doesn't think so. In fact, he believes that sometimes stonewalling the press is the only sensible response.

"I doubt that many people in life would want to be staked to a position based on what they said in an impromptu press interview," says Bulger. "But lawmakers are all of the time.

"I honestly believe this," he continues, "we have a right to say 'no' to them. Just as they say 'I must keep you at arm's length lest I be co-opted by you,' we ought to be able to say the same thing. There is a real danger that we're being co-opted by them."

Bulger's complaint against the press transcends the usual gripe that reporters want to know too much, too often, too soon. He contends, instead, that because publishers and station owners have political points of view, reporters are little different from any of the other competing interest groups lawmakers daily contend with. They are only more dangerous, Bulger adds, because they have the ability to make their views widely known.

"I'm insufferable on this issue," Bulger laughs. But not without reason: In the mid-1970s as South Boston, under a federal busing order, simmered on the verge of racial conflagration, Bulger noticed that the city's press habitually classified a racial incident as any white-on-black violence.

Garry Boulard, a freelance writer from New Orleans, writes regularly for *State Legislatures* magazine, the *Los Angeles Times,* and the *Christian Science Monitor.* This article is reprinted from *State Legislatures* (June 1996): 15.

But the far more frequent black-on-white crimes, he argues, were written up only as simple criminal statistics from the daily police blotter.

That dichotomy, Bulger suggests in his memoirs, also infected the media's coverage of busing: "*Boston Globe* reporters, editorial writers and columnists who savaged us for resisting busing kept their children away from it," he writes. "Robert Turner, a *Globe* columnist who was particularly vitriolic toward us, enrolled his own children in Milton Academy, an outstanding school. Tom Wicker of the *New York Times* was asked, 'Why is it you advocate forced busing for our children, but then put your own children in private schools?' He answered that he would not sacrifice his children for his political beliefs!"

Nearly 20 years later, Bulger's relationship with the press hardened. A four-month investigation into whether he was improperly involved in a downtown Boston real estate development turned up no wrongdoing on his part, an event worthy of notice on Page 17 of the *Globe.*

Bulger notes, however, that before his exoneration, the *Globe* published nearly 20 stories on the investigation, "most of them on Page 1."

Lawmakers, Bulger advises, can enjoy productive relationships with the press by being honest and helpful—and inaccessible when so inclined. "The press is not the voice of the people, 'vox populi,' as they like to put it. They are entirely self-appointed," Bulger adds. "The constitutionally proper voices are from those who are elected. Lawmakers need to keep that in mind."

Angels in the Newsroom

by Christopher Conte

When the city council in Norfolk, Virginia, took out a full-page newspaper advertisement to gripe that leaders in the neighboring city of Virginia Beach had negotiated a regional water deal behind its back, the local newspaper had a ready-made story. It was dramatic, and it pitted well-known community figures against each other. But the *Virginian-Pilot* made an unusual decision: It buried the battle of the political heavies deep inside the paper, and instead led with a story about how members of civic groups in both cities wanted the politicians to set aside their differences so Virginia Beach could get the water it needed.

There were no journalism review articles about the *Virginian-Pilot*'s decision, but it's easy to imagine what they might have said. Had the paper implicitly editorialized by seeking out minor figures and giving their views prominent coverage just because it agreed with them? Was it playing down an important political conflict in order to engage in some civic boosterism? Was it naively ignoring the real decision-makers? Had the paper gone soft?

Editor Cole Campbell answers no to all these questions. "The citizens were be-ing far more reflective than their leaders were," says Campbell; by addressing the issues reasonably and constructively, the civic leagues were helping citizens work through their views on the water controversy. And that, Campbell argues, would contribute more to shaping public opinion—and hence, to resolving the water controversy—than the posturing and chest-beating of rival city council members.

Welcome to another day in the trenches at the *Virginian-Pilot*, where editors and reporters are practicing a new brand of journalism. "Public" or "civic" journalism, as it is called, seeks to restore grassroots democracy to America—and in the process recapture a vanishing audience for the news business. To that end, newspapers and television stations all around the country are convening public forums, pounding the pavement to seek out the views of ordinary citizens, giving readers more of a voice in news and editorial pages, and ac-

Christopher Conte, a longtime writer and editor for Congressional Quarterly and the *Wall Street Journal,* is a freelance writer specializing in communications issues. This article is reprinted from *Governing* (August 1996): 20–24.

tively enlisting citizens in a search for solutions to society's problems. "We aim," explains Tom Warhover, the *Virginian-Pilot*'s regional editor, "to put the 'participatory' back in 'participatory democracy.'"

All this should come as a welcome relief to government officials and others who see the press as too negative, too sensational and too irresponsible. But many journalists consider civic journalism dangerous. The movement has been variously branded a marketing gimmick and a presumptuous bid to set the political agenda. Critics contend that it destroys the idea that reporters should stand apart and tell the unvarnished truth, in favor of a feel-good, touchy-feely journalism that offends nobody—and makes no difference. Speaking for many conventional journalists, William Woo, editor of the *St. Louis Post-Dispatch,* worries that the reform movement could undermine traditional news values such as "objectivity, detachment, independence [and] the courage to print stories that are unpopular and for which there is no consensus."

This is a debate about more than journalism, however. Public journalism is part of a broader effort to strengthen civic life in America. It has attracted support from philanthropies—most notably, the Pew Charitable Trusts, which has provided news organizations more than $6 million since 1993 for public journalism projects, and which publicizes their efforts tirelessly through its Pew Center for Civic Journalism in Washington, D.C. The movement to reform journalism also parallels efforts of a growing number of local officials who say individuals and communities must develop greater capacity to solve their own problems because government can't afford to meet all their needs.

Civic journalism has little chance of succeeding, however, unless political leaders and citizens, as well as journalists, meet the challenge it presents: Will political leaders accept citizens as genuine participants in decision making rather than malleable tools to be either ignored or manipulated by sound-bites, negative ads and inflammatory "wedge issues"? And will citizens become truly deliberative—even if that means supporting a journalism that is more issue-oriented and thoughtful, but also, quite possibly, less entertaining?

At its most basic level, civic journalism seeks to reconnect with people who have dropped out of public life. That's no easy task for news people, whom many Americans have come to see as part of an uncaring political elite. Nevertheless, reporters and editors at the *Spokesman-Review* in Spokane, Washington, set out last year to rebuild some bridges to people on what they came to call the "ragged edge" of mainstream society.

Spokane is a good place for such a project: Its circulation area in eastern Washington and Idaho includes Ruby Ridge, where Randy Weaver had his disastrous shoot-out with federal authorities. It is home to a melange of former hippies, survivalists, secret militia members, struggling ranchers and timber industry cast-offs. Nothing in the experience of the newspaper people—all "baby boomers, white, middle class, and married to professional spouses," according to editor Rebecca Nappi—prepared them for the alienation they encountered. Nappi had to spend hours on the telephone just trying to persuade people to talk. Later, when a rumor circulated that reporter Jeanette White was a CIA agent, a man threw a fake punch at her; you're not CIA, he declared, after she showed no signs of self-defense training.

To build trust and start a community-wide dialogue, Nappi persuaded six area residents to write their own stories for a package of articles that explored why some people have become so angry and alienated. The guest columns helped shatter some stereotypes, and suggested that people have more nuanced views than standard sound-bite stories often acknowledge; one gun-control opponent, for instance, conceded that "a good case can be made for regulating guns" because "many among us … haven't displayed sufficient wisdom or discipline." He also suggested that America's gun problem arises from the fact that too many young people are denied "a good education with its promise of work and dignity."

Since the series ran, there have been some tentative signs of a new dialogue between deeply estranged parts of society. Government employees have asked the paper for a similar presentation of their lives and views. The paper has agreed. Meanwhile, it is conducting a survey to determine why people don't vote and trying to persuade a local talk-show host to let it present its findings on his program in hopes of building dialogue between the two audiences.

Public journalism is about more than just getting people to talk, though. It's about creating a particular, well-mannered kind of discussion, in which participants earnestly seek to find common ground. News people, the theory goes, have a special responsibility to make such discourse happen. Journalists should serve as "advocates for the kind of talk a mature polity requires … a useful dialogue, where we can know in common what we cannot know alone, and where the true problems of the political community come under serious discussion," writes Jay Rosen, director of the Project on Public Life and the Press, which is sponsored by the Kettering Foundation,

the Knight Foundation, the American Press Institute and New York University.

This implies correcting some bad journalistic habits, including a tendency to stress conflict and play up the extremes in debate, and to view public affairs from the perspective of insiders interested mainly in questions of strategy rather than from that of citizens concerned about the underlying moral issues. When Virginia Senator John Warner refused to endorse fellow Republican Oliver North in a 1994 race for the U.S. Senate, for instance, the *Virginian-Pilot* didn't dwell on the likely impact of the decision on Warner's or North's political future; rather, it invited readers to discuss when loyalty should give way to independence in politics. Similarly, to help readers sort out problems ranging from school bond issues to the future of Social Security, the *St. Paul Pioneer Press* is preparing a series of articles that will examine the responsibilities of different generations for each other. And in 1993, when rowdies were taking over a neighborhood park in Charlotte, North Carolina, the *Charlotte Observer* invited readers to suggest what should be done, but it said it would only print constructive suggestions.

To some, such unbounded faith in public discourse seems naive. "There seems to be this belief that U.S. society is a meritocracy played out on a level playing field, where political decisions are made according to rules laid down by the Marquis of Queensbury," notes Robert McChesney, professor of journalism and mass communication at the University of Wisconsin. "Civic journalism shows too little interest in the real world of organized politics and social ideologies. To the contrary, civic journalism deals with atomized individuals. Notions of class conflict and inequality are nowhere to be found." McChesney says a

From Lapdogs to Watchdogs

Slowly, the political climate in New Jersey is changing. And one of the biggest changes is the media, especially the aggressive new muscle-flexing by *The Star Ledger* of Newark.

For generations, the *Ledger* was the one element politicians could count on. Its credo was an unstated promise that if you run for office, the *Ledger* will not go out of its way to hurt you. Furthermore, if you get elected, the *Ledger* will make sure your views are well represented in the paper.

The *Ledger* was the voice of the status quo. Most of its reporters were expected to be chummy with their sources. And to keep the *Ledger* friendly, an elected official was expected to make sure that any important policy initiative would find its way into print there before any rival publication got wind of it.

At its most ludicrous, this journalistic symbiosis often meant that governors and their aides kept the *Ledger* happy by leaking the contents of a press release one day before issuing the release to other statewide media.

It wasn't that the *Ledger* was biased; it would print both sides of the story. But it was not aggressive. Governors, especially, knew that if they called the right person in the *Ledger* hierarchy, their calls would be answered.

But that benign approach to reporting went far beyond the pages of the *Ledger*. As the state's largest newspaper, the *Ledger* covered every aspect of state government. Rival newspapers may have wanted reporters to be more independent—but they also wanted them to have the same scoops as the *Ledger*.

Those days, thankfully, appear to have ended. The *Ledger* is changing its tune, with new editors and new reporters. Its once sleep-inducing editorials now bristle with "kick-their-butts" bravura.

Source: Excerpted from Jim Goodman, "From Lapdogs to Watchdogs," *New Jersey Reporter* (May/June 1996): 43, 45.

harder-hitting journalism, one that is more overtly political and that takes more seriously the old journalism objective to comfort the afflicted and afflict the comfortable, would do more than civic journalism to re-energize politics.

Some of the most innovative civic journalism projects can be found right in McChesney's back yard, where the *Wisconsin State Journal,* along with public and private television stations in Madison, have turned the televised forum into an art form. The "We the People" programs, often originating from government buildings, are rich in the symbolism of participatory democracy. In a 1994 mock trial, for instance, a "jury" of citizens heard "testimony" from two congressmen, a state legislator and an economist on health care reform. (The verdict: A single-payer system would be best.) Some sessions have actually attracted the largest television audience for their time period.

The televised events are just part of the picture. Before they are held, the news organizations sponsor "town meetings" where citizens can discuss the issues among themselves and hone questions for the later sessions with leaders. Separately, the *Wisconsin State Journal* periodically convenes meetings of community leaders to discuss ways to address issues highlighted in the newspaper.

Although discussions at all three levels can be substantive, there is a note of artificiality to this idea of democracy as docudrama. "It's designed to suggest that a real dialogue has taken place, but nothing ever comes of it," says John Nichols, a columnist for Madison's scrappy afternoon paper, the *Capital Times*. Nichols, who dismisses public journalism as a "marketing ploy," faults the town meeting organizers for randomly selecting citizen participants rather than choosing activists who really could make politicians "quake in their boots." And he says that convening community leaders puts the newspaper in all-too-cozy a relationship with Madison's power elite.

Still, Madison Mayor Paul Soglin says public journalism has made a difference. After the *Wisconsin State Journal* ran "City of Hope," a series of articles on urban problems, businesses effectively assumed responsibility for financing a city program to provide "job coaches" for at-risk teenagers, and the "leadership group" agreed to develop "career ladders" to help people advance beyond low-paying jobs. Moreover, while Soglin says he initially was concerned about the newspaper setting the agenda in the leadership group meetings, the newspaper has limited its role to that of facilitator. And in one notable case, civic journalism actually thwarted the newspaper's own political preferences: After the newspaper ran a series of articles and held town meetings on how to deal with suburban sprawl, voters elected a new slate of county supervisors who favored land use controls, even though the newspaper had endorsed the

pro-growth incumbents. "I am convinced their land use project changed the county board," Soglin says.

Many conventional journalists say convening public meetings commits the journalistic sin of making the news rather than just reporting it. But even worse, they say, is the emphasis public journalists put on finding solutions to social problems. "News reporters are supposed to explore the issues, not solve them," says Michael Gartner, chairman and editor of the *Daily Tribune* in Ames, Iowa, and a former president of NBC News. By linking news people with specific causes, he says, public journalism "ultimately will cost a newspaper its most precious asset—its credibility."

Leaders in the public journalism movement go to some lengths to show that they remain true to the principle that the press shouldn't engage in advocacy outside of the editorial pages. "We certainly don't presume to reform journalistic practices," says Rebecca Rimel, president of Pew Charitable Trusts. "But we do hope the news media will embrace practices that re-engage the public in the democratic process." And public journalism advocate Arthur Charity writes in *Doing Public Journalism,* a primer on the new journalism, that the ethical standard for the new journalists is to "advocate democracy without advocating particular solutions"—that is, to help people in their search to address problems without telling them what they should do.

The *Charlotte Observer* followed this maxim in a celebrated 1994 civic journalism project on life in troubled inner-city neighborhoods. Alongside conventional feature stories, the paper published lists of what community leaders said the neighborhoods needed. It subsequently reported on volunteer efforts designed to meet those needs. Partly to protect reporters' desire to maintain their professional detachment, the *Observer* hired a public relations expert to work with community people in drawing up the lists and to knock on doors persuading community residents to attend televised forums on neighborhood issues.

"What they did in Charlotte was quite traditional, except that they took their journalistic effort one step further," says Edward M. Fouhy, director of the Pew Center for Civic Journalism. "They weren't advocating, but they were pointing the community in the direction of a solution."

In some cases, though, attempts by public journalists to blend traditional journalism values with a more proactive stance have produced rather bizarre results. Last year, the *San Jose Mercury News* found itself in the awkward position of encouraging citizens to become politically involved and then restricting what it would let them do.

It all started innocently enough. When the paper published an investigative series on special-interest influence in the state legislature, it invited readers to contact it if they wanted to do something about the problem. Some 200 citizens accepted the offer. "Many of them were champing at the bit," recalls Assistant Managing Editor Jonathan Krim. "Some wanted to lobby for an initiative to limit campaign spending." That was too overtly political for the newspaper, however. Krim says *Mercury News* editors decided to restrict the group to "non-partisan" activities in order to make sure that "our position wasn't compromised."

Ultimately, the readers came up with what Krim describes as a "generic statement of accountability," which they asked legislators to sign. Even that rather bland activity left Krim uncomfortable. "We were pushing the envelope" of what journalists should do, he says, adding that he wishes in retrospect that the effort had focused more

exclusively on public education.

Experiences like that make civic journalists particularly wary of wading into political activism. They find it safer to deal with unorganized individuals or unofficial organizations, and to gauge the impact of civic journalism according to its impact on "social capital"—that is, the capacity of communities to address their own problems.

Lewis Friedland, an assistant professor of journalism at the University of Wisconsin, says the Charlotte neighborhoods project has had a "tangible, measurable" effect in increasing social capital: Volunteer efforts in the covered neighborhoods have increased, the pace of housing rehabilitation has stepped up, the mayor quickly acceded to public demands to build a community center in one neighborhood, the city heeded previously unmet calls to clear an overgrown lot where there had been a rape, and more. (Friedland's research, which was funded by Pew, is yet to be published.)

Charlotte's assistant city manager, Del Borgsdorf, agrees that the news coverage helped produce these results, but he does not view the project as an unqualified success. Televised public meetings on problem neighborhoods, he says, sometimes took on the tone of a "media inquisition," with some people who had never been active previously grabbing the limelight and making unsubstantiated charges against city government. In some cases, officials were stampeded into making decisions without the usual deliberation; the new community center, for instance, wasn't justified based on the underlying demographics and probably wasn't the community's biggest need, according to Borgsdorf.

Moreover, Borgsdorf worries about how enduring the changes at the *Observer* will be. Some of the key reporters have since moved on to other things, he says, and the paper has returned to the habit of demanding that government come up with programs to solve all problems. "The media raised expectations that whole neighborhoods should deliver what was needed, and then scored the government on the results," he concludes.

The *Observer* has tried to keep paying attention to the neighborhoods (it recently appointed a poverty and welfare reporter, for instance). But lack of resources in this era of downsized newsrooms and shrinking budgets limit what it, or any newspaper, can do. Indeed, the biggest obstacle public journalism faces may be that it costs a lot of money: It takes much more time and effort to figure out the amorphous public than to cover a handful of officials, and it's much harder to present news stories that depict all sides of an issue than to follow the simplistic convention of looking just for two, radically divergent sides.

Foundation money helps only marginally because it is available just for special projects, not the routine daily business of reporting the news. But an active citizenry needs higher-quality daily reporting more than voluminous special series, staged media events or well-publicized civic works projects. "The public isn't looking for newspapers to become a different kind of institution, or to be places where people can come together to solve problems," notes Richard Harwood, a Bethesda, Maryland, public affairs researcher and public journalism advocate. "They're looking for newspapers to produce better journalism—not to provide answers or solve their problems."

Harwood has worked with a number of newspapers to train reporters in "public listening," a technique for interacting with ordinary citizens designed to prevent stereotyping them or oversimplifying their views. He urges reporters to look for ambivalence, to stress the grays of public opinion, and to try to get beneath the emotionally charged "icons" of public discourse to people's underlying values. He says reporters should pay attention to areas of agreement, as well as conflict. And he urges them to listen closely for the connections people draw between seemingly disparate issues. Recently, Harwood worked with the *Wichita Eagle* to develop tools for listening to whole communities; in Wichita, he found, there were four different kinds of neighborhoods, and taking the pulse of each one required a different approach.

No newspaper has tried harder than Norfolk's *Virginian-Pilot* to apply the lessons of public journalism to daily reporting. It generally doesn't do splashy, elaborate projects. While it joined some other news organizations in running public forums on crime legislation last year, its only regular, overt public journalism exercise is to convene small "community conversations," in which reporters discuss specific issues with small groups of people. The real test of how well the paper does its job is to be found in little things, according to editor Campbell. "How often do you have a strong citizen orientation in the paper, framed in a way that engages people as political players, not consumers?" he asks. "That's how you measure success."

The *Virginian-Pilot*'s efforts, whether they involve helping a self-initiated citizens' group form to discuss school issues or seeking the views of civic leaders when politicians engage in parochial bickering, are just part of a larger mosaic. Norfolk and surrounding towns, known collectively as Hampton Roads, have a strong tradition of civic involvement. The Department of Neighborhood Services for the city of Hampton, for instance, sponsors a free, 10-class "college" to train activists in community organizing, public speaking and building partnerships with private businesses. In Portsmouth, a private, nonprofit corporation is helping a small black neighborhood rehabilitate homes, and a cultural diversity committee brought in consultants to help citizens meet in living rooms to consider race relations.

Government backing is crucial to the success of such citizen initiatives, says Toni Whitt, a *Virginian-Pilot* reporter who described the phenomenon in a 1995 article. "Where the programs have succeeded, government has offered its support, encouraging and nurturing the groundswell," she wrote. "Where government erects roadblocks, public involvement almost always collapses, creating more citizen apathy and dissatisfaction."

Alone, the press may be unable to foster healthy citizen participation, but it can help, not only by illuminating how people view issues but also by prodding people to sort out inconsistencies in their views. As Warhover, the *Virginian-Pilot* regional editor, puts it, "We bring the politicians' questions to the people, and the people's questions to the politicians. We can do a lot to bridge the gap."

Virginian-Pilot reporter Karen Weintraub engaged in some bridge-building this spring, when she examined widespread anger among Virginia Beach voters at the city's leaders. The citizens, she wrote, accused their city council of allowing runaway development that threatens the city's suburban ambiance. But the leaders felt falsely accused; they were powerless to prevent much of the growth that had occurred in recent years because it had been allowed by permits granted many years earlier.

Less than two weeks later, Weintraub wrote that the Virginia Beach Planning Department was seeking public comment on possible revisions to its comprehensive plan. Weintraub could have given the announcement the perfunctory treatment frequently accorded such a notice, but instead, she made a big deal of it. This was an opportunity, she told readers, to "change your city's future; to decide which empty lots become city parks and which turn into shopping centers; to suggest where new homes should be built or farmland preserved." Was she just setting up readers for another disappointment, asking them to buy into a process that might not make much difference and, in any event, would not show results for years to come?

"It's a leap of faith," concedes Weintraub. "But what's the alternative?"

The Disappearing Family-Owned Newspaper

by B. J. Roche

The [Berkshire] *Eagle* is the latest in a string of independent family-owned newspapers in Massachusetts that has gone over to corporate ownership in recent years, each for different reasons. The *Salem Evening News* was bought out by Ottaway Newspapers, ... a subsidiary of Dow Jones, after ... two branches of a family trust couldn't agree on a course for the paper.

The largest corporate owners in Massachusetts today aren't even a newspaper company: Fidelity Investments ... now owns more than 100 papers, mostly weeklies, in suburbs surrounding Boston.

Indeed, the family-owned newspaper seems to be headed the way of the black-and-white television. Fewer than 400 family-owned papers remain in the country by one estimate, but newspaper consultant Jack Authelet says each sale occurred for a different reason, ... [noting] the sell-off of the Ingersoll chain ... was forced by bad investments.

"Ingersoll got involved in junk bonds and lost everything," he says. "If the Millers hadn't lost their senses and gone into real estate, they'd still be publishing papers...."

One [consistent] factor ... is ... the tendency of third-generation ownership to undo what the first and second generations had created. "You take any business and look at the third generation, and they've screwed it up," says one journalist.... "There are too many cousins and brothers and aunts and uncles."

Just as corporate ownership can take away a local identity, it can also bring resources that rejuvenate a newspaper, Authelet says, citing *The Middlesex News,* now owned by Fidelity, as an example.

"What happens to papers is as diverse as the reasons why people want to sell," he says. "In some cases, you had some tired old publishers, and it's been refreshing to see a group come along and breathe some new ideas into a publication."

"The bad thing is that in a lot of these instances, where the bottom line becomes the overriding concern, you have people other than journalists making the decisions," he adds. "You have bankers making decisions, corporate officers making decisions, and this doesn't always equate to the best decision for Main Street U.S.A."

B. J. Roche teaches journalism at the University of Massachusetts, Amherst. This article is reprinted from *CommonWealth* (Spring 1996): 18.

V. STATE LEGISLATURES

In theory, state legislatures fulfill the representative democracy function in state government. Each legislator represents a particular district with particular interests. Legislators then meet in the state capital to meld the interests of the districts they represent with the interests of the state as a whole. The results of this tugging and hauling are the state budget, state policies, and occasionally a constitutional amendment.

In practice, however, state governments operate somewhat less democratically. Not everyone can afford to run for a seat in the state legislature, nor can many afford the time and loss of income that a legislator faces while serving in the legislature. So there tends to be a bias in just who serves based purely on economics: those who can afford to serve do, those who cannot don't. The resulting shortfall deprives a legislature of well-rounded representation of all the people of the state.

Further, subject-area specialists both within and outside the legislatures have an inordinate amount of power over legislators. This power relationship is concentrated toward those legislators who chair or are on money committees: finance or revenue, and appropriations. Because of their heavy workload, individual legislators increasingly must rely on these experts—their peers and lobbyists—for guidance on how to vote. Thus, in the basic operating processes of the legislature, some individuals, both inside and outside the legislature, wield more power than others.

Finally, once the legislation has been signed into law, the governor and the administrators of state agencies and programs are largely on their own to interpret and implement the laws. The courts often become important in helping define what a legislature really meant in passing certain legislation when conflicts arise. Or they can determine that the legislature was wrong in what it decided and declare a legislative act unconstitutional or void. In effect, the state legislature is only the starting point for action in the states. Once legislators have made their decisions, it is up to others to interpret, carry out, and resolve the issues created by legislation.

One Person, One Vote

Until the 1960s, everyone in a state was not equally represented in the legislature due to geographical bias. State legislatures determined how district lines were drawn and thus who would be represented in the legislature and to what extent. Legislatures used various devices such as the gerrymander (excessive manipulation of the shape of a legislative district to benefit a certain incumbent or party) or silent gerrymander (district lines were left intact despite major shifts in population).[1] Both types of legislative legerdemain resulted in underrepresentation of minorities and those living in the cities.

As a result of this misrepresentation, the U.S. Supreme Court ruled in the landmark decision *Baker v. Carr* (1962) that federal courts had the power to review legislative apportionment in the states. Two years later, in *Reynolds v. Sims,* the Court ruled that both houses of a state legislature must be apportioned on the basis of population—that is, "one person, one vote." And in the *Davis v. Bandemer* case (1986), the Court gave political parties standing in court suits over apportionment if a particular political party felt gerrymandered unfairly. And which party won't feel treated unfairly if it does not get the legislative apportionment plan that helps it the most? In *Colgrove v. Green* (1946), the Court indicated that it wanted to stay out of the "political thicket" of apportionment; forty years later it jumped squarely into that thicket.

Redistricting is always one of the most politically charged issues that state legislatures find on their agendas, since it directly affects the legislators themselves and is so overtly political. Each party tries to maximize its potential strength in future elections, and concurrently reduce the power of the opposition.

In the latest round of redrawing the lines following the 1990 Census, several of the states were compelled to create districts with enough minority strength to ensure that a minority representative would be elected. In essence, some of the states were compelled to use a "racial gerrymander" to increase the number of minorities in Congress and in state legislatures. The result has led to a new legislature computer game called "shapes," which replaces the older and neater game of "blocks."[2] "Blocks" used counties, townships, cities, and voting districts as the building units (or "blocks") for creating districts. In "shapes," computers are used to create new districts that maximize the representation prospects of minorities.

While use of blocks usually resulted in neat, box- or rectangularlike districts, the latest shapes to emerge from the computers are considerably more difficult to define. The Texas legislature created what looks like a snowflake district in Houston and the Illinois legislature developed a district that has been likened to an earmuff in Chicago. The North Carolina legislature added the so-called "I-85" district that sits astride an interstate highway running from Durham to west of Charlotte and has been likened to a snake.

The basic redistricting game remains the same: trying to provide equal representation for all citizens. But in some cases the legislatures had to work harder to ensure that some citizens got the representation they should have. Without such torturous and directed line-drawing activities, some minorities would remain submerged in majority-dominated districts. Put simply, their candidates would never win. However, some argue that this type of redistricting actually reduces the overall power of such minorities because their presence in other districts is reduced in order to "pack" them into a minority-majority district.

This situation is slowly being resolved by the U.S. Supreme Court, as lawsuits challenging racial gerrymandering in several states are on appeal. The plaintiffs in these cases are generally members of the majority white race arguing that in creating districts in which minorities will win, the legislature has violated their rights. In June 1995, the Court struck down Georgia's congressional district map as racial gerrymandering violating the Constitution's guarantees of equal protection under the law.[3] In 1996, North Carolina's "snake" district was rejected by the U.S. Supreme Court. The Court directed the North Carolina legislature to redraw the district before the 1998 elections.[4] The partisan split control legislature was able to develop a new plan with new district lines for the 1998 elections.

Much is made over how distorted the shapes of some districts are, but there are larger questions involved. Should this so-called racial gerrymandering be declared unconstitutional, just as other forms of gerrymandering have been? Is there a legitimate community of interest gathered within these shapes, similar to those in towns, counties, and cities?

Legislative Reforms

The original reapportionment decisions coincided with a general revival of state government during the mid- to late 1960s. The revival came at a time when the states sorely needed a new, more positive image. Numerous publications described the apparent failures, unrepresentativeness, and corruption of state governments.[5] It took national legislation such as the Civil Rights Act of 1964 and the Voting Rights Act of 1965 and U.S. Supreme Court decisions to force state governments to fulfill their responsibilities to those they represented.

In the 1970s and 1980s, state after state passed laws that drastically reformed state legislatures and improved their public image. Some of the most important of these reforms include providing offices for legislators, creating greater staff capability for the legislature and for individual legislators, installing newer technology to assist and monitor legislative action, removing some restrictions on schedules and sessions while tightening deadlines for action, moving to longer annual sessions, and providing for longer terms.

In the 1990s, more changes are afoot as voters in many states have made their state legislatures the target of the initiative process. Reform now is aimed at restricting rather than enhancing legislatures. In many states, the term limit movement has taken direct aim at the state legislatures. The 1990 term limits initiative in California "also cut the legislature's operating budget by 38 percent. Layoffs of staff began soon after, and California's staff has been cut substantially."[6]

Why are voters targeting their legislatures? One reason might be the continuing decline in public esteem of state elected officials. A recent analysis of state polls asking citizens about the performance of their state legislatures found more indicating the legislature was doing a fair or poor job than indicating it was doing an excellent job.[7]

Another reason for a decline in citizens' views of how well legislatures operate is the increasing number of states in which scandals have been found. The roster of states with such problems continues to grow.[8] A December 1996 Gallup Poll asked a nationwide sample of adults how they "would rate the honesty and ethical standards" in a variety of fields. State office holders ranked fourth from the bottom of a list of twenty-six fields, with only 13 percent of the respondents rating them very high or high—just ahead of car and insurance salespeople and advertising professionals.[9] Alan Ehrenhalt suggests that the trend toward negative campaigning may also be a factor. The negativity of campaign rhetoric often leaves voters with the feeling that they are selecting the lesser of two evils when they make their decision.[10]

But some observers argue that a major cause for the decline in public support has a budgetary policy base to it. In the 1980s, the economy grew and state revenues outpaced state expenditures. It was easy to make decisions with an ever-increasing pot of money available. New or additional taxes were not needed to provide more for citizens. Beginning in the late 1980s and continuing into the 1990s, however, the states and their elected leaders began facing hard times as the economy faltered nationally and, in some states, catastrophically. The decision calculus changed dramatically as legislators and governors were forced to raise taxes even as they cut back on state services.[11] Now in the mid-1990s the cutting mood in the legislatures continues, especially following the 1994 elections, even though revenues are healthier in many states.

Separation of Powers

State legislatures do not operate in a vacuum. In most instances they are uneasy partners with other actors in state government. Other parts of state government, not just the legislatures, were reformed in response to the "indictment" of the states in the 1960s. Gubernatorial powers were strengthened to make governors the chief executives of the states in fact, rather than just in theory. However, these reforms did little to reduce the natural conflict between the executive and legislative branches that is built into state constitutions.

The U.S. Constitution and state constitutions share a fundamental principle: separation of powers. Consider, for example, this article from the Colorado Constitution that clearly separates legislative, executive, and judicial authority:

Article III. Distribution of Powers. The powers of the government of this state are divided into three distinct departments, the legislative, executive and judicial; and no person or collection of persons charged with the exercise of powers properly belonging to one of these departments shall exercise any power properly belonging to either of the others, except as in this constitution expressly directed or permitted.

Executive Branch Appointments. Appointments are perhaps the area of greatest tension between the executive and legislative branches of state government. Legislatures often have a constitutionally mandated power to confirm gubernatorial appointments. They can cause the governor problems with this authority by refusing to confirm appointments.

In some states, legislatures have the statutory or constitutional authority to make appointments to boards and commissions; they even can appoint their own members to these positions. Only four states strictly ban legislators from serving on boards and commissions. Eleven states allow legislators to serve on advisory bodies only. This "legislative intrusion" into the executive branch has been challenged successfully in Kentucky, Mississippi, and North Carolina.

Legislative Veto. A second area of tension lies in the increasing use of the legislative veto—a procedure permitting state legislatures (and the U.S. Congress) "to review proposed executive branch regulations or actions and to block or modify those with which they disagree."[12] In lieu of legislative veto legislation, some states have enacted laws regarding review of administrative rule-making procedures.

In the early 1980s there was a rapid rise in the use of the legislative veto—up to forty-one states by mid-1982. However, the tide then turned against this legislative bid to gain increased control over the executive branch. Courts, both state and federal, invalidated the legislative veto as an unconstitutional violation of the separation of powers principle.[13] And voters in several states rejected their legislature's use of a legislative veto.[14] In the 1990s, two state high courts—Idaho and Wisconsin—have reopened this power for their legislatures, albeit with some restrictions.[15]

The State Budget

With all of the action focused on the state budget, it is no surprise that power politics is also involved. In some states, governors and legislative leaders are locked in a struggle over who will control the state's finances. Because of uncertainty over projecting next year's revenues, the need to cut back on expenditures, or even whether or not to raise taxes, budgets are being adopted much later than in the past—some well into the budget year. Governors want increased power and flexibility over budget making, while legislators find themselves forced to make difficult decisions with little time for deliberation.

Further, when governors and legislatures argue over the budget, delays in providing funds for programs and local governments occur. This leads to the embarrassing situation of the governor and legislature fighting budget battles in broad daylight with a seeming "inability to make even the most basic decisions on time."[16]

Part V explores different aspects of state legislatures. Jennifer Babson of *CommonWealth* provides a case study of the "bill killer committee" in the Massachusetts state house. Charles Mahtesian of *Governing* takes a critical look at whether reform really works in state legislative bodies. And Alan Rosenthal of *State Government News* points out the fine ethical line state legislators must walk.

Notes

1. The term "gerrymander" originated in 1812, the year the Massachusetts legislature carved a district out of Essex County that historian John Fiske said had a "dragonlike contour." When the painter Gilbert Stuart saw the misshapen district, he penciled in a head, wings, and claws and exclaimed: "That will do for a salamander!"—to which editor Benjamin Russell replied: "Better say a Gerrymander"—after Elbridge Gerry, the governor of Massachusetts. Congressional Quarterly's *Guide to U.S. Elections,*

2d ed. (Washington, D.C.: Congressional Quarterly, 1985), 691.

2. See Kimball W. Brace and Doug Chapin, "Shades of Redistricting," *State Government News* 34:12 (December 1991): 6–9.

3. *Miller v. Johnson* (1995).

4. *Shaw v. Reno* (1996).

5. See, for example, Frank Trippett, *The States—United They Fell* (New York: World Publishing, 1967).

6. Alan Rosenthal, "The Legislative Institution—In Transition and at Risk," in *The State of the States,* 2d ed., ed. Carl E. Van Horn (Washington, D.C.: CQ Press, 1993), 127.

7. Karl T. Kurtz, "The Public Standing of the Legislature," National Conference of State Legislatures, August 1991.

8. To learn more about this problem, see "Evaluating State Legislatures," *State Policy Reports* 9:4 (January 1991): 8–13; Rob Gurwitt, "Deadly Stings and Wounded Legislatures," *Governing* 4:9 (June 1991): 26–31; and Jeffrey L. Katz, "Sipping from the Cup of Corruption," *Governing* 5:2 (November 1991): 27–28.

9. Leslie McAnemy, "Honesty and Ethics," *The Polling Report,* January 13, 1997, 8.

10. Alan Ehrenhalt, "An Embattled Institution," *Governing* 5:4 (January 1992): 28.

11. Rosenthal, "The Legislative Institution," and Thad Beyle, *Governors and Hard Times* (Washington, D.C.: CQ Press, 1992).

12. Walter J. Oleszek, *Congressional Procedures and the Policy Process,* 3d ed. (Washington, D.C.: CQ Press, 1988), 297.

13. The Supreme Court case was *Immigration and Naturalization Service v. Jagdish Rai Chadha* (1983).

14. New Jersey in 1985, Alaska and Michigan in 1986, Nevada in 1988.

15. "Idaho Court Says Legislature May Veto Administrative Rules," *State Legislatures* 16:6 (July 1990): 14; and "Wisconsin Finds No Separation of Power Violation in Statute Authorizing Legislative Committee to Suspend Administrative Rule," *State Constitutional Law Bulletin* 5:6 (March 1992): 1–2.

16. Linda Wagar, "Power Play," *State Government News* 35:7 (July 1992): 9.

A Look at the Legislature's Most Mysterious Committee

by Jennifer Babson

Rep. David B. Cohen concedes that his committee does not frequently command the public spotlight.

"When I was first elected, I don't think I knew there was a 'Bills in the Third Reading,'" the Newton Democrat laughs. Perhaps that is due to the fact that the House committee Cohen chairs holds no public hearings; no official meetings among its three members; and operates in quiet efficiency in a basement office in the Statehouse.

The committee is charged with vetting bills—those that have already made their way through the committee system—for their state constitutionality before they are permitted final consideration on the House floor. It functions, in part, as a legal copy editor for state legislators (some of whom may not be well-versed in the particulars of Massachusetts code). Does a bill reference the wrong section of the law? Maybe the definition of the measure "does not make sense," as one House counsel put it. Or perhaps the bill is littered with the kind of grammatical errors that would make a third-grade teacher blush. Members need not worry, says Cohen, an attorney, because the committee will clean those things up. (The Senate has its own version of the panel.)

While the committee has reported hundreds of bills to the floor within this House session alone, that leaves hundreds of others, according to some estimates, that have yet to emerge from Third Reading. If a measure not destined—due to content or poor drafting—for the House floor lands in Third Reading, the panel has three ways of dispensing with the bill. "We can hold onto it," Cohen says, until the end of the session (two years), when it automatically expires; the committee may file a special report asking that it be discharged of further action on the bill (a sign that Third Reading has serious problems with it); or the panel may send it back to committee with a request that changes be made. (The committee itself is permitted to make technical changes to bills.)

Third Reading has earned the reputation as a "graveyard" of sorts for legislation that House leaders have little interest in putting to a final, recorded vote. The

Jennifer Babson is associate editor of *CommonWealth*. This article is reprinted from *CommonWealth* (Spring 1996): 11–12.

House counsel, who reports to Speaker Charles F. Flaherty, plays a central role, along with Cohen, in determining whether a measure will receive the Third Reading stamp of approval. Cohen says the committee does not keep track of how many measures fail to make it out of Third Reading. The committee's defenders point out that few other states require, as Massachusetts does, that state representatives file bills on behalf of constituents who petition them to do so. This leads, defenders say, to an avalanche of legislation, the bulk of which lawmakers do not have time to consider.

But critics contend the committee has become another tool that leaders use to shape the agenda of the House. "The idea is to have a committee whose role is to make sure the bills are in proper form," says Paul Fitzgerald, executive director of Common Cause Massachusetts, a nonprofit watchdog group. "The problem occurs when you don't use that to go through the process but you use it to control the process." One could say the committee has a high success rate: Rarely does a measure reported out of Third Reading fail to win final passage in the House.

But "sometimes bills languish in there forever, because representatives don't real-ize that they need to bring it to the attention of the committee chairman," says Rep. Carol A. Donovan (D-Woburn), who served as vice-chair of the committee last year. If the Speaker desires an immediate floor vote on a bill that has not yet been reported out of Third Reading, at least one member of the panel must be present to report the bill from the committee with the stroke of a pen. "One of us had to be at all of the sessions," says Donovan. "If the Speaker or Majority Leader wanted something, we had to be there." And unlike in the Senate, which recently saw a series of internal rules reforms, bills in the House are not required to be placed on a floor calendar prior to their consideration. They may be brought up at any time.

The movement of some bills straight from Third Reading to a floor vote and passage during informal House sessions (in which measures deemed "noncontroversial" may be passed by a voice vote of the members who are present) has irked some lawmakers. But Cohen says criticism, which he claims is infrequent, comes with his job: "If I bring up a bill too quickly, I'm subject to the complaint that it has been greased," Cohen says. "If I take too much time, I'm sitting on it."

The Sick Legislature Syndrome and How to Avoid It

by Charles Mahtesian

One quick look at the Minnesota legislature tells you that it is a state-of-the-art political institution, all fitted out for the interactive democracy of the next century.

There is gavel-to-gavel televised coverage of every session, something very few states provide. Voters can use the Internet to peruse bill texts and bill status, committee schedules, press releases and biographies of the members.

Every Friday, *Session Weekly,* an informative and readable journal published by the nonpartisan House Public Information Office, reports on the highlights of each week's activity. All of this is provided to the public free of charge.

The same brief glance at Tennessee's legislature suggests that the Volunteer State is, one might say, a little amateurish. There is no televised coverage, and there is no Internet site. Tennessee is one of only two states that don't have one [as of February 1997]. In Nashville, they brag about how they rank 48th out of 50 in per-capita legislative branch expenditures. In fact, Tennessee spends less than half of what Minnesota spends—despite being home to a half-million more residents.

Over the past couple of decades, while Minnesota was winning national praise for innovations such as public campaign financing and gender pay equity, Tennessee's legislature went almost completely unnoticed until recently, when frivolous arguments over a Ten Commandments resolution and the teaching of creationism attracted nationwide ridicule.

It probably won't surprise you to learn that last year, one of these two bodies conducted an efficient, productive and thoroughly civilized legislative session, something it has done every single year during the 1990s. Or that the other has sunk into a humiliating morass of bitter partisanship and personal scandal.

What will surprise you is which of these legislatures is which.

In the past four years, voters in Minnesota have been bombarded with tawdry tales of errant members nabbed for shoplifting, fraud, drunk driving, spousal assault and spreading false rumors about constituents. A scandal surrounding the misuse of state phone card privileges led to

Charles Mahtesian is a staff writer for *Governing.* This article is reprinted from *Governing* (February 1997): 16–20.

the resignation of the House majority leader and the eventual ouster of the speaker in 1993. All in all, lawmakers there have exhibited a stunning knack for discrediting their institution, accumulating a body of offenses that equals, if it does not surpass, some of the more egregious transgressions of their colleagues in other states.

By last fall, all sense of collegiality had vanished from the Minnesota House. Since nearly all of the turmoil had occurred on the Democratic side of the aisle, Republicans took the opportunity to portray the ethical chaos as the arrogant excesses of an entrenched majority. Governor Arne Carlson's spokeswoman herself openly mused about the "thieves and drunks" of the state legislature.

Meanwhile, the Democratic caucus itself was in full-scale revolt against its speaker, the combatively partisan Irv Anderson. Two of Anderson's fellow Democrats took their criticism to the editorial pages of the *St. Paul Pioneer Press,* blaming Anderson for gridlock and calling for his removal. Within a week of last November's elections, he was unceremoniously dumped from the speakership.

As for the voters, they apparently found the Republican tactics almost as unappealing as the scandals themselves. Democrats actually survived the election with one more House seat than they had before it. But the voters made their feelings clear. They not only stayed home from the polls in record numbers, but overwhelmingly approved a ballot measure permitting recall of virtually anyone holding elected office. The entire episode suggests one compelling lesson: If the Minnesota legislature is the state of the art, there must be something wrong with the art.

In Tennessee, meanwhile, the year concluded as inconspicuously as it began.

There were few surprises at the ballot box, and legislators' personal foibles remained largely out of the public eye. The 1996 legislative product was steady, if unspectacular; nearly all interested parties received a little of what they wanted with a minimum of rancor. Republican Governor Don Sundquist's welfare reform package passed, but with more than 40 amendments. Business and labor both claimed small victories on workers' compensation. State employees received a raise that was not quite what they asked for, but about what they could reasonably expect. "We all don't get what we want with every piece of legislation that passes," says House Speaker Jimmy Naifeh. "We need to remember that half a loaf is better than none."

In short, it was a typical year in the Tennessee legislature, displaying the balance that has enabled it to compile a consistently impressive record of substantive work throughout the 1990s. While most states were engaged in futile hand-wringing over exploding Medicaid expenditures, Tennessee created TennCare, the nation's most ambitious Medicaid overhaul. Long before higher education accountability issues were on the national radar, Tennessee established a performance-based funding mechanism that linked dollars to outcomes—the first of its kind in the nation. Over the course of the decade, the Volunteer State has enacted a wide-ranging K–12 education package and comprehensive campaign finance, ethics and lobbying legislation.

And it has done all that while holding to a level of comity and bipartisanship that is foreign to most chambers these days. "In Tennessee," says Senate Speaker John Wilder, who by statute also holds the position of lieutenant governor, "we don't have to shut down the government before we sit down and talk."

Three Flavors of State Legislatures:
Professional, Hybrid, and Citizen

Professional (10)	Hybrid (23)	Citizen (17)
California	Alabama	Arkansas
Florida	Alaska	Georgia
Illinois	Arizona	Idaho
Massachusetts	Colorado	Indiana
Michigan	Connecticut	Maine
New Jersey	Delaware	Mississippi
New York	Hawaii	Montana
Ohio	Iowa	Nevada
Pennsylvania	Kansas	New Hampshire
Wisconsin	Kentucky	New Mexico
	Louisiana	North Dakota
	Maryland	Rhode Island
	Minnesota	South Dakota
	Missouri	Utah
	Nebraska	Vermont
	North Carolina	West Virginia
	Oklahoma	Wyoming
	Oregon	
	South Carolina	
	Tennessee	
	Texas	
	Virginia	
	Washington	

Note: Professional: full-time, large staff, relatively high pay, stable membership; Citizen: part-time, small staff, low pay, high turnover; Hybrid: somewhere between professional and citizen.

Source: National Conference of State Legislatures.

Even under Sundquist, a more partisan figure than any of his recent predecessors, the Republican governor and the Democratic legislature have exhibited a pronounced ability to coexist. Of all the freshman Republican governors who came into office in 1994 facing sizable Democratic opposition, Sundquist arguably has registered the most success in enacting his agenda.

That is no coincidence. Because while Tennessee's legislative system is far from perfect, it speaks to the value of simple qualities such as civility that have been largely lost in the legislatures that have rushed headlong toward professionalism. The Minnesotas and the Californias of American politics aren't laughing at Tennessee anymore. What they want to know is how they can get some of that old-fashioned decency back.

California, the flagship of legislative professionalism, remains the most dramatic exhibit. Stable leadership is nonexistent there. Within the last year and a half alone, five different speakers have held the House gavel. The sense of angry partisanship reaches beyond chamber doors and into the electoral arena, where opposition members are targeted for recall for the slightest provocation. Within the capitol, the halls are choked with representatives of special interests—1,100 registered lobbyists at last count—all narrowly focused and a constant reminder of the high stakes of modern legislating.

Not all of the 10 state bodies classified as "professional" by the National Conference of State Legislatures bear all of these symptoms. But enough of them do to make the pattern unmistakable. Professionalism creates an institution filled with able, full-time legislators, talented staff and generous resources. And yet many of these institutions become hopelessly polarized, from the back benches to the rostrum. It isn't difficult to find professionalized legislatures elsewhere in the country that have shown symptoms of the Minnesota problem in one way or another.

In Pennsylvania, for example, the Senate shut down for much of 1993 because the result of a single special election threatened the razor-thin Democratic numerical advantage. Few were surprised by this tactic: The previous year, Republicans had pulled a similar stunt for fear one of their own would switch party allegiance. It is the cutthroat competition for control in a close partisan situation that explains why, during the past decade in Pennsylvania, ethically tainted members from both sides of the aisle have routinely escaped discipline.

In New York, sharp-elbowed partisanship between legislative leaders virtually guarantees an annual budget standoff. Since a threesome comprised of the governor, the Democratic Assembly speaker and the Republican Senate leader dominates in Albany, there is no effective mechanism for resolving the partisan differences. Last year, New York set a new record by delivering a budget that was 103 days past due.

Illinois is not much different in its partisan ferocity. In 1996, for example, when Republican Governor Jim Edgar offered a wide-ranging school finance package amidst an all-out GOP effort to retain its recently acquired House majority, his proposal was immediately rejected and scorned by his own party. The potential political consequences, it seems, were too great. And Democrats were too close to winning back the House for Republicans to want to take the risk. (As it turned out, the Democrats won the House back anyway.)

Meanwhile, there are signs that the "sick legislature" syndrome is spreading to states that have been relatively free of it thus far. In Florida, where Republicans took control in 1996 for the first time since Reconstruction, Democrats insisted on challenging the credentials of six victorious GOP legislators. Republicans, in turn, registered two challenges of their own. During the legislature's organizational session, a group of lawmakers angrily objected not only to the content of the opening prayer but to the composition of the veterans' delegation that led the Pledge of Allegiance.

The irony was hard to miss. Only recently Florida had been recognized as the 10th and latest state to join the ranks of fully professionalized legislative bodies.

Not everyone in the Minnesota legislature accepts the notion that the onslaught of professionalism is at the root of the recent years' embarrassments. But an increasing number of members, past and present, are beginning to acknowledge that professionalism, partisanship and incivility are linked to each other in some unholy way. "The legislature was less partisan when it was more of a part-time body," says John Brandl, a former leader in the Minnesota House and Senate who now teaches at the Hubert H. Humphrey Institute in Minneapolis. "People are becoming so dependent on their position in the legislature and so self-protective that they can't see the institution for what it is."

There is no simple explanation for how Minnesota got that way, but there is a history, and it stretches back at least as far as 1979—the year the Minnesota House was split evenly between the two parties. Democrats, seizing on campaign practice violations against newly elected Republican Representative Robert Pavlak, moved to expel him, then took advantage of his absence to seize control of the chamber, 67 votes to 66.

To a Republican caucus comprised mainly of first-term members, it was a jarring introduction. And they have never forgotten it. "That was my eye-opening to Minnesota legislative politics," says Steve Sviggum, the current GOP House leader. "That was the absolute worst power politics I've ever seen."

Over the course of the 1980s, with party control up for grabs, those same tensions hardened into a conviction on both sides that they were entitled to pursue their goals by any means necessary. "As each party assumed power," political scientist Royce Hanson wrote in 1989, "it used its organizational and procedural power to humiliate the minority, producing a thirst for revenge among the members who could hardly wait for their turn in power to get even."

The growing partisan hostilities of the Minnesota House are reflected in simple physical changes. At one time members chose their seats on the House floor by se-

niority, regardless of party. Now the parties face each other across a dividing aisle. And the members' offices, once scattered haphazardly through the legislative building across from the Capitol, are now on two different floors, one for the Democrats, one for the Republicans.

About the only remaining link to an earlier era in the Minnesota House is the continued presence of Irv Anderson, the Democrat who engineered the Pavlak expulsion ploy in 1978 and served as speaker during the party's recent time of troubles in 1995 and 1996. Anderson missed most of the changes of the 1980s after losing his bid for reelection in 1982, but he returned to the chamber in 1990, and by 1993 he was the presiding officer. A gruff, acerbic and brilliant tactician from International Falls, the coldest city in America, Anderson acceded to the speakership in 1993 promising a kinder, gentler, "new Irv." But by last April, the updated Anderson did not seem at all different from the vindictive and iron-fisted leader both parties remembered. He ran the institution with the same single-minded goal he had emphasized in his earlier tour of duty: maintenance of partisan control at any cost. Republican parliamentary concerns were routinely ignored and dismissed. Their committee placement requests went unheeded.

In the end, whatever Anderson's motives were, his campaign strategy worked—Democrats held the House. But he paid for it by losing the speakership.

There is one difference between Tennessee and Minnesota that you won't pick up just by listening to the rhetoric or watching the proceedings on the floor. It is in the composition of the membership.

In Minnesota, NCSL classifies at least 30 members as "full-time legislators," and that is certainly fewer than the actual number, because many who do little else besides legislating still list some other occupation for the record. There is, in addition, a sizable contingent of government employees, teachers and labor officials. In Tennessee, only one legislator lists his occupation as full-time. The largest number are farmers or lawyers, or are drawn from the ranks of business. A 1993 NCSL study ranked Tennessee second in the nation (after Alaska) in the percentage of business owners serving as legislators.

None of this is to say that any one profession is better suited to lawmaking than another. But it is hard to avoid noticing some degree of correspondence between professionalism and partisan acrimony. If professional legislatures attract more talented and better-informed members—and few dispute that they do—it is equally certain that these same members have difficulty avoiding partisan collisions with each other.

Members who have devoted lives and careers to legislative service have a tendency to bristle at any perceived threats to it. In moments of conflict, they are all too aware that a reversal of fortune is only a controversial vote and one election cycle away. "There's more members who see their position as their full-time or primary occupation," says Minnesota's Robert Vanasek, who served as House speaker from 1987 to 1991, "and one of the consequences is that thinking about reelection is much more on their minds."

Within the framework of the professional legislature, there is a certain inevitability to those partisan confrontations, because a body filled with capable legislators and skilled staff is unlikely to content itself with passing innocuous resolutions. Minnesota's 1995–96 regular session alone saw the introduction of 6,185 bills that touched nearly every industry, interest and enterprise in the state, ranging from wind-power energy to wine-tastings at bed-and-breakfasts.

Not only do interest groups grow more active and more sophisticated but some of the largest and most influential of these groups gradually evolve into appendages of the state parties—or perhaps vice versa. "It's not that we can't do things," says Senator John Marty, the 1994 Democratic gubernatorial nominee. "It's that there are pressures stopping them."

In the Minnesota legislature, a liberal, labor-dominated Democratic conference collides with a Republican conference of anti-tax zealots, anchored in affluent suburbs and rural areas where anti-tax and low-spending pressures are the greatest. Between one caucus grounded in the notion of an activist government and another committed to de-funding and dismantling it, consensus has been almost impossible to find. The two parties are no longer merely at odds, they are now diametrically opposed to one another. "The worlds they are representing," observes University of Minnesota political scientist Frank Sorauf, "are increasingly divergent and homogeneous."

Witness the wildly disparate assessments of the 1996 legislative session offered by each party's leaders. "We did what we promised to do last January," Speaker Anderson declared in April. "Pass legislation that makes streets safer, government more accountable, jobs more rewarding and education more effective." If that was indeed the outcome, then Republicans missed it altogether. "The people of Minnesota were the losers," concluded Steve Sviggum. "This was a frustrating session for those of us who expect accountability and responsibility in government."

Women in State Legislatures, 1969–97

Year	Percentage of total
1969	4.0
1971	4.5
1973	5.6
1975	8.0
1977	9.1
1979	10.3
1981	12.1
1983	13.3
1985	14.8
1987	15.7
1989	17.0
1991	18.3
1993	20.5
1995	20.6
1996	20.7
1997	21.3

Source: Center for the American Woman and Politics (CAWP), National Information Bank on Women in Public Office, Eagleton Institute of Politics, Rutgers University.

Tennessee passed a partisan milestone in 1995, but it did so in a remarkably civilized way. Late in the year, two party switches handed Republicans a tenuous one-vote Senate majority. The first thing the GOP did was to allow John Wilder, the Democratic Senate speaker, to remain in the job he had held since 1971. Then, with control of the chamber up for grabs in the coming general election, they actively discouraged GOP opposition to Wilder in his home district.

As implausible as those decisions might have seemed in most other states, in Tennessee they barely raised eyebrows. Wilder was simply reaping the returns on his own style of stewardship. It was he, after all, who had initiated the practice of naming Republicans as committee chairs while they remained in the minority in the mid-1980s.

Even the most partisan senator would agree that Wilder harbors an abiding preoccupation with maintaining the chamber's civility and a collegial approach toward policy making. Last year, when the legislature passed a resolution naming a new state golf course after Wilder, the joke went around that one of the rules of the new course would be to require bipartisan foursomes.

The House, too, has benefited from an unusual degree of leadership stability. Since 1973, when Ned McWherter began a 14-year run as speaker before serving two terms as governor, only three individuals have presided over it. McWherter, the dominant legislative presence in Tennessee over the past generation, believed in an independent legislature that was entitled to full partnership in the state governmental process. And he continued to believe it after he had left the speakership for the governor's office. "McWherter recognized," says Bill Purcell, the former House majority leader, "that the enhancement of the legislature was good for the executive."

Indeed, it has been. After agreeing to cede authority to McWherter for the creation of the controversial TennCare program in 1993, lawmakers have been careful to avoid picking it to death in their oversight capacity. They have worked in relative harmony with both McWherter and his Republican successor, Sundquist, on a whole range of other major issues in recent years, including prison system reform, school finance and welfare and the delivery of children's services.

In Tennessee, unlike in Minnesota, members still arrange themselves on the floor the old-fashioned way, by region instead of by party. "In my 10 years in the House," Purcell says, "there were only two issues that broke down along party lines. Literally, only two out of thousands."

The chamber's longtime lobbyists agree. "There's not a whole lot of ideological difference between the majority of legislators," says Dick Williams, a veteran of 24 years as chief lobbyist for Tennessee Common Cause. "Most of them still don't view themselves strictly as Republicans or Democrats."

The House is not as imbued with quite the same bipartisan spirit that Wilder nurtures in the Senate. Some complain that Speaker Jimmy Naifeh wields a heavy gavel. But even Republicans concede that Naifeh shows no interest in humiliating or embarrassing the opposition. If there are grievances, there is an opportunity to air them for an hour and a half every Wednesday, when the leaders from both parties in the House and Senate meet with the governor to flesh out issues. "It gives us an opportunity to talk if someone has their feathers ruffled," says House Republican Leader Steve McDaniel. "If you ever stop communicating, it would be like if a husband and wife stopped talking—things would get pretty bad. After all, we are a family."

You don't often hear that kind of talk in Minnesota these days. It would be a tropical winter day in International Falls before Irv Anderson and Steve Sviggum ever described themselves as members of the same family.

Not that there aren't a few signs of a turnaround at the Minnesota state capitol. After the turbulent 1996 session and the brutal fall campaign, there at least seems to be a recognition that the notions of consensus and bipartisanship are worth recovering, if it is not too late. To signify his intentions, newly elected Speaker Phil Carruthers announced this year that his first move would be to decentralize authority. He says he envisions a body that is "more participative, less bitter, less top-down, with an emphasis on less partisanship." His goal, he says, is to involve both parties in the process.

At the same time, there are those who insist that stronger medicine is needed. A number of elected officials, including GOP Governor Arne Carlson, are backing the idea of scrapping the current system entirely and replacing it with a unicameral legislature, like the one that exists in Nebraska.

In Tennessee, legislators would find that idea hard to comprehend. Their professed interest is in protecting a system that they believe works. Still, there are some warnings about the dangers of creeping partisanship: The past few years have witnessed an increased number of intense campaigns and the growing use of tax issues as a partisan wedge. Naifeh has been challenged by aggressive opposition at home over the last two elections. Indeed, some legislators of both parties are predicting the next session will be the most partisan in years.

If that is the case, though, neither Speaker Naifeh nor Republican leader Steve McDaniel is losing much sleep over it. At a recent meeting between the two, they even joked about the predictions of conflict. "I never said that," Naifeh told the Republican.

"Neither did I," McDaniel replied.

Political Protocol: Legislative Campaigns

by Alan Rosenthal

The career of another outstanding legislator is currently at stake. Few public officials have given as honorable and effective service in the legislature as has Roger Moe of Minnesota. A senator for 26 years, including 15 as majority leader, Moe was indicted for having violated state law by his "use of employee services or public equipment for political purposes." There is some question as to the Ramsey County attorney's judgment in pressing the grand jury for an indictment in a case that many observers believe is trivial.

Some state laws provide that public facilities, including employees, should not be used to assist in a political campaign. The intentions of such laws are laudable—to ensure that taxpayer dollars are not spent on election campaigns (other than public financing), and to limit the advantage incumbents would have over challengers by tapping into state resources.

Because of the nation's anti-politics and anti-institutional mood, we are attempting to root out politics from legislative bodies. There is increased competition between Democrats and Republicans for control, and either party has a chance of winning a majority in most legislative chambers. Winning may not be everything, but losing is nothing.

Not many years ago, campaigns for legislative office were the business of state, county, and local parties. These party organizations have been superseded by the legislative parties—the majority and minority party caucuses. Caucus and legislative party leaders raise funds and allocate money and services to candidates in the most competitive districts. They introduce bills and amendments that force the opposition to go on record against a popular proposal or a substantial interest group. They assist legislative members and enhance their electoral prospects by making them look good in their districts.

Vigorous two-party competition is just what we want in a healthy democracy. We've got it. But we also are suffering from some of its excesses—extreme partisanship, political jockeying and turning the legislative terrain into an electoral battlefield. Add to all of this partisan staffing,

Alan Rosenthal is a professor with the Eagleton Institute of Politics at Rutgers University. This article is reprinted from *State Government News* (September 1996): 16.

How a Bill Becomes State Law

This graphic shows the most typical way in which proposed legislation is enacted into law in the states. Bills must be passed by both houses of the state legislature in identical form before they can be sent to the governor to be signed or vetoed. Of course, the legislative process differs slightly from state to state.

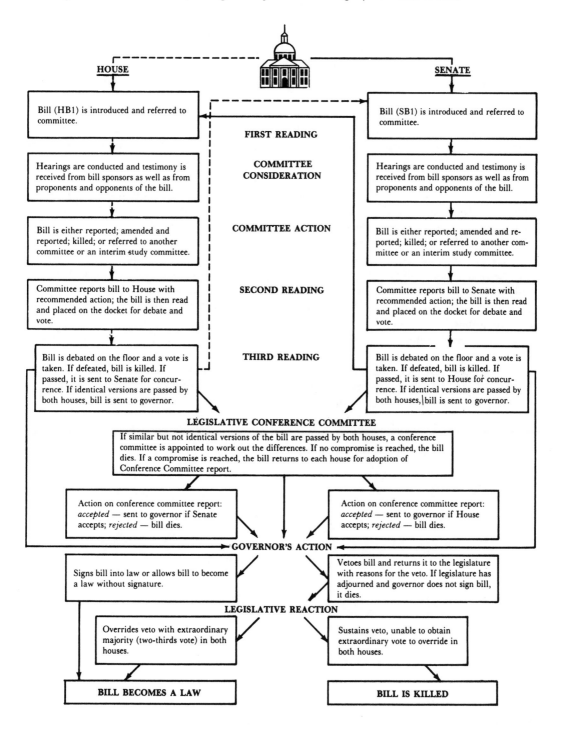

HOUSE

SENATE

Bill (HB1) is introduced and referred to committee.

Bill (SB1) is introduced and referred to committee.

FIRST READING

Hearings are conducted and testimony is received from bill sponsors as well as from proponents and opponents of the bill.

COMMITTEE CONSIDERATION

Hearings are conducted and testimony is received from bill sponsors as well as from proponents and opponents of the bill.

Bill is either reported; amended and reported; killed; or referred to another committee or an interim study committee.

COMMITTEE ACTION

Bill is either reported; amended and re-ported; killed; or referred to another committee or an interim study committee.

Committee reports bill to House with recommended action; the bill is then read and placed on the docket for debate and vote.

SECOND READING

Committee reports bill to Senate with recommended action; the bill is then read and placed on the docket for debate and vote.

Bill is debated on the floor and a vote is taken. If defeated, bill is killed. If passed, it is sent to Senate for concurrence. If identical versions are passed by both houses, bill is sent to governor.

THIRD READING

Bill is debated on the floor and a vote is taken. If defeated, bill is killed. If passed, it is sent to House for concurrence. If identical versions are passed by both houses, bill is sent to governor.

LEGISLATIVE CONFERENCE COMMITTEE

If similar but not identical versions of the bill are passed by both houses, a conference committee is appointed to work out the differences. If no compromise is reached, the bill dies. If a compromise is reached, the bill returns to each house for adoption of Conference Committee report.

Action on conference committee report: *accepted* — sent to governor if Senate accepts; *rejected* — bill dies.

Action on conference committee report: *accepted* — sent to governor if House accepts; *rejected* — bill dies.

GOVERNOR'S ACTION

Signs bill into law or allows bill to become a law without signature.

Vetoes bill and returns it to the legislature with reasons for the veto. If legislature has adjourned and governor does not sign bill, it dies.

LEGISLATIVE REACTION

Overrides veto with extraordinary majority (two-thirds vote) in both houses.

Sustains veto, unable to obtain extraordinary vote to override in both houses.

BILL BECOMES A LAW

BILL IS KILLED

which grew in the 1970s and 1980s. These staffs often define progress in partisan terms and may be tempted to involve themselves in political campaigns.

During the last six years, two incidents brought the issue of public facilities to the forefront. In "Computergate" in New Jersey, a grand jury investigation resulted in a statement from the jury critical of the Legislature's failure to distinguish between legislative work and campaign work. The Legislature afterward formulated rules to separate the two. These rules have been followed without incident since. In "Staffgate" in Washington [State], the Public Disclosure Commission (PDC) found violation of the law that prohibits the use of public facilities "for the purpose of assisting in the campaign." Each of the caucus staffs in both chambers was fined $100,000, while supervisors in each unit were fined $2,500. The Legislature and PDC negotiated an agreement on off-limits practices, which have been in place for several years.

In neither state were legislators indicted. New Jersey's law was unclear and the state deputy general in charge of the investigation did not appear to be scalp hunting. Washington's PDC saw its job as making institutional progress rather than doling out individual punishment. The PDC, however, took a beating in the press for not pressing a case against legislators.

Some people advocate a complete separation of legislative and campaign staffs or the complete elimination of partisan staffs. That would be a mistake. Partisan staffs contribute to the process, and their campaign involvement can enrich their contribution. But campaigning should be on the staff's own time, not the state's time. Legislatures must adopt standards of conduct regarding the use of public facilities, and many already have done so.

It is possible to distinguish the impermissible from the permissible, acknowledging that gray areas will persist and that de minimis allowances will have to be made. The experiences of New Jersey, Washington and others demonstrate that the problem can be handled. And it can be handled without changing the nature of the basic relationship between the legislature and its staff—and without singling out individual legislators for punishment.

VI.   GOVERNORS AND THE EXECUTIVE BRANCH

As the head of state politics and government and the elected representative of the people, governors must perform a wide variety of duties. They greet visitors, travel to other states and even other countries to lure new businesses to their states, rush to the scene of disasters to demonstrate concern, prepare annual and biennial agendas for government activity, and, on occasion, discuss important issues with the president. From state to state the record varies on how well these and other gubernatorial responsibilities are fulfilled. Some governors are reelected to another term, others are excluded from service, and still others are elected to higher office.

Since its weak beginnings after the overthrow of colonial rule, the American governorship has grown in power and influence. The extensive reforms of the past three decades are becoming evident throughout the executive branches of the fifty states. As Larry Sabato reported more than a decade ago, "Within the last 20 years, there has been a virtual explosion of reform in state government. In most of the states, as a result, the governor is now truly the master of his own house, not just the father figure."[1] Many of the powers that were restricted have been expanded, and governors now have new powers at their command, such as the ability to reach the people directly through the media and to serve as the key state official in the intergovernmental system of grants and programs.

Like any office or position, the caliber of the individuals who seek and then serve as governors varies considerably. Most states have been able to say "goodbye to good-time Charlie" and hello to "a thoroughly trained, well regarded, and capable new breed of state chief executive."[2] This does not mean that all governors have spotless records. In 1988, Evan Mecham (R-Ariz., 1987–88) was impeached by the state House, convicted by the state Senate, and removed from office. In April 1993, Governor Guy Hunt (R-Ala., 1987–93) was convicted "of diverting $200,000 in inaugural funds for personal use" and was automatically removed from office.[3] In October 1993, Governor David Walters (D-Okla.), in a plea bargain, plead guilty to a misdemeanor charge of violating a state campaign finance law in his 1990 election, and thereby avoided being tried on more serious felony charges.[4] In 1996, Governor Jim Guy Tucker (D-Ark.) announced that he would resign after being convicted on twenty-four counts of felonious conspiracy to commit bank fraud in connection with the Whitewater investigation and Governor Fife Symington (R-Ariz.) was hit with a twenty-three-count federal indictment relating to the financing of his real estate enterprises from 1986 to 1991.

In the 1990s it is not clear whether the governors are better or not. But one thing is very clear: the governors of every state are facing fiscal problems of a magnitude not felt before in the states.[5] At the beginning of the decade these problems were tied to the recession, as economies faltered, state revenues fell, and programs had to be cut back while taxes had to be raised to keep the budget balanced. Now, mid-decade, governors are still faced with the need to cut both government agencies and programs—and taxes.

But with the shift in program and fiscal responsibility from the federal government to the states, governors and other state leaders have been put into the spotlight. They are the leaders who now must address the domestic side of our policy agenda. While they are in the process of cutting both revenues and programs, they will soon be faced with additional, as-yet-unknown responsibilities devolving from the federal government. There is one thing they all agree on: the government should not try to balance the federal budget and the federal deficit on the backs of the states.

Governors and the State Ambition Ladder

An interesting aspect of the governorship is its place on the "ambition ladder" that eager politicians climb to attain higher and higher levels of success. Clearly, the governorship is the top political office in the states, though there have been instances where the true political leader was a U.S. senator. For example, in Louisiana in the 1930s Huey Long moved his power base from the governor's chair to the U.S. Senate, and in Virginia U.S. senator Harry Byrd ran the famous "Byrd Machine" for several decades earlier in this century.[6] On the whole, though, few offices hold as much promise of political power as does the governorship.

Governors may be all the more powerful if their party also controls the state legislature, though if it holds too many legislative seats, ideological and personal splits in the party can arise and diminish the governor's ability to control. However, as noted earlier, more states have a political power split than a political power concentration that could enhance the governor's position.

With both potential and actual political power available, it is no surprise that the governorship is a coveted position at the apex on most states' political ambition ladders. Certain pre-gubernatorial positions are particularly valuable while climbing the ladder: state legislative office, other statewide elective office, law enforcement work, and local elective office. More recently, those holding congressional or U.S. senatorial office are shifting toward the governorship, as are some individuals who have had no previous elective position at all. Moving up from a local position, usually as mayor of a large city, has not been built into this ladder. For example, in the 120 gubernatorial elections conducted between 1987 and 1996, just 2 of 26 large-city mayors running achieved the governorship.[7]

But what is the next step after the governorship? Is it a higher elective office? Three of our four most recent presidents were governors—Jimmy Carter (D-Ga., 1971–75), Ronald Reagan (R-Calif., 1967–75), and Bill Clinton (D-Ark., 1979–81, 1983–92). Reagan indicated that "being governor was the best training school for this job [of being president]."[8] In 1997, there were thirteen former governors serving as U.S. senators and one serving as a U.S. representative.

Most former governors enter the private sector, usually to develop a lucrative law practice. These governors must give up what former governor Lamar Alexander (R-Tenn., 1979–87) called "the very best job in the U.S.A."[9] Is there life after being governor? The National Governors' Association (NGA) asked some former governors what had happened to them since leaving office. Yes, there was life, but the quality of that new life can be determined only by the individual. By planning early for the transition, NGA suggests, the governors "can also help ease their own adjustment to the 'good life.' "[10]

Campaigning for Governor

Being elected governor is not as easy as it once was. One reason is the new style of campaigning that has led candidates to create their own organizations instead of relying solely on their political party. Opinion polls, political consultants, advertisements tailored to specific audiences in the major media markets, direct mailings, telephone banks, and air travel are extremely expensive, and full-time fund-raisers often are needed to help gubernatorial candidates wage winning campaigns. Without the party to alert the faithful and bring in the straight-ticket votes, candidates must create what Sabato calls their own "instant organization" or "party substitute."[11]

This way of building a campaign organization is obviously expensive, and indeed the cost of running for governor has escalated greatly in recent years. But to be competitive, a candidate must raise considerable funds for his or her campaign. For those with private wealth, or access to wealth, this hurdle can be overcome more easily than for those without such resources. For these latter, conducting a campaign for the governorship requires continuous fund raising, or the campaign will be impaired.

In addition, gubernatorial races are more competitive. Awareness of the importance of state government and of the key role of the governor in state politics has increased the number of candidates for the office.

Finally, there has been a decline in the number of opportunities to be elected governor. All but two states allow governors to serve four-year terms and only one limits a governor to a single term.[12] In addition, the power of incumbency gives a sitting governor a considerable advantage in any reelection campaign. The result is that fewer new governors are being elected in the states. Between 1900 and 1910 there was an average of 3.3 new governors elected in each state; in the 1980s, the average across the fifty states was 1.1 new governors elected per state.[13]

One Among Many

The governor is not the only official in the executive branch of state government who is elected statewide. The states elect more than five hundred officials, including forty-three attorneys general, forty-two lieutenant governors, thirty-seven treasurers, and thirty-six secretaries of state. The legislatures appoint some state officials, mainly in the postaudit function, and the lieutenant governors in a few states have some appointive power. This means that governors have little or no power over some parts of state government, except their own power of persuasion or the power they can create through the budget.

Fragmentation of executive branch leadership complicates the politics between the actors involved. In the early 1980s, for example, the governors and the lieutenant governors of California, Missouri, Nebraska, and New Mexico were pitted against each other over the issue of who is in charge of state government when the governor is out of state. Can the lieutenant governor make appointments to office or the bench (patronage)? Call a special session of the legislature? Issue pardons? And who receives the governor's salary while he or she is absent?

More recently, some governors have had difficulties with other elected officials: in Virginia, the governor and lieutenant governor fought over the budget surplus and taxes; in Idaho, the governor and lieutenant governor squabbled over regulating the amount of timber exported from the state; in Georgia, the fight was between the governor and the attorney general, with the two officials battling over the state's open meetings law and personnel matters; and in North Carolina, the governor and attorney general fought over the governor's right to contract leases and appoint certain officials.[14]

Executive branch fragmentation has other consequences. Perhaps most importantly, it restricts what governors can accomplish in high priority areas such as education. A gubernatorial candidate may pledge to improve primary and secondary education, but, once elected, have difficulty fulfilling this goal because other elected officials with responsibility in the education policy area may have different views on what should be done.

Recent federal court decisions have begun to restrict a chief executive's ability to remove or fire government employees, an action often needed to open up positions for appointing the executive's own team. After a series of cases restricting the power of patronage, the U.S. Supreme Court took direct aim at the gubernatorial power of patronage.[15]

In 1990, the Supreme Court decided narrowly in *Rutan et al. v. Republican Party of Illinois* that state and local government violates an individual's "First Amendment rights when they refuse to hire, promote or transfer ... [an employee] on the basis of their political affiliation or party activity."[16] This case, which focused on the patronage process of the Illinois governor's office, highlights a basic tension in these situations. There is a tension between the right of employees to be protected for their political beliefs and the need of an executive to put into place individuals who will seek to

achieve the goals for which that executive was elected.

The most significant restriction on a governor's ability to be governor is the relationship that he or she has with state legislators. There are many types of advice and counsel that governors give each other on this relationship; consider these comments by incumbents to newly elected governors in 1982:

Don't necessarily judge your success by your legislative score card.... Avoid threatening to veto a bill. You just relieve the legislature of responsibility for sound legislation.... A governor successful in managing the selection of legislative leadership gains a Pyrrhic victory.... It's too easy to dismiss one or two legislators because there are so many. You do so at your own peril.... Legislators will complain about your spending too much time with the staff, but what they really mean is you don't spend enough time with them.... If someone urges your support on a bill by saying it's a "merely" bill, sew your pockets shut; there are no "merely" bills.... Legislators will learn that press coverage comes from opposition to the governor.[17]

Part VI provides a close-up view of the governorship as we move through the latter 1990s. Jerry Brekke in *Comparative State Politics* provides a case study of the process of impeaching a secretary of state. This is followed by a series of short analyses by Alan Ehrenhalt and Charles Mahtesian of *Governing* and Jack Van Der Slik of *Illinois Issues* depicting the different styles of being governor in the states.

Notes

1. Larry Sabato, *Goodbye to Good-time Charlie: The American Governorship Transformed,* 2d ed. (Washington, D.C.: CQ Press, 1983), 57.

2. Ibid., xi.

3. "Alabama Gov. Hunt Guilty; Office Now Folsom's," *Congressional Quarterly Weekly Report,* April 24, 1993, 1035.

4. "Oklahoma: Walters Pleads Guilty to Misdemeanor," *The Hotline,* October 22, 1993, 15.

5. For an in-depth discussion of the fiscal problems facing governors in ten states, see Thad L. Beyle, ed., *Governors and Hard Times* (Washington, D.C.: CQ Press, 1992).

6. V. O. Key Jr., *Southern Politics in State and Nation* (New York: Knopf, 1949), 19–35, 156–182.

7. Tony Knowles of Anchorage in Alaska (1994) and George Voinovich of Cleveland in Ohio (1990). See Thad L. Beyle, "The State Elections of '96," in *Toward the Millennium: The Elections of 1996,* ed. Larry Sabato (Boston: Allyn & Bacon, 1997), 198.

8. "Inquiry: Being Governor Is Best Training for Presidency," *USA Today,* September 11, 1987, 11A.

9. Lamar Alexander, *Steps Along the Way: A Governor's Scrapbook* (Nashville: Thomas Nelson, 1986), 9.

10. "Is There Life after Being Governor? Yes, A Good One," *Governors' Weekly Bulletin,* August 8, 1986, 1–2.

11. Larry Sabato, "Gubernatorial Politics and the New Campaign Technology," *State Government* 53 (Summer 1980): 149.

12. The two states with two-year terms for their governors are New Hampshire and Vermont; only Virginia restricts its governor to one term.

13. See Thad L. Beyle, "Term Limits in the State Executive Branch," in *Limiting Legislative Terms,* ed. Gerald Benjamin and Michael J. Malbin (Washington, D.C.: CQ Press, 1992), 164.

14. "People: Some Governors Get No Respect," *Governing* 1:2 (November 1987): 67.

15. The cases involving local governments were *Elrod v. Burns* (1976), *Branti v. Finkel* (1980), and *Connick v. Myers* (1983).

16. Cheri Collis, "Cleaning Up the Spoils System," *State Government News* 33:9 (September 1990): 6.

17. Thad L. Beyle and Robert Huefner, "Quips and Quotes from Old Governors to New," *Public Administration Review* 43:3 (May–June 1983): 268–269.

Impeachment Under the Missouri Constitution

by Jerry Brekke

What are impeachable offenses? The American practice has been to answer this question through the political process. Thus, it is generally accepted that legislatures have the right to determine what are impeachable offenses. Most state constitutions follow the national pattern of having the house of representatives vote the impeachment charges and having the senate conduct the impeachment trial. Missouri followed this procedure in its earlier constitutions, but under the present (1945) constitution, the Supreme Court of Missouri conducts the trial. The exact language states that "all impeachments shall be tried before the supreme court, except that the governor or a member of the supreme court shall be tried by a special commission of seven eminent jurists."[1] The concurrence of five of the seven members of the supreme court or special commission is needed for conviction.

The grounds for impeachment under Article VII Section I are for "crime, misconduct, habitual drunkenness, willful neglect of duty, corruption in office, incompetency, or any offense involving moral turpitude or oppression in office." These are quite standard impeachable offenses. How-ever, the fact that Missouri places the responsibility for determining guilt on the supreme court or a special court commission is an important distinction from the process provided by the Constitution of the United States and most state constitutions.

The Supreme Court of Missouri had an opportunity to apply these provisions in a 1994 case that involved the office of secretary of state. Secretary of State Judith Moriarty was charged and convicted in circuit court of a misdemeanor. She had violated election laws by backdating paperwork to get her son on the ballot for a seat in the Missouri House of Representatives. The jury recommended that she receive no jail time but that she pay up to a $1,000 fine. The judge followed the recommendation of the jury and fined her $1,000.

After the circuit court found Moriarty guilty, Gov. Mel Carnahan called [for] her impeachment, and the house voted articles of impeachment under the constitutional grounds of misconduct. Moriarty was

Jerry Brekke is a professor of government at Northwest Missouri State University. This article is reprinted from *Comparative State Politics* 17:6 (December 1996): 23–25.

charged with the creation of a false declaration of candidacy, which falsely showed that her son appeared in the presence of an election official and signed, subscribed, and swore the declaration of candidacy. The thrust of the law on which the charges were based requires that any person wishing to run in a primary election for state office must file a written declaration of candidacy in the office of secretary of state by a certain date. This must be done in person. The law expressly forbids the printing of any candidate's name on a ballot "unless his written, signed and sworn declaration of candidacy has been filed."

The supreme court agreed with the circuit court, finding that Moriarty had failed to prevent and failed to repudiate conduct that created a false declaration of candidacy. Moriarty's son had been given privileges and special treatment not available to any other person seeking public office.

The Supreme Court of Missouri in its written decision convicting Moriarty of the charges also commented on the impeachment process as it exists in Missouri.[2] The court noted that the Missouri procedure was unusual: only in Nebraska does the supreme court play a similar role. The supreme court stated that its role in the impeachment process must be that of a court and not as a substitute political body. Missouri's constitutional impeachment process combines a political function (impeachment by the house) with a judicial function. The court stated it would convict only where there was actual misconduct as the law defined it. This "misconduct" was defined as doing an unlawful act, doing a lawful act in an unlawful manner, or failing to perform an act required by law. It would not include errors in judgment, acts done in good faith, or good faith exercises of discretion. Since the secretary ignored the clear directives of a law for which the secretary bore ultimate responsibility for enforcement, it was exactly the sort of misconduct for which the constitution required impeachment and removal from office. The standard of proof required to convict was by clear and convincing evidence. The court by unanimous decision found such evidence in the Moriarty case.

In the Moriarty case, the Supreme Court of Missouri has provided a partial answer to the question of what are impeachable offenses under the Missouri constitution. Conviction under the misconduct offense is not a political decision, but rather a legal question where the court will demand clear and convincing evidence of a violation of law. Charges brought under other impeachable offenses such as incompetency or willful neglect of duty may force the court to reconsider the Moriarty precedent. However, it is clear that in Missouri what constitutes an impeachable offense is no longer exclusively a political consideration.

Notes

1. Constitution of the State of Missouri, Art. VII, sec. 2.

2. Matter of Impeachment of Moriarty, 902 S.W. 2d 273 (Mo.banc 1994).

The Debilitating Search for a Flabby Consensus

by Alan Ehrenhalt

… A few recent leaders have professed something like the Margaret Thatcherite dictum: You make friends until you have enough, and then you stop.

The most candid exponent of this idea in recent years has been William F. Weld, the Republican governor of Massachusetts. "If we are going to do things in a different way," Weld said not long after his inauguration in 1991, "maybe we can't have everybody on board. Maybe we can't have consensus government." And he set out to prove he meant it. When it came time to honor public employee labor contracts negotiated by his Democratic predecessor, Weld simply repudiated them. "They are not my people," he declared. "They are not my constituents." It was a sentiment that Margaret Thatcher could applaud.

But in the years since, Weld hasn't had the luxury of separating friends and enemies quite as neatly as Thatcher did. Faced with lopsided Democratic majorities in both the state House and state Senate, he soon learned to broaden his definition of friendship. When he wanted a capital gains tax cut, he secured Democratic votes for it by supporting a 55 percent legislative pay raise. He cozied up to William Bulger, the Democratic Senate president, whom he had denounced in 1990 as a symbol of sleazy government. "He tells funny jokes," Weld once explained, "and I laugh at them." Weld is a politician who has written his own corollary to the received wisdom of the sandbox: Not everybody needs to be your friend. But if your friends don't constitute a majority, make a few more.

Not all of the current governors understand this quite as clearly as Weld does. Gary Johnson took office last year [1995] as Republican governor of New Mexico proclaiming that he was not an ordinary politician and had no intention of compromising his principles to cooperate with a bunch of careerist Democratic officeholders who had brought the curse of bloated government upon the Land of Enchantment. The result has been an ineffectual administration, a string of overridden vetoes and a two-year shouting match between the governor and the legislature that has brought the entire state to the brink of exhaustion. Johnson had ab-

Alan Ehrenhalt is a staff writer for *Governing*. This article is reprinted from *Governing* (October 1996): 7–8.

sorbed the useful idea that it pays to know who your friends are and who your enemies are. But he never learned Weld's corollary: It also pays to know how to count....

The most impressive gubernatorial achievements of recent years have all been pulled off by politicians with a keen instinct for building a majority and a clear willingness to draw the line once that majority was secure. Ned McWherter, as governor of Tennessee in the early 1990s, steered through a massive expansion of state health insurance coverage not by persuading everyone in the state to like it—much of the medical community still does not—but by finding the votes to pass it and letting the critics be critics. If McWherter

had waited for an overwhelming statewide consensus, TennCare would not exist.

It is hard to find many Ned McWherters in American politics these days, let alone political leaders with the skill of Franklin Roosevelt. That could be due to a decline in the quality of raw material, but I don't think so. I think it has more to do with the detailed polling information now available to officeholders at virtually every level. Roosevelt didn't know for sure in the summer of 1936 whether his approval rating was 53 percent or 61 percent; he simply understood, based on a lifetime of political experience, that he had quite a few more friends than enemies. And so he was not only confident of reelection but also free to start drawing some lines in the sand....

Roy Romer:
The Conciliator-in-Chief

by Charles Mahtesian

Frustrated to the point of exasperation, in a last-gasp try to hammer out an agreement on grazing rights on federal lands in 1993, Colorado ranching interests put out an appeal for Governor Roy Romer's assistance. Romer was no champion of their cause, but ranchers knew that ... he had extensive contacts within the new Clinton administration. His rural background gave him some familiarity with the issues. More important, they trusted him.

Romer brought Interior Department Secretary Bruce Babbitt out to Colorado for weekly meetings with environmentalists, farmers and ranchers. Within three months, they came to an accord on an alternative rangeland management plan that became known as the Colorado model.

In his three terms as governor, Romer's uncanny knack for finding common ground and brokering deals between warring factions has become the hallmark of his tenure. "He has the depth to understand the complexities of the issue and the conviction of a solution-oriented consensus builder," says Reeves Brown of the Colorado Cattlemen's Association. "He's the consummate collaborationist."

... Romer's hand has been forced by his circumstances. He is a Democrat in a Republican-friendly state and [is] hampered by relatively weak constitutional powers. When he takes his legislative agenda to the Capitol, he [faces] two hostile chambers that dominate the budget process.

For that reason, much of his success has occurred outside the legislative realm. At the national level, Romer won notice as a lead Democratic negotiator on welfare and Medicaid reform. Ultimately, Congress scrapped the compromise struck between Republican and Democratic governors, but Romer emerged with a reputation among his colleagues as one who could zealously guard his party's interests without poisoning the negotiation process. [In January 1997 Romer became President Clinton's choice to chair the Democratic National Party.]

... Romer's style is deceptively simple. His first trick is obvious—he listens. But those who have worked with him also report another shared observation: Nobody gets everything they want.

Charles Mahtesian is a staff writer for *Governing*. This article is reprinted from *Governing* (December 1996): 28.

Jim Edgar's Dilemma, or the Perils of "Third Way" Leadership

by Jack Van Der Slik

What do you do when you're the leader, but nobody is following? Five and a half years into his governorship, Jim Edgar might well ponder that question....

So why can't Republican Jim Edgar parlay his own political popularity, and his party's 1994 legislative election sweep, into policy? The problem is partly one of style. Edgar illustrates the perils faced by what Stephen Skowronek, a Yale political scientist, calls "third way" political leaders.

Republican Ronald Reagan represented one leadership style. He was an iconoclast who fashioned a new orthodoxy from his belief that government was the problem, not the solution. He sought to deconstruct government and its overweening regulation. In Illinois' 1994 gubernatorial election, Democrat Dawn Clark Netsch represented a second way. She was the defender of an older government-can-do-it orthodoxy. An activist, Netsch argued for more progressive taxation to fund the state's needs, particularly in education.

Edgar hugs the middle. He is no ideologue and no visionary. He repudiates no orthodoxy, conceives no new paradigms. He is above all intellectually cautious. As befits his personal style, Edgar goes about government problem-solving like a knowledgeable mechanic who works without philosophical blueprints.

This style was suited to Edgar's first term, when the state was faced with the fiscal need to retrench. Good at saying "no" and holding down spending, Edgar did his best work while frustrating the Democratic legislative majorities during those four years....

And Edgar proved himself a master of political strategy throughout his re-election campaign. He skillfully met the candidacy of Dawn Clark Netsch, who in her primary victory projected the image of a "straight shooter." By September Edgar had morphed her persona into a tax-and-spend liberal who is soft on crime. She would shrink from capital punishment; he would build prisons and shorten the appeals process while holding the line on spending. He won by nearly a 2–1 margin.

Despite such successes, the weaknesses in Edgar's leadership style have become

Jack Van Der Slik is a political scientist and director of the Legislative Studies Center at the University of Illinois at Springfield. This article is reprinted from *Illinois Issues* (July 1996): 6–7.

more apparent during the second term, when his own party controls the legislature.

Working without fixed principles, third-way executives like to poach on the territory of their opponents. That can work when control of the government is split between two parties and bipartisan deals are the currency of exchange. President Bill Clinton has played the third way with great political success since Republicans took control of Congress....

Illinois' suburban Republican legislative leadership wants a business agenda with a seasoning of social conservativism. But Edgar, despite a larger platform to promote his centrist agenda, remains handicapped in policy negotiations because he has little talent for advocacy.

His public appearances are wooden. State of the state and budget speeches, meant to communicate an agenda, are rhetorically banal. Additionally, the pressroom is not his natural habitat. His news conferences are never knockouts. When caught in the halls by the youthful press corps, Edgar is defensive. His answers are peppered with caveats, stipulations and conditional limits. He uses more words to say what he does not mean than to express what he wants or intends to achieve. At political events, he dutifully works the crowd, but with ritualistic discipline, not engaging élan. A Washington reporter likened his low-key style to George Bush "without charisma."

When playing the insider's game, Edgar bargains better defensively than offensively. His tight-knuckled negotiating sessions are no fun for anybody, including himself. In casual moments he acknowledges the burden of stress and his wife's concern about his health. Former Gov. Jim Thompson, in contrast, liked to make such sessions a rollicking good time for all.

Without the ability to communicate a message or attract consensus, but wanting a legacy, Edgar's governance thus far has amounted to a timid mix of pilot projects, task forces and trial balloons. The governor has given us a committee to study long-term care for the elderly, a task force on schools and a commission on gangs. The charter schools experiment is for 45 schools out of more than 2,500. The solution to governance, he says, is "better government, not bigger government." But as Walter Mondale once asked, "Where's the beef?" ... [T]he ultimate success of third-way leadership rests in achieving consensus, on drawing the margins to the center. Indeed, whatever the style, the success of a political executive rests in his ability to exercise leadership.

The Man Without a Party

by Alan Ehrenhalt

... No state ... has elected a governor quite like [Independent Angus] King. Alaska's Walter J. Hickel and Connecticut's Lowell P. Weicker Jr., the other two independent governors of the 1990s, weren't truly nonpartisan figures. They were longtime Republican officeholders who felt more comfortable running without the party label. King is different. Although he was a registered Democrat for most of his adult life, he never ran for any office before 1994, and he had spent most of the previous decade as nonpartisan moderator of a statewide public affairs talk show.

More important, King doesn't fit the stereotype of the independent politician as ornery loner. Lowell Weicker compared the American two-party system to the one-party Soviet monolith, and urged its overthrow. Ross Perot never manages to talk about the two major parties without conveying the sense that he considers them sleazy and contemptible. King, on the other hand, professes no interest in replacing the two major parties. He expects them to survive long after he is gone. "I'm not an anti-politician," he insists. "I'm very comfortable as an independent. But you can't

run this as an oligarchy. You have to work with the parties."

In short, unlike many of the people who run for office as independents, King has no particular desire to let off steam or throw bombs. What he wants to do is govern. The interesting question is whether, as a man without a party, he can find a way to do it....

King went out of his way to send the message that he aimed to be different ... from any Maine governor of recent times. He began dropping in on legislators of both parties, inviting them to his office, slipping into committee hearings to see what was going on. "I'm in the office late at night," says Paul Jacques, the House Democratic leader, "and there's a shadow in the doorway. It's him. Or the phone rings and this voice says, 'Hi Paul, it's Angus.'"

None of this required any particular strain on the new governor's part. "I'm a collaborationist," King likes to say. "I love getting people around a table and working things out." That task was made easier for

Alan Ehrenhalt is a staff writer for *Governing*. This article is reprinted from *Governing* (October 1996): 26–28, 30–31.

him by the peculiar outcome of the 1994 legislative elections. As a result of those elections, Democrats control the House by the tiniest of margins, while Republicans hold the Senate almost as narrowly. It has been an arrangement made to order for a centrist looking to play a broker's role. "It's almost a perfect situation for him," says Maine's Democratic secretary of state, Bill Diamond. "It demands compromise."...

By the beginning of [1996], even some politicians who had questioned King's capacity to govern as an independent began admitting they had underestimated him. "He's a much more controlling man than I realized," one veteran state legislator confided to a newspaper reporter. King just kept on speaking in quiet, soothing tones. "I like the guys, by and large," he insisted. "They are essential. I can't make policy by myself."...

Despite any fiscal traps the legislature may choose to set for him, the fact remains that Angus King is phenomenally well liked by the general public. [In March 1996], the Roper Center for Public Opinion research polled the state's voters and found that 85 percent approved of his performance. "Angus King is among the most popular, if not the most popular, of all 50 governors," the center concluded.

Whatever his governing limitations as an independent, King is perceived as several steps above his quarrelsome partisan predecessors on the simple question of personal character. "Even if they disagree with him on the issues, they believe he's trying to do a good job," says Chris Potholm, a Bowdoin College political scientist who did King's campaign polling. "They also believe the Democrats and the Republicans are not helping him. There's a sense of quality there. People respond to that."

Legislators in both parties who are more than willing to stiff the governor in closed-door committee sessions are noticeably leery of challenging him on any highly visible public issue. "The way the public at large perceives him," says [Joseph G.] Carleton [Jr.], the deputy House Republican leader, "he's almost above the parties."

What Angus King is not above is a good old-fashioned publicity stunt. He meets cruise ships at the Canadian border to greet foreign tourists. He rides his Harley-Davidson motorcycle in biker rallies across the state. He sang "Honky Tonk Woman" at his inaugural ball. He brought a bagpiper into the Capitol to celebrate his signing of a supplemental budget. To an outsider, it seems to fit a little incongruously with the seriousness of King's overall approach to government and political reform. But to the Maine electorate, it somehow comes off as genuine, a natural way for a stressed-out chief executive to let his hair down and relax. And it reinforces King's image as an easygoing, approachable man of the people, a refreshing contrast with his two stiff predecessors, [Republican] John McKernan and Democrat Joseph Brennan....

VII. STATE BUREAUCRACIES AND ADMINISTRATION

Departments and agencies within each state carry out the laws passed by the legislature and approved by the governor. These departments vary in size and in responsiveness to executive control. Transportation, human services, corrections, education, and health usually are large departments with sizable budgets and staffs. These "big ticket" agencies perform services quite visible to the public, and governors and legislators alike pay close attention to them. Governors appoint the heads of these agencies with great care, and the legislatures often must confirm the appointments.

Many parts of the state bureaucracy, however, appear to be remarkably immune to the vagaries of legislative and gubernatorial politics. The key to successful bureaucratic politics is to keep a low profile. Governors come and go, legislators come and go, but some agencies keep on doing what they have always done with minimum intrusion from outside. State government encompasses so many agencies and activities that it is virtually impossible for the governor and the legislature to keep track of them all.

Between a Rock and a Hard Place?

State bureaucrats—this is not a derogatory term—often are torn by competing values: economy and efficiency on the one hand and political expediency on the other. In the world of politics, points often are scored for achieving an electorally advantageous goal rather than for saving money or doing a job efficiently.

Another problem is accountability. To whom are state employees accountable? To the governor, the legislature or particular legislators, the interest served by the agency, the public at large, themselves? The numerous lines of accountability give those in the state bureaucracy the opportunity to play one group against another and thereby do what they want.

In recent years important changes have been made that have improved the caliber of the states' work forces. The standards for hiring, promotion, and retention have been raised. Educational requirements are more exacting. In-service training has been upgraded. State employees who report wrongdoing in state government—"whistleblowers"—are better protected against retaliation. And more employees are covered by civil service and merit systems, which has reduced the number of patronage positions. Moreover, minorities now have better opportunities for employment and advancement within state government.

Another related development has been the growing political influence of state employee organizations. State employee groups and state employee labor unions have become stronger in almost all of the states. Like other interests, they lobby their own concerns and proposals before the governor and the state legislature—and with increasing effectiveness. What do they want for their efforts? Higher wages, better health and retirement benefits, and more recognition of their professional status. When it comes to preparing the budget, the most influential parties often are those who carry out the intent of the budget—namely, state employees.

Finally, we must note the dynamic growth of state governments over the last several decades. Since 1950 the number of state government employees has increased by 300 percent; only the increases in primary and secondary education employment were greater. While there was a consistent "core" of about forty administrative agencies in most of the states in the late 1950s, this had grown to over seventy-five by the mid-1980s.[1] So both the number of people working for state government and the number of agencies in which they work increased greatly.

However, in the last few years the fiscal woes of the states have changed these dynamics dramatically. Growth stalled with precipitous declines in many states' revenues. Cutbacks in state work forces, not growth, seemed to be the guiding philosophy for governors and legislators seeking to balance state budgets. Further, this trend affected state power structures. The strength of state employees was reduced as governors and legislators looked for new ways to cut back on the size of state governments and their budgets. The goals of seeking higher wages, better health and retirement benefits, and recognition of professional status within state bureaucracies gave way to trying to protect programs, agencies, and jobs, and trying to hold the line on the level of salaries and benefits. Hard times cut very sharply into state bureaucracies.

In the aftermath of the 1994 elections there were still more efforts to cut back state programs and state bureaucracies, and thereby the state budget. While the drive for cutbacks in the early 1990s was economic, by mid-decade it had become political, as the view in many state capitals of what state government should be changed. Now the situation is changing once again. State finances are in much better shape, and the need to cut back has lessened; in fact, what many politicians would like to do is cut back on taxes—a very popular political move. But looming in the near future are serious changes in how many federal programs are to be carried out. Policy makers in Washington are making changes in major programs such as welfare that will necessitate an increased state role. State-level policy makers may suddenly need to increase both the state government work force and state budgets as federal programs devolve down through the system.

Organizational Problems

How are state agencies organized? Some would argue they aren't. Governors trying to "run" state government or citizens trying to find out where to get help often are baffled by the apparent organizational chaos of the many departments and agencies. Periodically, the states reorganize their executive branch departments. This usually is done either to improve economy and efficiency, to clear up the lines of accountability so that the governor is the chief executive in fact as well as in theory, or to gain control over some agencies that are perceived as out of control—usually the control of the governor or of the legislature.

Not surprisingly, reorganization often is resisted by the agencies themselves and by groups with vested interests in the way things are. Those who know how the system works prefer the status quo and are extremely reluctant to learn new ways. And when the goal is to give the governor more power and influence, the agencies fight hard: they are far from willing to lose or share their power. Organizational battles are so difficult to mount and win that many governors and legislatures avoid them, believing victory is not worth the political costs.

Republican governors are particularly attracted to setting up economy and efficiency commissions to survey state government programs, organizations, and policies in an effort to find ways to save the taxpayers money. These commissions, which usually are made up of members of the business community and supported by an out-of-state consulting firm specializing in such studies, review a state's budget, governmental organization, and programs. The commission issues a well-publicized final report pointing out waste in state government and indicates three to four hundred suggested changes as to how the state could save millions of dollars.

Some of the suggested changes make sense, and others do not. They usually include some reorganization and consolidation of agencies, turning over some of what the agencies do to the private sector (privatization), eliminating some programs, charging or increasing user fees for some services, or transferring a program to another level of government.[2] One observer concludes that such studies have "been largely discredited" and may be more "a political than an administrative tool."[3] Even reorganizations have been criticized as doing more to spawn confusion "about program goals and work responsibilities" and sparking "political brushfires" that keep "managers from getting back to those basic issues of responsibility and accountability."[4]

Major executive branch reorganization efforts have occurred in twenty-seven states since the 1960s.[5] The goals usually articulated in these efforts were "modernization and streamlining of the executive branch machinery, efficiency, economy, responsiveness, and gubernatorial control."[6] Reorganizations are not apolitical events; they involve a battle for power among the branches of government. Aside from the built-in resistance that state bureaucrats

have to such changes, legislators often oppose them as well because reorganizations usually increase the power of the governor over the executive branch at the expense of the legislature.

Rather than seek major reorganization of the bureaucratic structure, state leaders may attempt partial reform when there is a pressing need to consolidate overlapping and confusing jurisdictions, or when they wish to tackle a particular problem facing the state by eliminating organizational barriers. This has been especially important in economic development, in the environmental area, and in the actual administration of state government.

Management and Personnel Changes

Where the states have made the most headway is in adopting new management techniques. Budgets no longer are worked out in the back rooms of statehouses by employees wearing green eye shades; they are part of a larger policy-management process headed by the governor.[7] The recent fiscal downturns experienced in the states forced governors to take an even firmer grasp of the process. Nearly all governors must operate under a balanced budget requirement. If there are any mid-year problems or revenue shortfalls, the governor needs to know about them immediately so he or she can take appropriate remedial action.

Changes in state government administration and personnel have been made, but not without considerable furor. Controversies over affirmative action (Should minorities have a leg up in hiring and promotions?) and comparable worth (Should men and women be paid equally for dissimilar jobs of similar skill levels?) bedevil state legislators and administrators. Politically, it makes sense to open up jobs for women and minorities; they are becoming more active in politics and their support often is needed to win elections. According to one observer of the state government scene: "We're going to have to move beyond the good ol' boy network to include in the profoundest way the good ol' girls and the good ol' minorities."[8]

A recent study of state government agency heads suggests that women in state government are circumventing the so-called "glass ceiling" or administrative lid rather than trying to break through it. They are doing this by moving into expanded state government activities, such as consumer affairs and arts agencies, by involvement in governmental and political activism, and by reaching parity with men in terms of education, experience, and professionalism. "The administrative ballpark or ball game [has been] substantially enlarged. The park's gotten bigger."[9]

However, this does not mean that there are not some very strong and capable women heading major, main-line agencies across the states. In North Carolina, one very capable administrator, Janice Faulkner, has been the "go-to person" sent in by Governor Jim Hunt to clean up agencies wracked by ethical, management, and/or political problems. She worked wonders in redirecting the State Department of Revenue; then, as the appointed secretary of state, she restructured its activities. She was then prevailed upon to correct a series of major political and administrative problems in the State Division of Motor Vehicles. Just when she thinks it is time to retire, she gets a call from the governor.

Ethics

How government officials, elected or appointed, behave while in office is increasingly a topic of concern at the state level. We generally recognize a corrupt act—or do we? Handing cash to a public official to influence a decision would seem to be a corrupt act. But what about a public utility political action committee that contributes funds to incumbent legislators' campaigns so that legislators might look more favorably on revising the utility rate structure? Is that a corrupt act? Or is that politics?

Like beauty, corruption and ethical misbehavior often are in the eye of the beholder. Some states are trying to clarify this issue by establishing codes of ethics, a set of ethical standards, and ethics commissions. Several states have established inspectors general offices to probe into allegations of wrongdoing in state government. In some instances, the inspectors general have the authority to "identify programs or departments that *might be vulnerable* to corruption...."[10] Some observers suggest that these steps, along with measures to open up electoral and governmental processes and to develop accountability measures, "have ... been at least as significant as the other reforms" occurring in the states over the past few decades.[11]

How widespread are ethics and corruption problems in the states? Again, the question really is, just what is an ethical problem? One point worth considering is that, given the size of our state governments, the number of people working in them, and the amount of money involved in their ongoing budgets, there is amazingly little corruption. What we see are the flashy, individual cases in which a governor has made an ethical error, a legislator has accepted money for a vote, or a state government employee has taken money for favorable treatment. These cases of state government "bad news" dominate the media; the good news—that no corruption occurred today, or yesterday, or last week—does not make the evening news.

Part VII explores some of these and other controversies concerning state bureaucracies. Tom Brune and Jennifer Halperin in *Illinois Issues* find a gender gap in the many board and commission appointments made by their governor. John F. Lopez and Joe D. Tanner of *State Government News* debate how state merit systems might be fixed. And Alan Ehrenhalt of *Governing* takes a provocative look at corruption in the public sector and what can be done about it.

Notes

1. Deil S. Wright, Jae-Won Yoo, and Jennifer Cohen, "The Evolving Profile of State Administrators," *Journal of State Government* 64:1 (January–March 1991): 30–31.

2. Tim Funk, "Efficiency Study Commissions: Is an Old Idea a Bad Idea?" *North Carolina Insight* 11:4 (August 1989): 42–43, 46–50.

3. James K. Conant, "Reorganization and the Bottom Line," *Public Administration Review* 46:1 (January/February 1986): 48.

4. Les Garner, "Managing Change through Organization Structure," *Journal of State Government* 60:4 (July/August 1987): 194.

5. Keon S. Chi, "State Executive Branch Reorganization: Options for the Future," *State Trends Forecasts* 1:1 (December 1992): 13. South Carolina, which reorganized in the early 1990s, was added to this list.

6. James K. Conant, "In the Shadow of Wilson and Brownlow: Executive Branch Reorganization in the States, 1965 to 1987," *Public Administration Review* 48:5 (September/October 1988): 895.

7. See James J. Gosling, "Patterns of Stability and Change in Gubernatorial Policy Agendas," *State and Local Government Review* 23:1 (Winter 1991): 3–12; and Robert D. Lee Jr., "Developments in State Budgeting: Trends of Two Decades," *Public Administration Review* 51:3 (May/June 1991): 254–262.

8. Comment by Jesse L. White Jr., former executive director of the Southern Growth Policies Board and a public policy consultant, in "On the Record," *Governing* 4:8 (May 1991): 18.

9. Study by Deil S. Wright and Angela M. Bullard, reported in Liz Lucas, "Women Winning State Posts," *Chapel Hill* (North Carolina) *News,* May 7, 1993, 7, 12.

10. Cheri Collis, "State Inspectors General: The Watchdog over State Agencies," *State Government News* 33:4 (April 1990): 13.

11. Fran Burke and George C. S. Benson, "Written Rules: State Ethics Codes, Commissions, and Conflicts," *Journal of State Government* 62:5 (September/October 1989): 198.

Jim Edgar's Gender Gap—Men Rule the Shadow Government

by Tom Brune and Jennifer Halperin

Just months after Gov. Jim Edgar took office in 1991, he signed a largely symbolic law to show his commitment to giving well-qualified women a place on the boards and commissions that would serve his new administration.

Called the Gender Balanced Appointments Act, the law represented Edgar's promise to try to make appointments in a way that would result in roughly similar numbers of men and women serving on state boards and commissions. The act was significant mainly for its recognition of the gender gap between the parties. Increasingly, a majority of women appear to be voting Democratic, offsetting a shift among men to vote Republican.

Five years later, however, the law remains little more than a promise, *Illinois Issues* found in the first comprehensive outside analysis of a governor's appointments to the hundreds of boards and commissions that revolve around the state's cabinet-level departments.

It is a promise that Edgar failed to fulfill. He appointed twice as many men as women to boards overall, and three times as many men as women to boards that pay salaries, the analysis found. As a result of

his appointments, two-thirds of 30 key boards and commissions remain the special preserves of men.

Most of the boards with a balance of men and women members are related to the arts, such as the Illinois Arts Council, or social issues, such as the Human Rights Commission or the State Board of Education. Two key boards that defy this categorization are the Lottery Control Board and the State Board of Elections.

But the desirable boards for compensation or power have at least twice as many men as women appointees. Men reign exclusively over four powerful boards: the Capital Development Board, the Civil Service Commission, the Illinois State Toll Highway Authority and the State and Local Labor Relations Board. Eight other boards have only one woman member, and seven more have only two or three women members.

"I can't believe he can't find qualified women to fill positions on these boards,"

Tom Brune is a Seattle-based freelance journalist. Jennifer Halperin is statehouse bureau chief for *Illinois Issues*. This article is reprinted from *Illinois Issues* (October 1996): 16–17.

says Myrrha Guzman, an attorney with the Elmhurst-based Citizen Advocacy Center. "He's the one who signed the Gender Balanced Appointments Act into law; he's not even following his own law. I don't know how he can justify such low numbers." Guzman has confronted Edgar before about his failure to appoint women to the Illinois State Toll Highway Authority. Of its nine members, none are women.

The figures surprised most legislators and caught the governor's office off-guard, an indication that Edgar's staff doesn't keep track of the gender of his many appointees.

"It does surprise me, knowing the governor's disposition on women in government," says Edgar's spokesman, Mike Lawrence.

Not surprisingly, few in powerful positions knew of the Gender Balanced Appointments Act. State Sen. Steve Rauschenberger, a Republican member of the Senate's Executive Appointments Committee that approves the governor's appointments to boards and commissions, says he had not heard of it. He says the committee has not used that law as a criteria in judging the people whose names Edgar had submitted for approval. "I'm surprised to learn it's that high a proportion of men to women," he says.

Lawrence was surprised as well. "He has appointed more women and minorities to high-ranking positions than any other governor." But Lawrence also says he is "at a loss" to explain why the appointments to boards and commissions, particularly those that pay salaries and involve policy-making authority, are so lopsided. "There is no question he is committed to having women in key roles," says Lawrence. "My sense is that he'll be surprised and that will be one area he'll want to work on."

Lawrence says he saw Edgar take a more active involvement in the appointment of university governing boards a year ago than with many other boards. The result, he notes, is that 45 percent of those appointments were women.

Republican state Treasurer Judy Baar Topinka is aware of the act. "I would hope we could come closer to the 50 percent mark [for women]," she says. "I object to using quotas—I think they're demeaning and condescending. But I can't believe we don't have more qualified women out there who can serve on these boards."

One woman who does serve on a prestigious board—Ruth Kretschmer of the Illinois Commerce Commission says she isn't bothered by a lack of female company. "I've worked very well with my colleagues," she says. "Then again, I've always been in the minority. I was only the second woman ever appointed to the commission. I would have thought overall there would be more women, though."

Republican state Rep. Suzanne Deuchler of Aurora says the governor's numbers should be higher. "More than 22 percent [of appointees to salaried boards] could have been and should have been women," she says. "I think there are qualified women in every part of the state who could serve on these. Obviously, I'd like to see more of a 50–50 split."

Republican state Comptroller Loleta Didrickson, meanwhile, put the onus on women to improve Edgar's statistics. "It's no different than a lot of boards of directors for top-500 firms," she says. "It demonstrates that we need to make sure our professional groups are putting forward names and resumes. It's up to us to make sure we're out there on corporate boards and in government offices. You have to make your wishes known."

How Can We Fix the Merit System?: Point/Counterpoint

by John F. Lopez and Joe D. Tanner

[*Editor's note:* Following are two differing views on the value and future of the merit system. John F. Lopez's plea for technology enhancement and management decentralization is followed by Joe D. Tanner's lauding of Georgia's recent overhaul of the merit-based employment system.]

The merit-based employment system, while not unique to the state of Michigan, must be supported by a human-resource management program that meets unique state needs while fulfilling the requirements of the Michigan Constitution. But, rather than assume the merit system is broken, the question we should more realistically ask ourselves is "How can we fix our human-resource systems?"

The Michigan Constitution of 1963 created a Civil Service Commission to govern the merit system. Among its responsibilities, the commission is charged with determining "... by competitive examination and performance exclusively on the basis of merit, efficiency and fitness the qualifications of all candidates for positions in the classified service." Additionally, to protect the integrity of these merit principles, the commission must make rules and regulations covering all personnel transactions.

These governing rules and regulations created what was originally believed to be an effective system of controls and measures to ensure consistent application of personnel practices among state agencies. However, the very effort to standardize the merit system made it complicated and bureaucratic. Numerous procedures, endless forms and strict conditions became a normal part of human-resource management, resulting in processes believed by many to be too strict. Essentially, state hiring agencies were given the message that there was only one way to get the job done—our way in personnel.

Add to that frustration the fact that processes in administering the merit system are limited by our agency's technology of the mid-1970s, and you now have a merit system in need of some serious modifications. The state must change to keep pace with the advances in technology and real-time access that is fast becoming routine

John F. Lopez is state personnel director for Michigan. Joe D. Tanner is executive director of Georgia's Commission on Privatization of Government Services in the governor's office. This article is reprinted from *State Government News* (June/July 1996): 6–7.

elsewhere. Let's face it, the citizens of Michigan—and people across the nation—are becoming increasingly familiar with the immediate benefits of fax machines, electronic mail, cellular telecommunication, and other interactive technology, including computer "webs" and "kiosks."

Our society expects immediate gratification, and the competition is heating up with more and more organizations claiming their services are the best and are available at a faster and cheaper rate than their competitors. Time is money and in state agencies we've been wasting a lot of it by limiting ourselves to our existing requirements for processing data (use only our forms, use U.S. mail—or "snail mail"). Integrating technology into Michigan's merit system and providing real-time access to information will increase the efficiency and effectiveness of state human-resource programs.

Of course, implementation of new and improved technological procedures will affect the way we approach the merit system today. Those of us in the personnel agency will no longer perform human-resource management. A technological network will empower the individual doing the hiring in the state agency with the ability to perform many human-resource management functions. The state personnel agency staff will act more and more as consultants and facilitators to help hiring managers make informed decisions about their unique human-resource requirements. We will advise them on the use of our services and improve their ability to acquire the most effective work force.

There is no denying that efforts to decentralize the role of performing human-resource management will raise concerns with employees in personnel and in other agencies, concerns such as:

Increased responsibilities and workloads at the agency level—An increased responsibility will lie with the hiring managers and their agencies. We must, therefore, ensure that the improved processes are also simplified processes.

Increased competition for employment opportunities—With an increase in opportunities to apply and be considered for positions comes a definite increase in competition. Employee assessment and development programs must be examined with this in mind.

We in personnel must be prepared to address these and other concerns with a focus on training and facilitation, recognizing that this is opposite the more classic reactive focus on controlling and regulating. By educating people on personnel processes and keeping them involved at every step, we can share responsibility for improving the way we partner to uphold the principles of merit, fitness and efficiency. Collectively, we must pay attention to the writing on the wall that says staying where we are poses a far greater risk in the long run. The state risks a dramatic decrease in the number of highly qualified candidates for civil service positions as these people continue to be snatched up by more technologically advanced organizations that can meet their employment needs more quickly and efficiently.

***

Georgia Gov. Zell Miller on April 8 [1996] signed into law one of the most sweeping changes in the state's legislative history. This legislation represents a bold and dramatic revision of the law governing the rights and privileges of state workers under the merit system. Having served in the executive branch as a state agency head for 25 years, I feel strongly that this is more than just a step in the right direction for state government. It is an affirmation to the citizens of this state that we are serious about government reform. It is also an acknowledgment that dissatisfaction with government is at an all-time high, and we have chosen not to engage in minor surgery when major surgery is clearly needed.

Georgia's merit system has many shortcomings. The process of hiring a state worker in Georgia takes from three to six months. The disciplinary process for terminating an employee for negligence takes six months to two years. Getting a position properly classified is also a time-consuming and laborious process. Reductions in force during a fiscal crisis typically result in the best workers going out the door. Clearly, the merit system needs to be overhauled, not tweaked.

I have sat on three statewide task forces that focused on fixing the merit system. And we have nibbled around the edges of these problems for many years. The governor realized that dramatic reform was needed and not slow incremental change.

Georgia's newly enacted law requires that all positions filled on or after July 1 be placed in the unclassified service. Workers hired after that date will be employed at-will and will not be covered by the merit system. The law also decentralizes authority for personnel management to the agencies and moves the Georgia State Merit System into a consultative role.

This legislation was not developed lightly or without an awareness of the potential for abuse. Accordingly, the governor has developed a set of guidelines for implementing the provisions of his new law. His executive order is based on the advice of 15 line managers and personnel directors from 10 state agencies.

It requires agencies to make employment decisions free from political intervention or influence, as well as to develop sensible policies that will allow agency heads to make personnel decisions effectively. But we will be very careful not to recreate the very bureaucracy that we have complained about for so long. We don't want agencies to develop written policies that try to anticipate every single concern or situation that might occur. This kind of nit-picking regulatory mind-set is what gets us into trouble every time.

Georgia created its merit system more than 50 years ago to reduce widespread political abuses existing at the time. Those political forces, attitudes and behaviors have long since disappeared. Today, a broad array of federal and state statutes prohibit political coercion and bar employment discrimination. In addition, the media plays an important watchdog role over state practices. Most importantly, Georgia's legislative and executive branches are working closely together to improve government operations and to deliver quality services to citizens.

The merit system insulates state workers from workplace realities. Workers in the private sector understand that their job depends on personal performance and the financial condition of their employer. Sadly, the merit system creates an entitlement mentality in some state workers that, at best, yields mediocre performance and, at worst, produces litigious behavior. For example, two classified employees recently filed a class-action suit claiming that they are entitled to receive an annual salary increase so long as their performance is satisfactory. They assert that the governor and the Legislature are obligated to fund these increases even during times of budgetary restraint and downsizing.

Having served the citizens of Georgia as an agency head, I experienced firsthand the costly and corrosive effects of inflexible personnel regulations on programs and operations. We must get away from the notion that we can dramatically change anything in the public sector by tinkering around the edges. It is also imperative, if we are to restore the average person's faith and trust in government, that we get away from the notion that regulation is the key to better government. Common sense is the key.

The Costly Medicine of Corruption-Fighting

by Alan Ehrenhalt

Thirty years ago, in response to a flood of complaints against the ethical conduct of his inspectors, New York City Building Commissioner Charles Moerdler came up with one of the most innovative anti-corruption ideas in the history of local government. Moerdler proposed that the inspectors be issued new uniforms without pockets. If his men didn't have a place to stuff the money, the commissioner explained, they wouldn't be tempted to accept bribes.

This may strike you as a rather extreme example of treating the symptom rather than the disease. The city council felt that way, and wasted no time in turning Moerdler down. So the proposal never got a legitimate test, and there's no way to tell for sure whether it might have worked.

We do know one thing, however. We know that in the aftermath of Moerdler's defeat, some city building inspectors not only retained their pockets but continued to line them regularly. In 1972, the building department staff was making a reported $25 million a year in bribes, and after a subsequent investigation, 43 inspectors were indicted on kickback charges. More were indicted and convicted in 1978, 1979, 1980, 1981, 1986, 1989, 1992 and 1993.

I know all this not because I keep track of these things, but because I have been reading *The Pursuit of Absolute Integrity*, a contrarily courageous new book about corruption and corruption-fighting by Frank Anechiarico and James Jacobs, two New York law professors who insist on asking some of the simple questions that most of us manage to neglect most of the time.

Is there more corruption in local government than there was a generation ago, or is there less? Or do we have any idea? If we have no idea, are we sure it makes sense to invest all the effort we invest in building a massive corruption-fighting monolith.

New York City has a problem with crooked building inspectors. It has always had one. The same is true for police officers. For the past century, the New York police department has undergone embarrassing disclosures and blue-ribbon investigating commissions with predictable regularity just about every two decades: in 1895, 1913, 1932, 1954, 1973 and 1994.

Alan Ehrenhalt is a staff writer for *Governing*. This article is reprinted from *Governing* (February 1997): 6–7.

You might assume that New York's history of cyclical scandal in the police and building departments indicates a lack of corruption-fighting zeal on the part of the city government. In fact, the opposite is true. For more than half a century, New York has had a separate Department of Investigation aimed at rooting out malfeasance in all the other agencies—the closest thing to a secret police anywhere in American local government.

A generation ago, the DOI worked in fairly close cooperation with the managers of the agencies themselves, but over the years it has grown more and more independent, to the point where there are undercover DOI investigators probing away in offices all over the city's bureaucratic spectrum. In an ordinary year, the DOI sometimes investigates as many as 2,000 suspected cases of corruption among city employees or contractors, and generates several dozen arrests.

And the DOI is far from the only anti-corruption weapon the city has in place. New York City has strict conflict-of-interest rules, detailed financial disclosure requirements and an elaborate whistleblower-protection program. All in all, it is an impressive and sophisticated corruption-fighting apparatus. There is no question that, in a certain sense, it works. It is always finding more corruption.

But does government get any cleaner as a result? That is an entirely different question. All we really know for sure is that every new scandal generates its own cycle of investigation, enhancement of corruption-fighting weapons, new disclosures, still more weapons, and still more disclosures, ad infinitum. "With each scandal," Anechiarico and Jacobs argue, "the corruption-hunting cadre lobbies for an expanded definition of its mission. The inevitable result is that more corruption is uncovered."

In refusing to render a verdict on the net outcome, Anechiarico and Jacobs join a long line of researchers and practitioners who have declared themselves frustrated agnostics on the question of the effectiveness of corruption measures over time. Legal scholar (and now federal Judge) John T. Noonan published the definitive book on bribery in 1984, tracing the history of official corruption back to biblical times. But which way were things going? Were the 1970s more corrupt than the 1950s? "No one has done the work that can provide a rational answer to this question," Noonan admitted. Nor has anyone done it in the years since.

Anechiarico and Jacobs take Noonan's argument a step further. "The student of corruption and corruption-control is bedeviled," they complain, "by the absence of data or indicators of the corruption rate. No one knows for sure whether official corruption has diminished over time and, if so, how much of this reduction, if any, is attributable to the anti-corruption project."

But what worries the authors most isn't the lack of good data about corruption—it's the fact that the anti-corruption establishment keeps on expanding in its absence. If it's difficult to document changes in the corruption rate over time, it's depressingly easy to document the ways in which questionable corruption-fighting zeal makes everyday life in the New York City bureaucracy more and more intolerable. New York, Anechiarico and Jacobs say, "treats public employees like probationers in the criminal justice system."

Anti-corruption controls on contracting there have turned the process of awarding virtually any contract, dealing with anything from hospital construction to drug treatment, into an endless labyrinth of form-submissions and paper-shuffling that most sensible businesses prefer to avoid. The conflict-of-interest rules are so complicated as to be virtually unintelligible to most employees, who have to call the Conflict of Interest Board to find out whether they might be in violation.

The financial disclosure requirements involve three separate sets of forms, 12,000 forms a year submitted altogether, adding up to more than 2 million pages of information on the dollar-by-dollar financial life of the city's senior employees. Working for the city of New York, one bureaucrat confided, "is like going to the bathroom without a door on the stall."

And yet much of this paperwork is little more than symbolic: For all the millions of dollars spent setting up this disclosure system, only a handful of city employees have been disciplined for violating it. In one recent year, only 1,000 of the 12,000 submissions were even read by anybody. "Due to budget cuts," the authors say, "the Conflict of Interest Board does little more than babysit the filed forms."

New York City's approach to corruption is what Anechiarico and Jacobs call "panoptic," after the Panopticon, the multi-sided prison that British philosopher Jeremy Bentham designed for the express purpose of making sure every prisoner was under surveillance every minute of the day.

The panoptic approach assumes that the correct response to corruption is not to end patronage, as the civil service reformers of the 1880s wanted to do, or to recruit experts, as the Progressives of the early-20th century recommended. The panoptic approach is to watch the bureaucrats like a hawk, Bentham-style, and to swoop down on them at the first hint of trouble. This is how we end up with an octopus like the

New York City Department of Investigation.

In the view of Anechiarico and Jacobs, panoptic corruption-fighting is a brand of medicine with profound negative side effects. It may not be worse than the disease, but there's no evidence it cures the disease in the first place.

"Large governmental organizations, such as New York City's," they write, "are loaded with anti-corruption mechanisms. As years pass, however, the origins and purposes of these mechanisms are forgotten; they become permanent features of the government and its bureaucracy and contribute very little, if anything. After pursuing the vision of corruption-free government for almost a century, we have the worst of both worlds—too much corruption and too much corruption-control."

It's a provocative point, but where does it leave us? If panoptic corruption-fighting hasn't banished the evil from our midst—as it clearly hasn't—that's no argument for abandoning vigilance altogether. True, we have no good evidence of how many New York City employees would be on the take if the Department of Investigation closed down. Maybe the number would be about the same as it is now. I'm not sure I'd want to risk finding out.

Nearly all of New York's most onerous and intrusive anti-corruption mechanisms were put into place following scandals so horrific as to dictate drastic action, not only politically but morally. Most of the disclosure forms and Kafkaesque contracting procedures of the 1990s exist because of the revelation in the 1980s that multimillion-dollar contracts to supply computers to the Parking Violation Bureau had been awarded to a dummy corporation controlled by the Bronx Democratic chairman. What is the city supposed to do [to] protect itself from that sort of humiliation? Nothing?

Anechiarico and Jacobs do not argue that. What they argue is that local governments have a whole array of possible strategies against corruption that they haven't even tried—strategies that don't involve simply demanding more disclosure and wiring more informers with miniaturized listening devices.

The best way to summarize their case is to say that corruption can be fought with positive weapons as well as with negative ones. Cities can nurture a climate of public integrity by treating their bureaucrats better, paying them more, moving management decisions further down the line to give more employees a sense of participation. They can decentralize more functions of government so that the line managers consider themselves more than automatons moved around on a chessboard by a central authority. The NYPD actually began doing this a couple of years ago, under Chief William Bratton, and the results so far seem impressive. Decentralized police management doesn't explain the city's remarkable decline in crime in the mid-1990s, but it can't be unrelated to it, either.

Beyond all that, cities can commit some effort to doing the studies they have never bothered to do on just what effect corruption-control has on corruption over a long period of time. And they can begin the job of setting sensible priorities. "Zero tolerance" never has been a realistic policy, and never will be.

"While corruption is never 'acceptable' in a moral sense," the authors conclude, "some level of corruption is a sociological fact of life in all organizations—public, private, educational, or philanthropic. Just as retailers consider some amount of 'shrinkage' (theft) a cost of doing business, the public and the public sector need to realize that every instance of corruption does not require another layer of corruption-proofing."

VIII.   STATE COURTS

The third branch of state government, the judiciary, probably is the one part of state government with which most citizens would prefer not to have any dealings. State courts handle the crimes reported in the news—drunk driving, child abuse, robbery, murder, and rape. Personal disputes, divorce cases, and other civil matters also are tried in state courts.

Despite the importance of the judiciary in state politics, it is perhaps the least visible branch. One reason is because citizens want it that way; they want the courts to be above the hurly-burly of politics. The legislature may conduct its business in a circuslike atmosphere and the governor may crisscross the state to keep an impossible schedule of appointments, but the courts must be a model of decorum, a place where the rational presentation of facts and arguments leads to truth and justice. But often there are breaches in this hoped-for decorum: the actions of defendants, lawyers, witnesses, aggrieved individuals, spectators, and even, in some people's opinion, the media can be disruptive to the pursuit of justice.

The Court System

The several levels of state courts each have different responsibilities. At the lowest level are trial courts, where cases are argued and juries may be called to weigh the facts presented. Intermediate appellate courts, the next level in many state judicial systems, are where the decisions of the trial courts and other lower courts can be appealed. Finally, each state has a court of last resort. It is usually called the Supreme Court, but in Maine it is called the Supreme Judicial Court; in West Virginia, the Supreme Court of Last

Resort; and in New York, the Court of Appeals. Here, the final appeals to lower court decisions are made unless a federal question is involved, which then means that appeal to the federal appellate courts is possible.

State court judges rule on a variety of concerns. Part of their workload is administrative (for example, the probating of wills). Another part involves conflict resolution (for example, deciding which party is correct in contested divorce settlements and property disputes). And still another area of responsibility includes the criminal prosecution and appeals process.

In a broader sense, state court judges are policy makers. Court decisions, rather than legislation or constitutional amendments, often modify or set aside state policies. Courts are reactive institutions of government, and their decisions are limited by the nature and timing of the cases brought before them. Judges establish new norms of acceptable behavior and revise existing norms to match changing circumstances. Their interpretations of the law may or may not have the backing of the public or of the governor or state legislature. Nonetheless, what they say goes—that is, of course, unless it is overturned by another court decision or by another decision-making body. In some instances, court decisions simply are ignored because the judiciary has no bureaucracy of its own to enforce decisions.

Judicial Politics

The norm of separating partisan politics from the judiciary is part of our national and state political cultures. But judges must be selected in some manner, and inevitably politics become a factor.

The methods used to select judges vary from state to state. Sometimes judges are appointed by the governor and confirmed by the state senate. In Connecticut, the legislature appoints judges from nominations submitted by the governor. In Texas, judges are elected as Democrats or Republicans. Other states—Montana, for example—elect judges on a nonpartisan basis.

Some states have adopted a variation of the "Missouri Plan" to remove politics from the selection process as much as possible. In this process, a nonpartisan group such as the state or district bar association screens the many candidates and recommends the top contenders to the governor, who then makes the final decision. The argument is that merit will be the foremost criterion in the screening and nomination process.

The Missouri Plan also provides that when their terms expire, judges can "run again" on their record. The voters are asked: Should Judge X be retained in office? If the voters say yes, the judge serves another term. If the voters say no, the selection process starts anew. In this way, the judiciary is accountable to the citizens of the state.

In the mid-to-late 1980s, the world of partisan elective judicial politics was in considerable ferment. Political observers were startled in 1986 when three states—California, North Carolina, and Ohio—all had well-publicized, negative, and very expensive partisan races for their state's chief justiceship. In California, the conflict revolved around the reelection of the chief justice, who objected to the death penalty; in North Carolina, it concerned the governor's choice of a new chief justice; and in Ohio, it centered around the very partisan and controversial style of the chief justice.[1]

In 1988, the entire Texas Supreme Court was up for election. Issues in those races included the governor's appointment of a new chief justice, charges of impropriety, controversy over the selection of judges, and the fallout from the major Pennzoil-Texaco lawsuit.

These campaigns, which cost an estimated $10 million, had "the nastiest, most negative campaigning I have ever seen," one Texas legislator told North Carolina's Judicial Selection Study Commission. "If you are before a judge in Texas now, you've got to be worried if you are a Democrat and he is a Republican."[2]

Is justice for sale, as some critics suggest? Giving money to political campaigns, even judicial campaigns, is legal and "that's the problem," according to a Texaco spokeswoman.[3] One Houston lawyer suggested that "it looks just as bad for a lawyer to give a lot of money to a judge as for a judge to take a lot of money from a lawyer."[4] This is all cannon fodder for those wanting to remove the judicial selection process from electoral politics.

The federal government is also involved in the politics of the states' judiciaries. In early 1987, a U.S. district court judge in Jackson, Mississippi, ruled that Section 2 of the Voting Rights Act of 1965 applies to judges elected at the state level. At issue was the question of whether electing judges from at-large, multimember districts dilutes minority voting strength. The impact of the decision probably will mean that state judges will be elected from single-member districts, thereby offering the possibility of greater minority representation in the state judiciaries.[5]

In December 1989, a three-judge federal appeals court upheld the concept that the Voting Rights Act applies to judicial election districts.[6] So, in those states covered by the provisions of the Voting Rights

Act, any changes in judicial district lines or the addition of judges must be precleared with the U.S. Department of Justice before being implemented.[7] In April 1990, the Department of Justice threw out Georgia's system of electing judges because it was discriminatory against blacks. The problem with the system was the election of judges in broad judicial circuits by a majority vote, rather than by a plurality vote. This has the same effect as at-large elections often do: diluting the strength of minority groups.[8]

Sometimes the "minority" can be a political party. In January 1994, a federal district court judge issued a preliminary order declaring that all North Carolina trial level superior court judges be elected in their home districts rather than statewide. The case involved a Republican Party lawsuit charging that the practice of electing these trial judges statewide leaves "islands of Republicans ... unconstitutionally swamped in a sea of yellow-dog Democrats. Only one Republican has ever been elected as a superior court judge."[9] In the 1994 elections, the Republican judicial candidates won handily statewide, but the portion of this decision ensuring judicial elections to be counted in home districts allowed some Democrats to win!

Tides of Judicial Policy Making

A current issue in the states concerns who should take the lead in the judicial system—the federal judiciary interpreting the U.S. Constitution, or the state judiciaries interpreting the individual state constitutions. For decades, the loud cry of "states' rights" masked inaction by state courts on segregation, malapportionment, and other unconstitutional practices.

During the 1950s and 1960s, under a broad interpretation of the Constitution (especially the Fifth and Fourteenth Amendments), the U.S. Supreme Court moved to upset the states' intransigence and, in some cases, illegal activities. Led by Chief Justice Earl Warren (the governor of California from 1943 to 1953), the U.S. Supreme Court overturned state laws upholding segregation, forced state legislatures to apportion themselves on a one-man, one-vote basis following each census, expanded voting rights, legalized abortion, and broadened the rights of the accused in the state criminal justice system. The Warren Court set minimal standards for the states to follow in these areas and often reversed state court decisions that narrowly construed the rights of individuals.

In recent years, the U.S. Supreme Court has become more conservative in its decisions. It has even backed away from some of the minimal standards it set earlier. Several state courts have decided not only to uphold these minimal standards but, in a new form of judicial activism at the state level, to exceed them. Former U.S. Supreme Court justice William J. Brennan, Jr., once described this trend as "probably the most important development in constitutional jurisprudence today."[10] Ronald Collins, an expert on state constitutional law, estimated that between 1970 and the mid-1980s state high courts issued approximately four hundred decisions based on the higher standards of the state constitutions as opposed to the minimum standards established by the U.S. Supreme Court in interpreting the U.S. Constitution.[11] As New Jersey Supreme Court justice Stewart G. Pollock suggests, "Horizontal federalism, in which states look to each other for guidance, may be the hallmark of the rest of the century."[12]

Why does such activism develop in a state's supreme court? One study of six state supreme courts from 1930 to 1980 found that dramatic shifts by state high courts from a relatively passive role to an active role take place in a relatively short period of time and are due mainly to a change in the composition of the court. The appointment of a "maverick" judge to a state's supreme court begins a process in which that judge dissents from the previous consensual and passive court decisions, soon swaying some supporters to the minority position. With additional appointments of more activist-oriented jurists, the court changes direction. Of import is the fact that once a transition to activism occurred, none of these courts moved back in the direction of nonactivism, at least not during the period studied.[13]

However, there is a question as to whether federal or state court decisions will affect states more. In recent years the U.S. Supreme Court has been making significant decisions affecting state politics. For example, in the last decade the U.S. Supreme Court allowed losing political parties to challenge a redistricting plan;[14] thrown out mandated closed party primary systems, thereby allowing independents to participate in the party nominating process;[15] upheld local government affirmative action plans favoring women and minorities;[16] ruled against the time-honored patronage system of governors hiring political supporters;[17] upheld a state's mandatory retirement age limit for its judges;[18] and is knocking down state redistricting plans based on affirmative action or "racial gerrymandering."

Changes are now afoot at the U.S. Supreme Court. After nearly a quarter century of relatively conservative Court appointments made by Republican presidents, Democratic president Bill Clinton has the opportunity to appoint more moderate judges. With these appointments,

Court observers guess that the Court will begin moving away from its very conservative stances on a range of issues. For the states, the interesting question is whether or not this could signal a turn of the tide in judicial policy making toward Supreme Court involvement in issues that the state courts have been handling.

The state courts addressed some difficult issues recently. The area of criminal procedure is in ferment now as more citizens are seeking stronger and more effective punishment of criminals and protection of victims. The recent spate of special legislative sessions and new and tougher state criminal laws passed in response to rising crime rates ensures that state courts will be handling challenges to these laws and their administration. In 1996 the California supreme court knocked down that state's new "three strikes and you're out" law.

State courts are also involved in the process of addressing school finance issues. With so much of the K–12 education financed by revenue generated from local property taxes, parents are finding that where they live determines the quality of education their children will receive. As governors and legislatures fight over how to achieve an equitable solution, the state courts often end up trying to develop ways in which educational equity can be achieved. For example, shifting money from affluent communities to poor communities and from rich school districts to poor school districts are ways in which equity may be achieved. Such actions will lead to conflict with the other two branches of government and some divisive politics.[19]

The abortion fight has also shifted in part to the states as a result of the 1989 *Webster v. Reproductive Health Services* decision. Some state legislatures and governors have developed abortion policies with no middle ground on which prolife and prochoice advocates can agree. Such efforts go directly into the state courts. The author of a controversial abortion judicial decision in Florida found his retention election much more difficult as antiabortion groups sought to defeat him. He won, but the political message was clear: abortion politics can be lethal.[20]

Part VIII explores different aspects of the state judicial branch. Tom Gogola of *Empire State Report* looks at how criticism by the governor and the legislature may harm courts in New York State. Charles Mahtesian of *Governing* analyzes what state supreme court workloads are like—and how some justices respond. Neil Upmeyer of *New Jersey Reporter* discusses the career of that state's retiring supreme court chief justice. Finally, Steven D. Williams in *Comparative State Politics* describes how a sitting state supreme court justice met with an unusual defeat in a 1996 retention election.

Notes

1. Katherine A. Hinckley, "Four Years of Strife Conclude with Ohio Chief Justice's Defeat," *Comparative State Politics Newsletter* 8:2 (April 1987): 13.

2. Jane Ruffin, "Texan Warns N.C. Commission to End System of Electing Judges," (Raleigh) *News and Observer,* November 12, 1988, 3C.

3. Sheila Kaplan, "Justice for Sale," *Common Cause Magazine* (May/June 1987): 29.

4. Peter Applebome, "Texan Fight over Judges Illustrates Politics' Growing Role in Judiciary," (Raleigh) *News and Observer,* January 24, 1988, 14A.

5. "Mississippi Ruling Could Aid N.C. Suit on Judgeship Elections," (Raleigh) *News and Observer,* April 5, 1987, 32A.

6. The Voting Rights Act of 1965, extended in 1970 and 1975, banned redistricting plans that diluted the voting strength of black and other minority communities. The law suspended literacy tests and provided for the appointment of federal supervisors of voter registration in all states and counties where literacy tests (or similar qualifying devices) were in effect as of November 1, 1964, and where less than 50 percent of the voting age residents had registered to vote or voted in the 1964 presidential election. State or county governments brought under the coverage of the law due to low voter registration or participation were required to obtain federal approval of any new voting laws, standards, practices, or procedures before implementing them. The act placed federal registration machinery in six southern states, twenty-eight counties in North Carolina, three counties in Arizona, and one in Idaho.

7. "Federal Court Applies VRA to State Judicial Districts," *Intergovernmental Perspective* 16:1 (Winter 1990): 20.

8. Peter Applebome, "U.S. Declares Georgia Judge Selection Illegal," *New York Times* News Service, in (Raleigh) *News and Observer,* April 27, 1990, 3A.

9. Joseph Neff, "Ruling on Judges Cheers GOP," (Raleigh) *News and Observer,* January 4, 1994, 1A.

10. Quoted in Robert Pear, "State Courts Move Beyond U.S. Bench in Rights Rulings," *New York Times,* May 4, 1986, 1.

11. Cited in Lanny Proffer, "State Courts and Civil Liberties," *State Legislatures* 13:9 (September 1987): 29.

12. Quoted in Pear, "State Courts," 16.

13. John Patrick Hagan, "Patterns of Activism on State Supreme Courts," *Publius* 18:1 (Winter 1988): 97–115.

14. *Davis v. Bandemer* (1986).

15. *Tashjian v. Republican Party of Connecticut* (1986).

16. *Johnson v. Transportation Agency, Santa Clara County, Calif.* (1987).

17. *Rutan et al. v. Republican Party of Illinois* (1990).

18. *Gregory v. Ashcroft* (1991).

19. Lawrence Baum, "Supreme Courts in the Policy Process," in *The State of the States,* 3d ed., ed. Carl E. Van Horn (Washington, D.C.: CQ Press, 1996), 156–157.

20. Ibid.

Judging the Judiciary

by Tom Gogola

The separation of powers is like free speech and freedom of religion, a cornerstone of the American democratic tradition at the local, state and federal levels. The first three articles of the U.S. Constitution give the executive, legislative and judicial branches of government explicit but limited powers to ensure that one body can't out-muscle the others. This model is replicated in the New York State Constitution. But since Gov. George Pataki's election in 1994, the hackles of the state's judiciary community and its civil liberties establishment repeatedly have been raised, as the governor has made no bones about critiquing the judicial branch—particularly in the area of criminal justice.

From his 1996 legislative initiative, the Police and Public Protection Act, which proposed new search and seizure guidelines to the Legislature, to his outspoken criticism of the Court of Appeals to his removal of Bronx District Attorney Robert Johnson from the highly publicized Gillespie murder case, Pataki has embarked on a campaign to put the gubernatorial stamp on the judiciary. Fueling much of the governor's actions has been the voter-mandated drive to implement the 1995 death penalty statute, passed by the Legislature and signed into law by Pataki after a dozen years of Mario Cuomo's vetoes. That effort has led to several instances in which the governor has aired his "verdict" on murder cases and a number of occasions when he has taken to broad-siding the entire judiciary for "coddling criminals" based on a smattering of Court of Appeals rulings that remanded verdicts back to lower courts based on technicalities.

A telling tension between Pataki and Chief Judge Judith Kaye of the New York State Court of Appeals was evident last May on Law Day in Albany, when Pataki took the opportunity to wax philosophical on the reach and propriety of his critique of the judiciary. In an exchange with Kaye, the governor opined, "Does criticism of judicial ruling constitute an attack on judicial independence...? The answer, clearly, is no."

Kaye's rejoinder to Pataki was not so much directed at his fight to critique the bench—she in fact agreed that he had the

Tom Gogola is a freelance writer based in Long Beach. This article is reprinted from *Empire State Report* (September 1996): 43–48.

privilege—but instead broadly hinted at the propriety of the shrill and politically motivated baggage that, in her view, often accompanies such criticism. But the stakes go much deeper—straight to the core of the separation of powers maxim. "The larger issue is very important," says Norman Siegel, executive director of the New York Civil Liberties Union (NYCLU), which filed suit on behalf of Bronx voters in the Gillespie incident, "and that is the independence of the judiciary, and more specifically the Court of Appeals, because Gov. Pataki found fault on a number of occasions with the Court of Appeals and attempted to demonize it and undermine its authority. The concept of limited government is an essential characteristic of democracy and also our constitution."

On Law Day, Pataki took the high ground, quoting noted Federalist and New Yorker Alexander Hamilton, who believed strongly in a powerful executive and judicial branch, especially the executive. But when the power of the executive is such that it begins yanking judges from cases, is that power being abused?

According to Siegel, the answer is clearly yes. Pataki's behavior, he claims, is unlike that of any of his predecessors dating back to the 1960s. "In modern times, you have governors Cuomo, Carey, Malcolm Wilson and Nelson Rockefeller, so you've generally had either moderate or liberal Democrats or moderate Republicans. It appears, however, that the political climate has changed, and the approach on issues of this nature has hardened.

"In the Police and Public Protection Act, [Pataki] was trying to get … the Legislature" to adopt new search and seizure guidelines for the court, he says. But "the process for such an initiation is dictated by law. What you do is amend the state consti-

tution. [Pataki] was, in our opinion, trying to bash the Court of Appeals. As a lawyer, separate from my duties in the NYCLU, every time I go before Chief Judge Judith Kaye's court, I respect them, even if you lose. There is an attempt by the Pataki administration to undermine that, and that theme in itself is probably the most troubling thing coming out of his administration."

The chief judge says, "This is a new age. The level of criticism we have experienced is greater and not just from the governor." In the past, comments from governors and other high officials weren't directed at specific cases, she says.

"There was a deep wound that I bore when stories started appearing last year about the Court of Appeals about 'junk justice,'" Kaye says. She adds with a laugh, "but they've scabbed over, because it [has] been fairly quiet. I don't consider this a personal battle with the governor. We're not locked in combat. This has as much to do with what the press, particularly the tabloid press, has picked up on as anything the governor has said."

Martin Adelman, past chairman of the criminal justice section of the New York Bar Association, sees a greater danger than Kaye, at least publicly, is willing to admit. "I haven't encountered anything like this in 30 years of practice," he says. The problem with Attorney General Dennis Vacco and Pataki is that "they are result-oriented, not process-oriented, and the law is about process. We didn't elect this guy [Pataki] emperor."

On March 14, 1995, Angel Diaz, Jesus Mendez and Ricardo Morales of the Bronx allegedly went on a crime spree in their hometown that would come to have a crucial impact on the application of the death penalty statute in New York and would draw the battle lines between the duties and rights of local prosecutors, the Legislature and the governor.

The three men had been released from prison in 1994 after serving sentences stemming from armed robbery and robbery-assault. On the night in question, allegedly with 9 mm pistols in hand, they reportedly stole a car, robbed a pedestrian and wound up in a shoot-out in the Bronx's Grand Concourse. When the melee ended, Diaz, a police officer, and three bystanders were wounded. Officer Kevin Gillespie was dead.

Bronx District Attorney Robert Johnson, a tremendously popular black prosecutor elected by an overwhelming majority in 1991 largely because of his outspoken opposition to the death penalty—never got the opportunity to make a determination of the sanction he would seek, despite the death penalty statute's call for a 120-day investigatory period. Almost immediately, Republican New York City Mayor Rudolph Giuliani and Pataki, arguing that the wanton brutality of the shooting itself warranted a first-degree murder charge, called for the death penalty for Diaz, who was charged with shooting Gillespie. Pataki wrote Johnson to ask if there was any situation in which the district attorney could envision himself seeking the death penalty.

Johnson had made no secret of his opposition to the death penalty when it was enacted the previous year but claimed he wouldn't exclude categorically considering the sanction under the proper circumstances. "The door is slightly ajar," he said when the death penalty statute was enacted. "It is my present intention not to utilize the death penalty provisions in the statute."

Along with the prosecutorial discretion the statute outlines for seeking the death penalty, it also offered—for the first time—the option of life without parole.

Responding to Pataki's ultimatum that he declare his intentions by the day following the date of his letter, Johnson tersely informed the governor that he was unwilling to make any determination at that point because Diaz hadn't been indicted yet. Besides, he wrote, the discretion to seek any sanction was wholly within the local prosecutor's domain.

At that point, Pataki made the highly unusual move—even he admitted as much—of removing Johnson from the case based on his conviction that Johnson would never seek the death penalty. The governor appointed Vacco, who supports the death penalty, to take his place. Johnson took his case to the state Supreme Court, arguing that Pataki had overstepped his boundaries and had violated the letter of the death penalty statute. "There is also the uncomfortable undercurrent that Johnson is a black [district attorney] and the only one in the state," Adelman says. "Manhattan [District Attorney] Robert Morgenthau has had several death penalty cases and has elected not to pursue a first degree charge in any of these cases. You don't hear any noise from Pataki about Morgenthau."

The overheated rhetoric of "racism" from one side and Pataki's persistent and occasionally denigrating criticism of the state judiciary's liberal, "pro-criminal" stance further polarized the various players—with the Urban League and the American Civil Liberties Union lining up on one side, and the Police Benevolent Association and Pataki on the other—and underscored the issues involved: the limits of the governor's authority, the limits of prosecutorial discretion, and the question of who represents voters in the Bronx. Did the governor have the right or duty to step in and remove a duly elected prosecutor from a case even when the criteria for such action was not judicial misconduct, criminality, incompetence or conflict of interest but differences in policy and, indeed, in this case, a different moral outlook when it comes to the death penalty? Does a statutory option mean that a prosecutor must at least consider it when the facts of a case dictate?

The state Supreme Court would not rule on the spat, however, and Pataki had a de facto round one victory. Vacco now is angling for a first-degree conviction against Diaz, but the trial has yet to begin as Johnson has taken his case to the Appellate Division, though arguments have not been heard.

NYCLU also filed suit on behalf of five Bronx residents in late April arguing to have Johnson reinstated based on the fact that the governor's actions were outside the purview of the new death penalty law. As with Johnson's parallel lawsuit, the lower court said it wasn't justifiable, and NYCLU has gone to the Appellate Division, which will hear arguments this month. Regardless of the outcome, it almost definitely will wind up in the Court of Appeals. "In our opinion," says Siegel, "the case raises profoundly fundamental questions about the nature of democracy in New York and crucial constitutional and legal questions about the authority of the governor to remove a duly elected district attorney.

"The separation of powers has a subsidiary proposition," Siegel adds. "The governor cannot act beyond legislative policy. Pataki argued that Johnson failed to comply with the new death penalty law by refusing to consider it, yet the murder-one law doesn't require a [district attorney] to consider seeking it. He went beyond what the Legislature provided, and as far as I'm concerned, he superseded his authority."

Pataki had argued that Johnson's refusal to "faithfully execute" the statute gave him the right to remove the district attorney. "It's not the governor's intention to micromanage the district attorney[s] around the state," says Pataki spokesman Patrick McCarthy. "District Attorney Johnson precluded himself from the option to utilize the death penalty, and the governor was assuring that the statute be applied throughout the state."

The governor has an obligation to assign special prosecutors in these kinds of cases, McCarthy adds, "and he was well within his rights to do so in this case. The Governor really went through the proper channels in making sure this was done properly because he was sensitive to the issue of separation of powers, and he made sure he was taking reasonable, responsible and effective measures throughout the entire affair."

At the time of the Gillespie murder Pataki and Johnson already had locked horns over the death penalty in the case of Michael Vernon, a severely developmentally disabled young man charged with killing eight customers in a Bronx shoe store in late 1995 because a pair of special-order sneakers hadn't arrived yet. Johnson chose not to seek first-degree charges in that case—not because of his opposition to the statute, but because of Vernon's disability. The governor, realizing that calling for the death of a mentally ill, black 22-year-old wasn't going to win him any friends in the Bronx, ultimately said he accepted Johnson's decision "with serious reservations."

Executive branch "meddling" in the affairs of the judiciary or other executive branch officials is by no means a unique phenomenon. One need only to look to the Oklahoma City bombing last year that led President Bill Clinton and Attorney General Janet Reno to pounce on the death penalty option for the perpetrators before any indictments had been handed down. But there are very few cases in New York involving overstepping the Legislature's statutory allowances, according to Siegel. In preparing his appeal, he cites as a precedent a Carey-era executive order that overstepped a law outlining properly administered conflict of interest safeguards for executive branch authorities. Carey issued such an executive order forcing employees to submit detailed financial records. "The court said there were limits, and that the governor couldn't create mandates not already included in the statute," Siegel says.

Despite the rarity of removing prosecutors and thus calling into question the separation of powers maxim, Pataki may have enough support in other counties to ensure a death penalty conviction in the not-too-distant future. The *New York Law Journal* recently reported that Otsego County District Attorney William Gibbons was taken off a murder-one case by Pataki because he had hired a former public defender to be an assistant district attorney on the case. Vacco now is handling the case, which involves a parental double homicide.

Gibbons, who supports the death penalty, says however that the attorney general was brought in "at our request."

Supportive district attorneys in upstate Republican strongholds notwithstanding, Siegel nonetheless is concerned that in the Gillespie matter, "If Pataki wins in court, what is to stop him down the road from removing anyone?"

Further emboldening the GOP criminal justice juggernaut in New York was the Howard Baer brouhaha. In that episode, which swirled through the New York media whirlpool around the same time as the Gillespie murder, Baer, a Clinton ap-

pointee and a generally well-regarded liberal, ruled that police in the Washington Heights section of Manhattan conducted an illegal search when they assumed two men who allegedly walked up to a car with out-of-state license plates, shoved duffel bags into the trunk and then ran away when detectives approached, were engaged in drug trafficking. Despite the fact that detectives found the bags filled with drugs and that a woman driver confessed to being a drug runner for years, Baer threw the evidence and confession out, infuriating Giuliani, who began to beat the drum for Baer's removal from the bench.

Not surprisingly, the issue instantly was politicized as conservative firebrands stoked the fires about Clinton's liberal bias. One of Baer's more controversial rationales for throwing the case out particularly incensed the mayor: He claimed that citizens of Washington Heights were rightfully fearful of police brutality and extortion given that the neighborhood's precinct had been the site of some of the worst cases of police corruption since the 1970s. Baer eventually caved to the pressure and consented to a retrial, allowing the evidence and confession to be admitted.

Pataki was mum on the Baer flap while it raged, though he obviously was irked by it. He held his fire until April 1, when he released the following statement: "Baer's original ruling was at war with common sense and was an insult to New York City police officers."

Of a more recent vintage was the Guidice murder. In that case, Giuliani called for the death penalty for the killer of officer Vincent Guidice. The officer responded to a domestic violence call and, when he arrived on the scene, he severely gashed his leg on a piece of broken mirror glass. The wound proved fatal.

But under the capital offense statute as it exists, neither the evidence nor the circumstances were enough to warrant a first-degree murder charge, though the alleged perpetrator had in fact broken the mirror while fighting off the police. Though it was another case in the Bronx, this time the governor and mayor found an ally in Johnson, who had argued strongly against the court's decision to set bail at a relatively low $10,000 based on the fact that the man in custody, Anthony Rivers, had extensive prior convictions including a half-dozen bench warrants issued when he failed to appear in court to answer other charges. In early June, Pataki criticized the low bail, arguing that "confidence in our criminal justice system is diminished by decisions that flout common sense and good judgment." He praised Johnson for arguing essentially the same thing in court. Says Pataki spokesman McCarthy, "That underlines the fact that the governor takes this on a case-by-case basis," and not out of any particular animus toward Johnson or antideath penalty prosecutors.

The governor also reiterated his desire that legislators pass a bill he sent them in February that would for the first time in New York's history give prosecutors the same right defendants long have held to appeal "unduly low bail and sentencing determinations" set forth by judges. The federal government makes that allowance for prosecutors, but the number of cases in which there is an egregiously "pro-criminal bail" or sentence in New York is very low. "If you could find a few bad cases, that shouldn't be cause for turning over the bail and sentencing system in New York," Siegel says. "Again this is an attempt to intimidate and undermine the judiciary, in this case, the trial courts."

The introduction of the bail bill can be traced directly to the now infamous Judge Lorin Duckman flap. In that case, the criminal court judge had set a relatively low bail for defendant Benito Oliver, who had been arrested for beating his girlfriend in Queens. Oliver, who had a history of domestic violence as well as a rape conviction, was slapped with an order of protection ruling upon his release. He then allegedly killed his girlfriend.

Giuliani immediately began calling to have Duckman ousted from the bench, particularly because in another case the judge had sentenced Maximo Pena of Brooklyn to serve no jail time after being convicted of beating his ex-girlfriend. Pena was released but soon thereafter was arrested for allegedly dragging her down two flights of stairs and punching her in the face. After it also was exposed that the judge's record contained some questionable statements about domestic violence, Duckman was transferred to the civil division.

In response, Pataki called for the prosecutorial right to appeal low bail and sentencing determinations and also argued for the stiffening of penalties for those who violate orders of protection, making them felonies instead of misdemeanors. The Legislature granted his wish on the latter this August [1996]. The former, however, is stuck in the Assembly Codes Committee, whose chairman, Democratic Assemblyman Joseph Lenton of Brooklyn, reiterated through spokeswoman Sara Duncan his concern that the bill was a "radical" departure from the state's bail guidelines and thus needs further study before he will report it out of his committee.

The cumulative effect of the governor's reaching into the judicial arena led the New York State Bar Association's Special Committee on Judicial Independence—formed in April to "reaffirm the preservation of an independent judiciary"—to detail what is an appropriate critique of the judiciary and what crosses the line into onerous meddling.

The committee, which included several prominent Republicans and Democrats, reported, "It is not fair to make personal attacks against a judge because of disagreement with his or her rulings in particular cases. It is highly improper for public officials who have the power of judicial appointment to demand resignation or removal of a judge based upon his or her rulings."

While not speaking directly to any particular case that has or may come before the court, Chief Judge Kaye notes that "there are rules that say lawyers are supposed to support the justice system and educate the public in a positive way. You're certainly not supposed to trash it as a lawyer."

Pataki is an attorney, having earned his degree from Columbia Law School.

"Is there any modern applicability to these rules [lawyers are supposed to support]?" Kaye asks. "That is a tough, tough question because we are in a media age, with sound bites and cynicism, and an age where people really think they know the justice system. I've bemoaned for years and years that the Court of Appeals has been ignored, and wished people would better understand what the court does, and come see what we do. [The understanding] came, but not in the way I had hoped, an informed temperate analysis, with the emphasis on informed."

The question raised by civil libertarians and those concerned with the separation of powers is simple: What is the net effect of an activist executive branch inserting itself directly into the criminal court system? At worst, those critics argue, in addition to casting a pall over the entire judicial process by politicizing crimes for the benefit of elected officials, it gives defendants short shrift when it comes to due process by making them pawns in the chess game of public opinion. "There is absolutely no good way to put a positive sound bite on a reversal of a murder case," Kaye says.

Critics say it also gives too much power to the executive branch—which is unfettered by the ethical constraints that prohibit judges from commenting on a case-by-case basis. "If we begin a campaign of press conferences, etc., how can we sit in judgment?"

But if holding judges' feet to the fire makes the criminal justice system more responsible and responsive to the concerns of the electorate, what then is the crime? "The governor's primary responsibility is safeguarding and protecting the rights of individuals around the state," says McCarthy. New York "for too long has protected the rights of criminals more than the rights of victims."

Supreme Chaos

by Charles Mahtesian

When Chief Justice John Mowbray retired from the Nevada Supreme Court in 1992, ending more than a year's worth of embarrassing controversy and petty quarrels, the state's legal community felt exhausted but relieved. At last, people assumed, the court could settle down to a normal standard of behavior.

But it didn't. Life on Nevada's highest legal tribunal hasn't gotten any better since the Mowbray affair ended. If anything, it has gotten worse. At least the Mowbray business was relatively simple. Unpopular with several colleagues, who considered him too old and infirm to remain on the court after 25 years, Mowbray was essentially hounded out of office. His telephones were shut off prematurely, he claimed, and he was not even invited to his successor's swearing-in. In response, Mowbray chose the word "cesspool" to describe the court. "This is the kind of stuff those bums do," he said. "It is terrible."

The occasion of Mowbray's departure was a time for reconciliation if ever there was one. Instead, the court almost immediately began an equally bitter argument over judicial discipline that continues to fester more than three years after it first surfaced. Two of the judges believe that a third, in association with the state attorney general and a prominent Las Vegas law firm, conspired to leak documents to the press in order to embarrass the court. The first faction formed a special panel to look into the source of the leaks; a second faction ousted them from the panel.

"The soap opera in Nevada is not only appalling but amazing," says Ronald Rotunda, a legal ethics expert at the University of Illinois College of Law. "You'd think a friend would tap them on the shoulder and say, 'What are you doing?'"

Appalling and amazing the Nevada situation may be. Unique, it unfortunately is not. The 1990s have been a time when a depressing number of state high courts and justices have seemed inexplicably bent on disgracing themselves.

The Ohio Supreme Court, best known over the years not for its incisive opinions but for its partisan and combative atmosphere, replete with allegations of phone-tapping, case-fixing and payoffs, reached a

Charles Mahtesian is a staff writer for *Governing*. This article is reprinted from *Governing* (July 1996): 40–43.

new standard in 1991, when two feuding justices settled a difference of opinion in a wrestling match that resulted in cracked ribs for one combatant. Justice Andrew Douglas, who was knocked to the floor by Justice Craig Wright during an argument over the source of an unflattering news report, agreed not to press charges after Wright apologized.

But the most bizarre case is that of Pennsylvania, where after several years of judicial sniping, backstabbing and other varieties of aberrant behavior, the legislature felt compelled to intervene in the affairs of the seven-member state Supreme Court. The legislature impeached Justice Rolf Larsen following his conviction on charges that he used court employees to obtain prescription tranquilizers in an effort to keep secret his psychiatric treatment.

More sensational than the misconduct charges leveled against Larsen were the counter-accusations he directed against his colleagues on the bench. In an extraordinary 83-page document, Larsen alleged that two of the other Supreme Court justices were conspiring against him to further their own political ambitions and to block his ascension to chief justice. Strangest of all was Larsen's charge that a fellow justice once commandeered a vehicle in a Philadelphia hotel parking lot in an attempt to run him down.

As details of life on the high court trickled out during the impeachment proceedings, the state learned of a dysfunctional institution beset with petty rivalries and riven by mutual distrust. The Larsen debacle intensified pressures to move away from direct, partisan election of judges and toward a system thought to ensure a higher caliber of nominee—so-called merit selection. In that sense, Rolf Larsen inadvertent-

ly became the state's foremost judicial reformer.

But all Pennsylvanians had to do to see the limitations of that solution was to look across the border to New York, where Chief Justice Sol Wachtler—a gubernatorial appointee with impeccable legal credentials—was serving 13 months in prison for anonymously harassing a former lover by phone and for threatening to kidnap her child.

Wachtler was, by virtually unanimous agreement, a special case, a highly competent judge who suffered a mental breakdown. His troubles suggest nothing about other jurists. The fact remains, however, that for the past several years, more than a few high courts and individual justices have been, one might say, acting a little funny.

Mississippi Justice Chuck McRae avoided a one-year license suspension for drunk driving last year by pleading hardship—he insisted he could not earn a living without driving privileges. Illinois Justice James Heiple led police on an O.J. Simpson-style low-speed chase to his home last January after initially being pulled over for speeding. He was later charged with resisting arrest.

Some high court justices have been embroiled in much more serious legal problems. The last two chief justices in Rhode Island have been forced to resign under an ethical cloud, both accused of, among other things, running the state courts as personal patronage and graft mills. The latest to step down, Thomas F. Fay, pleaded guilty in 1995 to two felony counts and three misdemeanor charges of unethical conduct, stemming in part from allegations he maintained a secret slush fund to finance a lavish lifestyle. His predecessor, Joseph Bevilacqua, escaped impeachment by resigning after being censured for associating with felons and committing adultery in a motel owned by organized crime figures.

Last year in Oregon, a former court secretary filed a sexual harassment complaint against Justice Ed Fadeley, who compounded matters with some ill-chosen remarks speculating about what constitutes a sexual advance. Louisiana Chief Justice Pascal Calogero received embarrassing attention after it was disclosed that he had voted against the efforts of a New Orleans newspaper to obtain documents relating to a controversial college scholarship program. Calogero's three sons had all received secret scholarships from the program.

And so it goes. "I don't know if there is some kind of airborne disease out there," says Ronald Rotunda, "but it certainly is true that many state courts are under siege."

Just as every institution has had its share of scoundrels, state supreme courts have always had errant members. Whether there are any more or any fewer now is a matter of speculation. Some high court scholars argue that the issue is not more problem judges, just more media scrutiny. Indeed, the extensive newspaper coverage of Illinois Justice Heiple's January arrest was due less to its specifics than to his notoriety as the author of the controversial Baby Richard child-custody decision [in 1995]. "Thirty years ago, the incident may not have made the papers," says Patrick McFadden, a professor at Loyola University in Chicago and the author of a book on judicial election campaigns. "A lot of indiscretions by judges were pushed under the rug, especially if it didn't directly affect their cases."

Others insist that any way you look at it, the number of judges involved in extra-ordinary incidents is just a small fraction of the 325 high court justices spread across the 50 states. "If you consider the totality of state supreme court justices at this given period, and then think how many have gone haywire, I suspect the percentage is exceedingly low," says Tom Darr, director of administration and communications for the Supreme Court of Pennsylvania. "You're going to find a percentage of people anywhere who go haywire."

Courts are also inevitably going to contain, as all institutions do, knots of people who can't get along with each other. With workloads constantly increasing and state supreme courts forced to consider a whole raft of difficult and emotionally charged issues, the potential for internal strife may be higher than it was a generation ago. "You're putting together anywhere from five to seven human beings and asking them to decide on sensitive political and legal issues," says Jeffrey M. Shaman, a judicial ethics expert at the DePaul University College of Law. "It's only natural that you'll have some personality conflicts."

And when those conflicts come up, judges are far more willing than they once were to talk freely about them. The splintering of the Nevada court has occurred in full view of the public. So did the fighting a few years ago in Ohio, where during the height of the court chaos, several justices complained that their colleagues on the bench were conspiring with the press to make the court look foolish.

"Internal wrangling used to be hidden," says Patrick McFadden. "There was an ethos toward keeping disputes internal. I sense a greater willingness by judges to take their problems with colleagues public."

Where supreme court justices are elected, these tendencies toward conflict have been made worse in the past few years by intense political competition over the makeup of the court. In Michigan, Texas and Alabama, supreme court life has been all but defined in the 1990s by the feud that pits the state's business, medical and insurance interests, which want to limit damage awards in civil cases, and trial lawyers, who want to preserve the status quo. More often than not, the partisan sniping on this issue that predominates at campaign time simply spills over into the court's next session.

Alabama's Supreme Court candidates have been perceived for the past decade essentially as stalking horses for either the Business Council or the Alabama Trial Lawyers Association. The dispute reached a dubious peak in the 1994 election for chief justice, in a bitter contest between incumbent Sonny Hornsby and Perry Hooper Sr., a business-backed challenger.

In one injudicious encounter, the two candidates confronted each other on the steps of the high court building. Hooper denounced his opponent for "conspiring to ensure a liberal, trial-lawyer majority." Hornsby responded by calling Hooper a "bald-faced liar."

In the end, the voters found it hard to figure out who was telling the truth. The contest proved so close—Hooper won by less than 300 votes out of the 1.1 million cast—that it ultimately trickled up to the U.S. Supreme Court. After nearly a year of legal wrangling, Hooper took the oath of office last October. In the awkward meantime, Hornsby continued to serve as chief justice even though his term had ended and his pay had been stopped.

"When you elect your judges in popular elections, candidates must find ways to distinguish themselves," says Kate Sampson of the American Judicature Society.

"That opens the door to all kinds of mischief."

No one can claim any direct connection between the humiliating antics of a few courts and the significance of the legal work the system is doing. The fact is that over the past decade, state supreme courts have been more assertive policy players than at any time in their history, taking an activist role on countless issues that used to be decided only by Congress or the federal judiciary. State supreme courts have invalidated school financing systems, guaranteed funding of abortions for poor women and granted free-speech protection to obscenity.

In the 1990s, virtually every state supreme court spends part of each year wrestling with the most volatile issues of the day—privacy, religion, free speech, right-to-die, school funding and fair housing cases. "That makes for more scrutiny than in the past," says Charles Sheldon, a judicial scholar at Washington State University. "They're caught up in the litigation explosion. More of these contentious and constitutional issues are going to the courts."

None of the recent examples of shameful publicity are going to reduce the importance of state supreme courts or cripple them as instruments of policy. What these incidents may do is offer ammunition to those who dislike the work a particular court or group of justices is doing. In the old days, state judicial activism was more likely to cause muted displeasure than outright insult. In the current environment, the flurry of less-than-dignified behavior is making state courts easy prey for their ideological opponents.

In New York this year, after concluding that the state high court was overzealously protecting the rights of criminal defendants, Governor George E. Pataki introduced legislation to strip the court of some of its authority. A few years ago, that might have been a politically risky move to make. In the aftermath of the Wachtler episode, it was not.

The trend toward state supreme court disrespect has been noticeable even in states where there has been no major scandal or misbehavior. More than a dozen state judiciary-related bills were filed in New Hampshire for the 1996 session, all aimed at limiting court authority or establishing a new disciplinary review process. Arizona also witnessed the introduction of a slew of anti-judiciary bills, including several term-limit measures. So far, most of these efforts to rein in the judiciary have been unsuccessful. But it is hard to miss their point.

In Massachusetts, legislators on unfriendly terms with Chief Justice Paul Liacos repaid him last year by quietly inserting a budget amendment that attempted to bar him from using one of his two personal offices. Never popular with legislators to begin with, the chief justice compounded matters by publicly joking about the ethical problems surrounding the House speaker and Senate president.

A few months later, a coalition of liberal groups in Massachusetts waged a war of invective against Charles Fried, the former Reagan administration solicitor general nominated to the state high court. After a particularly nasty barrage of insults, one confirmation panel member summarized the prevailing climate in an exasperated defense of the nominee. "Charles Fried does not have horns and a long green tail," he said. "He's not a rapist, murderer or a pedophile."

Fried's ugly confirmation battle underscored the limitations—as well [as] the benefits—of high court merit selection. Choosing justices by appointment rather than election is presumed to remove politics from the process and ensure a higher caliber of judges. That is why about half the states use some variation of a merit-based system.

And the advantages are impossible to ignore. Despite the controversy over his nomination, Charles Fried, when finally confirmed, clearly added a superior legal mind to the bench. He did not have to run in a demeaning campaign for the job and was not viewed as the tool of a self-interested political coalition that paid for his candidacy. On the other hand, it would be a stretch to call his appointment non-political: It was Fried's partisan pedigree and ideological consistency that in large part attracted Republican Governor William F. Weld's notice.

The absence of judicial elections is no guarantee of blue-ribbon choices, as Rhode Island residents can attest to. Until a judicial reform package was enacted in the wake of the state's most recent scandal, the legislature selected high court judges on a cavalierly political basis, often from its own clubby ranks. Joseph Bevilacqua, serving as House speaker in 1975, simply had his colleagues confirm him as chief justice. His successor, former legislator Thomas Fay, was placed in office by then-House Speaker Matthew Smith, who in turn won appointment as court administrator. Smith was convicted of two misdemeanor counts in 1994, three months after Fay's guilty plea.

"There are political aspects to merit selection as well," warns G. Alan Tarr, author of *State Supreme Courts in State and Nation*. "Where there have been problems, the question is whether appropriate candidates have been put forward."

But if appointing justices on a "merit" basis is no guarantee of statesmanship, it is beginning to look more and more as if electing them on a partisan basis is a recipe for trouble. Direct election clearly played a significant role in creating the embarrassing spectacles in Alabama, Nevada, Ohio and Pennsylvania.

Judicial scholars nearly all agree that merit selection isn't a perfect method—just a demonstrably better one than the alternative. "There are a lot of arguments about different systems," says Patrick McFadden, "but it's fair to say that the election systems generate more oddballs than the merit systems."

End of an Era

by Neil Upmeyer

You needn't look beyond the borders of New Jersey to test the validity of President Bill Clinton's assertion that "The era of big government is over."

With fewer bureaucrats on the state payroll, government in Trenton is actually doing less than it was a year or two ago. Aside from cutting taxes, Gov. Christie Whitman's main claim of success, so far, is cutting government spending. While state spending rose at an annual rate of 12 percent during the booming 80s and 7 percent even during the recessionary years of this decade, Whitman can crow that on her watch, expenditures have grown only 1 percent a year—well below the rate of inflation.

But "big government" doesn't only refer to big spending on big bureaucracy. And on July 1st [1996], additional proof of the end of this era came with the resignation of Robert Wilentz, chief justice of the State Supreme Court. Wilentz served with distinction for 17 years, but his resignation in the face of a struggle against disabling cancer marks as clear a departure from big government as the new state budget that took effect the same day.

Democratic Gov. Brendan Byrne picked Wilentz in 1979 to be the new chief justice. At that time, Byrne reflected on qualities found among the three preceding chiefs, saying he was "looking for someone with the depth of a Weintraub, the authority of a Vanderbuilt and the compassion of a Hughes." In retrospect, Byrne still thinks he chose the right person. "It was a great appointment," he says. Echoing the words Wilentz had used to endorse Byrne during his first run for governor in 1973, Byrne calls Wilentz "a good and decent man."

"I chose him because of his outstanding reputation as a lawyer, because he was successfully running one of the largest law firms in the state and because he is beloved by everyone who knows him," says Byrne.

Byrne praises the "powerful intellect" Wilentz brought to the state's most controversial cases. "I didn't agree with the surrogate mother [Baby M] decision," said the former governor. "But it was well thought out."

Neil Upmeyer is president of the Center for the Analysis of Public Issues in Princeton, New Jersey, and editor of *New Jersey Reporter*. This article is reprinted from *New Jersey Reporter* (July–August 1996): 2.

Wilentz "is a towering intellect," said John Degnan, who served as Byrne's attorney general. "And he is a deeply compassionate guy—very concerned and caring."

That sense of concern and caring was the hallmark of Wilentz's career on the bench. "The Wilentz-led Court broke new ground in many areas of life, but always with a deep sense of social justice as the underpinnings," Whitman declared upon hearing his plan to step down.

Social justice may have been the motivation behind the court's most far-reaching decisions—but the imposition of his judicial authority proved controversial.

Wilentz, characterized by friends as an "activist" and by foes as "interventionist," established a new role for the Supreme Court by dictating policy in a way that blurred the lines of authority separating the Governor, the Legislature and the Judiciary. His tenure is marked by big government solutions to some of the state's most perplexing problems.

Seeking to correct the funding disparities that distinguish urban school districts from their wealthy suburban counterparts, Wilentz set the standard for an equitable remedy in the 1990 *Abbott v. Burke* decision—a financial commitment the Legislature has yet to meet and which now is being challenged by the Whitman administration.

And through two "Mount Laurel" decisions during the 1980s, the Wilentz court challenged the precept of "home rule" by attempting to force suburbs to take responsibility for providing affordable housing.

None of these decisions enjoyed popular support. One nearly cost Wilentz his job.

Even though he came from a political family (Wilentz's father was both the Democratic boss of Middlesex County and the state attorney general who prosecuted Bruno Hauptman for the Lindbergh kidnapping) and served two terms in the Assembly (Gov. Hughes called him "the best legislator in the country"), many considered Wilentz arrogant and aloof as chief justice and maladroit in his dealings with the Legislature.

Thus, the 1983 *Mt. Laurel II* decision—which sought to enforce the "fair share" principles defined in the original 1975 *Mt. Laurel* ruling by imposing a host of intrusive remedies to compensate for a town's failure to provide affordable housing—"exploded in the state like a giant hand grenade," wrote former Gov. Tom Kean in his book, *The Politics of Inclusion.* Wilentz, writing for the court, declared: "We may not build houses, but we do enforce the constitution."

It was "clearly an instance of judicial activism at its worst," Kean wrote. "An unrestrained court had stomped on the toes of the executive and legislative branches of government."

Yet, out of respect for the principle of judicial independence, Kean set aside his opposition to the *Mt. Laurel* decision and, in 1985, renominated his former Assembly colleague for a tenured position as chief justice. Kean endured a wave of criticism from GOP colleagues over the nomination to stand by his beleaguered nominee during rancorous debate over the confirmation, even cajoling the deciding vote from a Republican senator.

The controversy over *Mt. Laurel II* may, in fact, have foreshadowed the end of the era of judicial activism. Adoption of The Fair Housing Act, a legislative remedy to New Jersey's lack of affordable housing, led to a third *Mt. Laurel* ruling in 1986. *Mt. Laurel III* sanctioned creation of the Council on Affordable Housing to oversee "fair share" cases, thereby eliminating the policy-making role the court had assumed in *Mt. Laurel II*.

But the chief justice's resignation, in all likelihood, ensures that the era of activism in the Wilentz court tradition is over. It was his leadership that created the con-sensus for intervention. Absent that leadership in the new era of smaller, less intrusive government, it is more likely the court will sit on the sidelines, deferring to the Legislature and the Executive. And those who must rely on the strength of the court may suffer as a consequence.

The 1996 Retention Election of Justice White

by Steven D. Williams

Tennessee's Supreme Court is unique in two ways. First, the state constitution requires that each of the three grand divisions (East, Middle, West) be represented in the five-member court with no division having more than two members. Second, the Supreme Court selects the state attorney general, who, by tradition, is from the grand division with only one justice.

In 1971, the legislature adopted a modified Missouri Plan for the intermediate appellate courts and the state supreme court. In 1973, the Democrats in the legislature decided to return to a system of partisan elections for the Supreme Court justices. Other appellate courts were left under the modified Missouri Plan.

In 1994, Democratic governor, Ned McWherter, led the fight to reinstitute merit selection for the high court under the mischievously named Tennessee Plan. One of the provisions of the Tennessee Plan that distinguishes it from other state Missouri plans is that it provides for a judicial evaluation commission to appraise the work habits of all appellate judges. These evaluations are then to be sent to all major newspapers before a retention election. A poor evaluation allows party nominated and/or independent candidates to oppose a sitting judge in the August general election.

Republicans had always supported a merit plan for the Supreme Court because a Republican has never won a partisan Supreme Court election. But if a Republican governor appointed a Republican justice, the justice would very likely be retained in a yes/no election.

Many Democrats favored a return to merit selection for the Supreme Court as a way to do away with judges needing to raise campaign funds. Moreover, a merit plan would make it easier to recruit blacks and women to the high court.

Since no candidate has ever been defeated in retention elections for intermediate appellate courts, members of both parties seem to assume it would be very difficult to defeat a sitting justice in a retention election. However, on August 1 [1996] the voters of Tennessee discredited that assumption. A sitting justice, Penny White, was rejected by 55 percent of the voters.

Steven D. Williams is a professor of political science at Tennessee Technological University. This article is reprinted from *Comparative State Politics* 17:5 (October 1996): 28–30.

The campaign against Justice White started when Attorney General Burson publicly assailed his immediate employers, the Supreme Court, over a murder case. Burson was outraged that a three-member majority, including White, found that the rape and murder of an elderly woman did not fit the legal definition of torture or serious physical abuse as an aggravating circumstance to support the death penalty.

The revelation of this decision mobilized many victim-rights advocates, law enforcement officials, and prosecuting attorneys to voice their anger at the court. Tennessee Conservation Union President, John Davis, seized the opportunity to raise money and send out letters denouncing the decision. Soon Justice White's retention election became a referendum on capital punishment.

These events occurred simultaneously with two lawsuits that contested whether White could have a retention election because she had not been evaluated by the judicial evaluation committee. The State Supreme Court recused itself from these suits and Governor Sundquist appointed a special Supreme Court whose members were scattered across two continents and four cities. This court issued four opinions with each one trying to correct a problem with the previous opinion. Its final opinion was that White would have to run in a partisan election. This decision encouraged the Republicans to field a candidate, John King, to run against White.

Finally [a] U.S. district judge, Bernice Donald of Memphis, ruled in a suit brought by an intermediate appellate Court Justice, Holly Kirby Lillard, that Lillard was entitled to be on the ballot without opposition because this is what the Tennessee plan statute stipulated. Burson had opposed Lillard's request but after this decision, the attorney general decided that the same rules would have to apply to all justices. Leading Republicans then joined the attack on White by allying themselves with victim-rights advocates instead of the Tennessee Conservation Union. (The state Republican hierarchy is not fond of the Tennessee Conservation Union because it has attacked leading Republicans for being too liberal.)

White failed to exhibit a judicial demeanor in the face of these attacks. She criticized the Tennessee Conservation Union for its "extremist rhetoric" and suggested that prosecutors should "close them down." She publicly courted votes from public defenders and criminal defense lawyers generating unfavorable news coverage about the ethics of judges asking for support from groups who may have to appear before them in court.

Leading Democrats, such as former Gov. Ned McWherter, who had appointed White, came to her defense in radio ads. Trial lawyers and some women's groups openly supported her, as well. However, these efforts did not save White. She lost in 74 of Tennessee's 95 counties, including her home county in East Tennessee.

White's term of office will end in August of 1997. Then, presumably, a nomination commission will present names to Governor Sundquist, who will appoint a new justice.

In 1998, all five justices will be up for a retention election. Will the Penny White example act as a recipe to conduct a campaign to unseat any justice who can be classified as soft on crime?

IX.   LOCAL GOVERNMENT

Former U.S. House Speaker Tip O'Neill always reminded us that "all politics is local." This admonition cautions those who would read some national feelings or trends into voting results across the country. In much the same way, it is also true for many of us that "all government is local." People are more immediately affected by what goes on at city hall and the county courthouse than by what occurs in the statehouse or the White House.

Evidence of this is everywhere. Children attend local schools; local transportation systems help them get to school and their parents and others to work; local police and fire departments ensure our protection; city sanitation departments, or contractors hired by them, pick up our garbage and trash; recycling efforts are established locally; marriage licenses, divorce papers, and wills are filed with county courthouses; civil suits and criminal trials are carried out in those same courthouses; recreational facilities and programs are run locally—and the list goes on.

Just as each election and campaign was local or unique in O'Neill's view, so, too, is local government. A particular array of services and facilities provided to those living in one community may vary considerably from those provided in another. In some instances a state government mandates a certain level of service. Often, communities go beyond that level in areas such as schools or parks, if that is what the elected officials and citizens of the community want to support. The phrase "want to support" should be translated as what they are willing to be taxed for.

For those who have lived in several different communities in their lifetime, the observation that there are real differences between these communities in what they provide for their citizens is no surprise. This variation can be even more striking when compared across states. For example, someone accustomed to the efficiency with which communities in northern states cope with snowstorms is amazed at the chaos that reigns in southern communities at the mention of a possible snowfall, let alone what happens when the snow actually starts to fall.

Running Local Governments

The job of running local governments can be mind-boggling to those who have sought and won a local elective position. Not only are they faced with trying to satisfy the demands of their fellow residents, but they must also answer to the demands of governments higher up in the federal system. These officeholders may have run on a platform with specific goals and may have made equally specific proposals and promises, but once in office they find severe restrictions on their ability to seek, let alone achieve, these goals.

Local governments are creatures of the states and are given a variety of responsibilities and tools with which to work. Some of these governments, such as counties, act more directly as agents of the state in carrying out certain state responsibilities. Others, such as cities, towns, and villages, are established to act as the general, local government of responsibility within a specified area. Still others are set up as special districts with some very specific responsibilities. School and fire districts are examples of these. Special district governmental units work in the same geographical areas as general governments, which can result in great confusion and overlapping of perceived responsibilities.

Unlike the very basic constitutional provisions that demand separation of powers in our federal and state governments, local governments may in fact concentrate authority in their legislatures. Mayors and chairs of county commissions are often selected from among members of the city council or the county commission. And while some mayors are separately elected, just as are governors, they lack the array of powers and institutional support that most governors have at their disposal. Generally, the larger the city or county, the more likely it is that the chief executive is elected separately. In many cities and towns, the mayor is the local chief executive, heading the administration of city government. In other municipalities (and in an increasing number of counties), there is *no* elected executive. Instead, the local council or commission hires a professional manager to act as the chief executive official of local government.

Policies and budgets wind through a tortuous course at the national level, as the president and the two houses of Congress pull and push in an attempt to achieve their goals. Each has the ability to stall, even stop, initiatives. So, too, at the state level: the governor and the houses of the legislature struggle with each other over policies and budgets. A stalemate often results. Yet this is an anticipated product of a concept dear to our constitutional framers: the separation of powers.

There can be stalemate at the local level, too, but it is usually the result of political and policy differences within the one local legislative body, the council or commission. Even when a mayor or county chief executive is elected separately, all of these officials will often meet together and attempt to work out their differences. Only a minority of mayors have the power to veto council actions. Policy and budgetmaking are generally the responsibility of a single government body, and the participants are expected to work out their differences within it.

In a way, this is considerably neater and more efficient than the national or state models. But it is also more vulnerable to manipulation, lacking the protection of other institutional power bases to intervene or check misuse or abuse of power. In response, some states have established oversight agencies and processes as a check on such potentialities.

Yet all this is still only a part of the story. The governing boards of the special district governmental units operating in the area must also be considered. For example, school boards and transportation authorities make policy decisions that have budgetary and tax consequences that the general government must fold into its overall local government budget and tax structure. These special district units possess a separate base of real or potential power, which adds to the political calculus of the local governmental process.

At this level, much is made of the "weak" and "strong" mayor models, with the difference based on whether a mayor is elected separately or selected by vote of a governing body, and whether a mayor has sole power of appointment, veto power, and so on. What is important to remember is that individual mayors often define whether they are weak or powerful. While formal structure does define the formal bases of power, it leaves out the many informal bases of power that an individual may or may not bring to the office. It is common to find an individual in a structurally strong situation acting as a weak leader, and vice versa.

What are these informal bases of power? They can vary by individual, by city or county, and by situation. Among them are an individual's personality and style, the strength of the political parties within a locality, the ability to access and use the media to an advantage, the size of the voter mandate received at the polls and the size of the citywide or countywide mandate received from the voters relative to the district-by-district mandate of the local legislators, the strength of ties to major nongovernmental institutions and other power bases in a community, and the realization by those involved in the governing process that an individual "is going places" and could be (should be, probably will be) a candidate for higher office.

There is one other major distinction of local government that is not seen at either the national or state levels. A rapidly rising number of local governments are run on a day-to-day basis by professionally trained administrators. Even many of those localities with mayors or commission presidents as CEOs now employ full-time professionals as chief *administrative* officers. These administrators, with master's degrees in public administration or business in hand, bring to government a series of learned approaches and well-tested processes geared toward making government work as efficiently and effectively as possible. They are generally nonpartisan and outside of the regular political process and politics of the community.

However, because of their unique position in government, these administrators often gain considerable power at the local level. They know what is happening, what it costs, and how effective it is. They know where the problems are. They handle the budget and work with the bureaucracy and those served by it on a daily basis. And they take the lead in developing next year's budget. In a very real way, they set and spell out the agenda for the local elected leaders.

All this power notwithstanding, these administrators are also vulnerable to political changes within the community and among elected officials. They are responsible for any errors or miscues that occur in the government. It should be no surprise, then, that there is considerable turnover among these professional administrators, as only a very few have a strong political base of their own. Their power base is usually the vote of the council, commission, mayor, or commission president. When that support is gone, so, too, are they. While hired administrators are not out of the political system, they are very much a part of the politics of local government.

A Political Entry Point

Local government can serve as an entry point into the political system for those who are politically ambitious. While many enter local politics for specific reasons, such as to improve the schools or promote economic development or environmental protection, they often find their work as an elected official very rewarding. A strong performance can expand an official's political base and can open up the opportunity to seek higher office. In a few words, these local units in our system are at the base of the political ambition ladder in the states, and many individuals take advantage of this.

Being elected mayor of a state's largest city will automatically place that mayor's name on a list of potential candidates for higher office. If nothing else, other serious candidates for higher office will usually try to obtain the support of the mayor in their own quests. When there are

159

many good-sized cities in a state, however, being mayor of one may not open up such opportunities.

However, in California, the former mayor of San Diego, Republican Pete Wilson, was able to use his position as a starting point from which to move up the political ladder to a seat in the U.S. Senate and then the governor's chair. After winning re-election in 1994, he decided to move toward seeking the Republican nomination for president in the 1996 election, although the campaign turned out to be an unsuccessful effort that damaged his previous reputation as a consistent winner.

But there are other realities to serving as an elected official in local government. One is the closeness of the official to the problems and the people being served, a closeness so intense as to cause burnout in some. Another is being tagged with the problems or errors of others in the governmental unit—a sort of guilt-by-association situation. And all too often there is a need to obtain more revenue to finance citizen wants—a need that translates into raising taxes. All of these and others can quickly shorten an individual's political career.

Still, the ongoing flow upward to other levels of government of many locally elected officials keeps alive the notion that "all politics [and government] is local."

The People Problem

All of the above omit an important aspect of what goes on in local governments: the people and what they are about. Throughout our history the migration of people has been a major factor in our nation's development. This migration has also had a major impact on local governments. The cities have been the focus of those wishing to move off the land and into a different sector of the economy. They are also the destinations of those coming from other countries. Individuals feeling disenfranchised from the society, economy, and political culture around them made the cities their jumping-off boards for new starts. Then, as mobility increased and individual wealth grew, people began moving out of the cities and into the suburbs to get away from the growing problems of decaying urban areas.

In recent decades, two national regions became target destinations of migration. People living in the colder and harsher climates of the North and Midwest began to move southward and westward. Economic factors abetted these moves as the older Rust Belt economies began to falter just as the newer, Sun Belt economies began to grow and expand. Ongoing developments in transportation and information exchange continue to fuel the movement of people across the nation's landscape.

All this has a major impact on local government and public policy. At one extreme are those governments presiding over failing economies that have led to an exodus of wealthy and productive citizens, a rise in the numbers of people requiring assistance, and a continuing need to increase taxes just when the tax base is eroding. At the other extreme are governments coping with rapid and often uncontrolled growth that puts facilities and services, if even provided, at risk. Lack of tax revenues are not necessarily the problem here. Even where growth is generating more income in increased revenue, the problem is trying to direct this growth and make some sort of coherence out of how the future community should develop.

In between these extremes are a variety of situations with which local governments must cope. For example, there are one-industry towns that suddenly find their industry gone with nothing to replace it; small farm-to-market towns that find their youth departed and farms bought out by large landowners using migrant labor; strip city developments where the only way you know you have left one city and entered another is by the signs saying "Good-bye" and "Welcome to"; and cities where never-ending development around their edges leaves the one-time heart of their metropolitan areas depleted and empty, like the hole in a doughnut.

Many would argue that the states are where the action is. But try telling that to some local elected officials. States are relatively well-defined cultures with their own established systems of politics and higher education, and are easily found on the Rand-McNally maps. Cities and other local governments often lack such definition; if it *does* exist, it is usually in flux. That is what makes working in local governments, whether elected, appointed, or as part of the bureaucracy, so challenging.

Now there is worry in local government circles, considering the changes being made at the national and state levels recently, that there will be more action at the local level than officials can cope with. Governors have made a strong pitch to Republican congressional leaders not to balance the national budget on the backs of the states. Local leaders have a double fear facing them: that both the national and state budgets will be balanced on the backs of the local governments. Their worst dream is the adoption of tax cuts and program reductions at higher levels of government that will place unbelievable demands for services and programs, and the necessary tax increases to pay for them, on the desks of local officials.

The articles in Part IX focus on some of these very difficult situations at the local level. Alan Ehrenhalt of *Governing* demonstrates how the long-time control of local government by developers may be changing in one city. Rob Gurwitt of *Governing* looks at how one mayor turned a troubled city around. Charles Mahtesian of *Governing* analyzes the stress between the cities and their legislative delegations in state legislatures and in Congress. Finally, Terry O'Brien of *Empire State Report* makes an argument for local government mergers, consolidations, and annexations.

Are Developers Still Invincible in Local Politics?

by Alan Ehrenhalt

Many years ago, on the eve of a congressional campaign in Arizona, I spent a morning at the Pima County Courthouse in Tucson, talking to a county commissioner who was about to declare for the U.S. House. "I imagine it will be expensive," I said. "Do you think you can raise the money?" He looked at me like I was the dumbest reporter he had ever met. "Are you kidding?" he said. "With the zoning cases I've got coming up before this board? I won't have to lift a finger."

I left that room not quite as dumb as I had entered it. I had learned the simple but important truth that development is the heart and soul of local politics in America. Local *government* is about many diverse subjects: sewers and trash collection, bonds and cash flow, prisons and hospitals. But local *politics,* in any jurisdiction that is not economically stagnant, revolves around questions of growth and development. They attract not only the money but also the energy and the resources and the emotion. Development is to local politics what true north is to a compass. In the end, everything points there.

As time went on, I learned another equally simple and useful lesson: It isn't just development that dominates the agenda in most places, it's developers. The pro-development interests are the permanent players that any county board or city council has to reckon with week in and week out, year after year. Neighborhood activists and anti-growth forces drift in and drift away issue by issue, and usually lack the stamina, let alone the resources, to prevail on most arguments of importance.

The most forceful lecture I've ever gotten on that subject came one day in the living room of a house in Concord, California, in the San Francisco Bay suburbs, from an anti-growth crusader who thought his town was overdeveloped and who was trying to put a lid on new office construction. "There is no way to raise money," he complained, "except from developers and unions—the development and building industry. You could fire a cannon in a council meeting and not hit anybody but a developer. That's the only people who go."

And so it has been, for most of the past 50 years, in most American communi-

Alan Ehrenhalt is a staff writer for *Governing*. This article is reprinted from *Governing* (November 1996): 7–8.

ties, from placid courthouse towns to booming suburbs to big cities struggling to survive. The coalition that favors growth and development puts in the campaign money, turns out for the late-night meetings and manages to get its way most of the time.

Most of the time. But not all the time. If you assume that developers never lose, you will miss a good many of the changes and subtleties that are making American local politics in the 1990s an interesting spectator sport.

If you are in any doubt on that point, you might consider a visit to Little Rock. Nobody has ever accused the Arkansas capital of being anything but a business-friendly town: Over the past few decades, its city government has approved commercial and residential development requests with all the enthusiasm you would expect from a city council that officially calls itself a "board of directors." As in most communities, the local planning commission has been dominated by real-estate interests. In many cases, building new residential subdivisions has required the annexation of new land into the city limits, and these the board has approved with perfect consistency—145 of them in a row, to be exact.

Wherever you come from, this history is likely to sound familiar to you. But it is not much help in understanding why the entire Little Rock political system is embroiled in controversy right now over the annexation of 190 acres of rolling hills and lakes, just beyond the city's western border, land that a development company wants to convert into a subdivision called Capitol Lakes Estates.

There's nothing very unusual about the plans for Capitol Lakes Estates—in quality and character, it would be similar to dozens of other developments that have

been extending the borders of Little Rock westward for the past two decades or so. What's unusual is that the project's backers haven't been able to get it through the city government.

The annexation request came up in July [1996], and the board leaped wildly out of character by turning it down, 7–3. It came up again in September and once more in October, and both times the developer had to ask for a deferral because the votes still weren't there.

What's the problem with Capitol Lakes Estates? There's a micro and a macro answer to that question. The micro answer is that residents of the adjoining subdivision, Spring Valley Manor, itself annexed to the city only three years ago, are worried that all the new development would bring annoying traffic congestion and deny them the semi-rural lifestyle they thought they were getting when they moved in. Spring Valley residents have been a vocal and well-organized presence at every meeting in which the Capitol Lakes annexation has been discussed.

But that's only part of the explanation, and unless you live somewhere nearby, it's not the most interesting part. What matters more is that local government is changing in Little Rock, in ways that are relevant—or will be relevant—to hundreds of communities all over the country.

The legislative body that rubber-stamped those previous 145 annexations was a city board with all its members elected citywide, and with an essentially powerless mayor chosen from the board itself on a rotating basis. The members could live anywhere in the city, but in practice most of them tended to come from a few affluent precincts of northwest Little Rock and to speak for upper-middle-class voters and the local business elite. In 1993, however,

Little Rock switched to a combined at-large and single-member-district system, with only three members elected at-large and the majority coming from seven newly drawn wards, each containing about 21,000 people.

To say this has caused a revolution in Little Rock politics would be going a bit too far. But to say it has shaken up lots of traditional assumptions would be more than fair. The ward system has led to a sprouting of neighborhood activism, with 30 to 40 functioning neighborhood organizations and a Coalition of Neighborhoods that is a major player in citywide politics.

It has also led to a new crop of local board members who understand that their careers are as dependent on neighborhood support as they once were on support from developers and the chamber of commerce. Little Rock Vice Mayor Joan Adcock, sometimes called the matriarch of the neighborhood movement, is widely assumed to be readying a mayoral campaign with the grassroots organizations as her constituent base.

The old system was ideal for those interests that had the technical skill and the resources to run political advertising citywide—in other words, the business community. The new system, in which a ward candidate can win with about 4,000 votes instead of 30,000, places more of a premium on the door-to-door campaigning that the neighborhood groups have become adept at. The neighborhood groups have far more influence on board decisions than they ever had in the past. "It was essential that we bust up the at-large system," says Jim Lynch, the Coalition of Neighborhoods founder.

It was against this background of political change that the fight against Capitol

Lakes turned out to be not only a crusade by its angry neighbors but a cause célèbre for the Little Rock neighborhood movement. Part of it was genuine concern about the prospects of future developmental sprawl, but some of it seemed to be activist back-scratching, based on the theory that when one neighborhood wants something, the others should just help out as a way of showing solidarity.

In any case, the Spring Valley protesters found the whole system receptive to them in a way it never would have been before 1993. "If I'd been doing this five years ago," concedes O. C. "Rusty" Sparks, the Spring Valley leader, "the door would have been slammed in my face." Now he jokes to reporters that he shows up at board meetings "with a sack of candy in one hand and a cattle prod in the other."

It seems likely that the Spring Valley people and the developers eventually will reach some sort of accommodation and that the 190 contested acres will become part of Little Rock, even if it doesn't happen on exactly the same terms the original blueprint called for. In the process, though, the neighborhood forces will have made their strongest argument yet that they are the power brokers of the new order that is emerging.

That will be one more reminder that in politics, as in the rest of life, the law of unintended consequences can be counted on to exact its revenge. The single-member districts that are being drawn in cities all over the country these days aren't being drawn to thwart the growth machine—they're aimed at getting more minorities and women elected to office. And they are doing that. Three of the seven wards created in Little Rock in 1993 now have black or female representation.

None of the creators of Little Rock's

ward system argued that it would create neighborhood power brokers or frustrate the growth coalition. In fact, the developer of Capitol Lakes Estates was one of the drafters of the reform. Now he and much of the city's business community are struggling to cope with the effects of a change they would just as soon undo.

In the end, I doubt that ward elections will lead to a genuine revolution in the life of Little Rock, or of any community in America that decides to try them. In the long run, government decisions still bend to those interests with the resources and stamina to maintain a permanent presence in the corridors, and in most places, that will continue to be the growth-and-development coalition more often than it will be the neighborhood activists. In the somewhat shorter run, however, there are quite a few chambers of commerce out there that will be finding local politics far more strenuous than they have ever known it to be in the past.

The Mayor as Showman

by Rob Gurwitt

It would be a stretch to say that Hartford, Connecticut, has turned its ailing economy around. It would even be a stretch to say that it is safely on its way to doing so. Poverty and joblessness, abandoned housing and neighborhood distress are still too prevalent throughout Connecticut's capital to boast of certain rejuvenation.

But the city's disposition is something else again. Over the past few years, its spirit and sense of confidence have undergone a striking revival. City government, Hartford's residents, its neighborhood groups, its business leaders and, most notably, its suburban neighbors—all have been overtaken by an almost buoyant belief that reversing the city's decline is possible.

The man responsible for this mood swing is Mike Peters, Hartford's mayor. Part fixer, part showman and part civic conscience, Peters was elected in 1993 at a time when it appeared Hartford was destined to lose itself in the civic chaos and community indifference that are the hallmarks of cities going down the tubes. The city hated the suburbs, the suburbs despised the city, the neighborhoods resented the business community, the business com-

munity ignored the neighborhoods—and everyone vilified City Hall.

In the years since Peters took over, though, Hartford has begun to gather its forces. Peters has little formal power as mayor: The city council, on which he does not even have a vote, sets policy, while the city manager oversees the operations of government. But Peters' immense popularity has given him great sway, if not outright control, over city government. Together, he and the city council have cut the budget every year since he took office; they have tried to drive hard bargains with Hartford's public employee unions; and they have tackled head-on Hartford's role as a regional social-service reserve by preventing the siting of new facilities in residential neighborhoods.

Even more notable, however, has been Peters' success at persuading many of the people who have a piece of Hartford's fate in their hands to feel obliged to do something constructive with it. He is a genuinely funny man, with a homespun, up-from-the-streets charm and dynamism that have giv-

Rob Gurwitt is a staff writer for *Governing*. This article is reprinted from *Governing* (December 1996): 31.

en him the ear of everyone from the city's black leadership and neighborhood groups to insurance conglomerate CEOs and suburban bluebloods.

This has yielded tangible accomplishments. The business community has stepped up to fill in funding gaps on youth programs and summer jobs, and to work with the city in crafting some job programs for welfare recipients. Suburban politicians have not only lent their resources—detailing road crews, for instance, to help Hartford fill its potholes—but have helped the city try to boost its state funding and have rallied around its efforts to keep the National Hockey League Whalers in the city. Perhaps most important, suburbanites no longer view Hartford as an alien landscape to be avoided at all costs. "When people are talking good about the city they live in," Peters says, "people on the outside hear about it. Good things start to happen."

It has become commonplace to say that city governments cannot tackle urban problems alone, that salvation lies in communal effort. This is, however, difficult to organize in the best of circumstances; it is near impossible when the city ranks among the poorest in the country. If Hartford under Mike Peters has yet to boast a new set of downtown monuments, à la Cleveland, or a major infusion of corporate largesse, à la Detroit, it may have something equally valuable as it continues to struggle against great odds: a model of political leadership that puts a premium on mustering the good will and energy of its citizens and neighbors.

Semi-Vendetta: Cities and the New Republican Order

by Charles Mahtesian

When Republicans swept both legislative chambers and the Illinois governorship in 1994, there was enough hand-wringing and anxiety among Chicago partisans that GOP Governor Jim Edgar felt compelled to address them. Yes, the Republicans would be in full control of state government for the first time in 22 years. But there was nothing to fear, he announced. The newly ascendant legislative leadership also tried to assuage nervous Chicago advocates. "Give us two years," insisted the new House speaker, Lee Daniels, "and we'll show you it's good news for the city of Chicago."

Hardly anybody in Chicago believed that, especially considering the two suburban Republicans who were poised to take over the legislature—Daniels, the longtime and long-suffering House minority leader, and his counterpart on the Senate side, James "Pate" Philip, a cranky conservative salesman from affluent Du Page County with a history of Chicago-bashing three decades long. "A lot of people in the city thought the sky was falling," says Timothy Bramlet, president of the Taxpayers' Federation of Illinois. "They thought they were going to get killed."

So did plenty of other urban Democrats in state legislatures all over the country. Nearly all of them feared the worst from a new crop of Republican governors and legislators; some talked as if a horde of suburban and rural Huns had overrun the statehouses. The universal assumption was that large cities such as Chicago, Cleveland, Detroit, New York and Philadelphia would suffer greatly or be neglected in their fiscal and social needs. Before the 1994 vote even took place, New York City's Republican mayor, Rudy Giuliani, was worried enough to endorse the Democratic nominee for governor, Mario Cuomo.

Eighteen months later, it is safe to say that the sky has not exactly fallen. No Republican governor or legislature has shown much interest in humiliating big cities purely for revenge or sadistic pleasure. On the other hand, it is also clear that there is a GOP blueprint for metropolitan America, that it is taking shape in many of the nation's statehouses and that it involves a rearrangement of power unlikely to bring

Charles Mahtesian is a staff writer for *Governing*. This article is reprinted from *Governing* (June 1996): 30–33.

much comfort to the traditional forces of urban Democratic politics. One fact is beyond dispute: The days when a city such as Chicago could come to a capital such as Springfield with an attitude and a wish list are over.

Until relatively recently, the sheer numerical strength and cohesiveness of a legislative delegation such as the Chicago Democrats made it possible to achieve a good many of the things the city wanted in the legislative arena. That's why the Illinois statutes are littered with specific references and exemptions to cities of more than 500,000 residents—Chicago being the only city that even comes close to qualifying.

But population losses and the resulting reapportionment of legislative seats slowly eroded Chicago's capitol clout. In 1948, the city contributed about 48 percent of the state's general election vote; by 1990, that share had shrunk to 21 percent. Now, only about a quarter of legislative districts are city-based, and it shows. "The city is playing a little bit more of a defensive game," says Mary Sue Barrett, a former lobbyist for the city and policy aide to Mayor Richard M. Daley. "The city of Chicago is approaching Springfield these days with a heavy dose of realism and probably diminished expectations."

It is the older industrial cities that are feeling those losses most acutely right now, but others are feeling them too. A scenario not too different played itself out last year in Washington State, where the 1994 election brought in a huge House Republican majority and increased suburban power. "Even Seattle," says Republican political consultant Brett Bader, "is no longer the big dog in the legislature the way it used to be."

In Illinois, as in other states where Republicans claimed control, the newly crowned GOP majority wasted little time in asserting its intentions. Within weeks of the opening of the 1995 session, nearly 100 bills were introduced that would have limited or stripped power from various city boards, districts and offices and shifted it to the state or suburbs, where Republicans could better monitor developments. Cook County, which in some legislators' minds was not much different from Chicago, its largest city, also proved to be a target. Property tax caps were imposed on Cook County—bringing it in line with the rest of the Chicago suburbs—and the county property tax assessment appeals system was completely restructured.

None of those moves came as much of a surprise to Chicago or Cook County legislators. But within a few months, the Republican legislative leaders came out with something considerably bolder: an idea to create a regional authority that would oversee O'Hare International Airport and the two other Chicago-area airports.

What was so attractive about airport management that would make the party of less government eager to create more of it? Several things. Besides a $90 million ticket-tax revenue stream, O'Hare offered thousands of jobs and potential contracts. Then there was the issue of siting another major airport for the Chicago metro area, with all its accompanying jobs and contracts. Mayor Daley was pushing for an airport that, at the very least, was located within Cook County limits. Suburban Republicans already had their own site selected in the cornfields of Peotone, in Will County, toward the outskirts of the metropolitan area.

Republicans insisted the move to create a regional authority was a means of addressing long-standing suburban concerns about noise, air pollution and runway expansion at O'Hare. Mayor Daley and other city officials viewed it differently. They saw it as a partisan grab for money and power. "Of course they are coming after us," Daley announced. "They're coming after the airports, they're coming after the Water Reclamation District, they want everything they can get."

Maybe so, but Daley beat them to the punch. While negotiating with Republicans over the proposed new authority, Daley cut a clandestine deal with the city of Gary, Indiana, to create his own bi-state airport authority—one that cleverly took legal precedence over any entity created by a Republican-controlled legislature. "Daley," said one Republican legislator, "just pulled the pin on the grenade and flung it into the suburbs."

In response, furious legislators acted with a rancor they had so far been careful to avoid. They went after both the Chicago city council and Daley personally, passing a retroactive bill to rescind the aldermanic and mayoral pay raises that had only recently been approved by the city council and the Cook County board. But the Republican bill never became law. Even Governor Edgar found the reprisal a bit heavy-handed, vetoing it as "vindictive" and not in the best interests of city-state relations.

The airport skirmish was a clue to the Republicans' foremost priority in power, not just in Illinois but in other states as well. They wanted to begin asserting authority over all the expensive public works projects that big cities such as Chicago have spent the last few decades collecting. Now that power has shifted to the suburban counties, suburban Republicans want commensurate control over lucrative regional assets such as airports and stadiums and any other facilities where the money and jobs are.

If there are going to be expensive new regional projects, Republicans want to decide where they will be sited, who will govern them, who will control the jobs and the revenue stream. As for existing public works assets, GOP legislators have an interest in them as well. "When you create a public works project, you're obviously creating jobs, you're obviously creating economic development," says Myer Blank, a senior research associate with the nonpartisan Civic Federation of Chicago. "It's where that economic development is going to happen that becomes the political battle."

It would be a mistake to view this mainly as a matter of anti-urban retribution. It is really just a 1990s version of old-fashioned spoils politics. It is happening in New York, where Republican Governor George E. Pataki announced plans [in 1995] to move hundreds of state jobs out of predominantly Democratic New York City districts and into upstate Republican areas. Angry Democrats labeled the move "geographic patronage." In Pennsylvania, Governor Tom Ridge recently won a court battle to oust Democratic holdover members of the Delaware River Port Authority after more than a year of trying. A patronage haven charged with doling out millions in economic development projects and contracts, DRPA was considered by Republicans to be beholden to the wishes of one of its board members—powerful Democratic state Senator Vincent Fumo of Philadelphia.

In attempting to wrest control of patronage, contract and revenue-rich regional economic assets such as the airports and port authorities, Republicans in both states are merely playing the time-honored game of political hardball perfected by the big cities themselves, back when their own swaggering clout enabled them to do so.

The new Republican majorities have done more, of course, than redistribute power and patronage. They are working considerably harder than the previous Democratic legislatures did to make cities live within their means. "They are asking more questions about where the money goes," says Sam Staley of the Buckeye Institute for Public Policy Solutions, an Ohio-based free-market think tank. "There is more of a willingness to question whether some of the problems of cities are self-created. That they are not always victims of circumstances."

Here, too, however, it would be difficult to make a case for widespread outright meanness. Republicans have not so much pulled the plug on aid to the cities as they have merely continued political and spending trends of recent years. While there may be less overall aid to the cities, it is largely a reflection of the same shrinking budget pie that determined decisions even under recent Democratic control. There is less money available, not just for cities but for nearly anything besides anti-crime initiatives, prison construction and health care entitlements.

Mass transit is a good example. Funding is down, in Illinois and in the other states where Republicans have returned to power. And some of that may be due to the fact that suburban legislators are more interested in highway construction than in covering the operating deficits of the Chicago Transit Authority or Philadelphia's Southeastern Pennsylvania Transportation Authority. Still, even urban lobbyists concede that there has been no real revolution here. "The city wasn't able to get money for schools and mass transit before," says Mary Sue Barrett, now with the Metropolitan Planning Council in Chicago. "Many of these issues have been around

for so long and not much progress was made in the old system. I can't say anything is different under the Republican regime."

If there is a state where Republicans can be said to be going after city interests with a truly hard-nosed attitude, it is New York. In New York City, 103,000 people were removed from the welfare rolls during Governor Pataki's first year in office. "Everyone in New York state recognizes that when you talk about general assistance and AFDC, you are talking about the city," says Margaret Weir, a senior fellow at the Brookings Institution, a Washington, D.C.-based think tank. "And it's going to be tougher and tougher for the Democrats to protect."

In most other states, however, new Republican majorities have not so much reversed Democratic social policy as they have simply proceeded with it. Under a GOP governor and legislature in Ohio, for example, 1995 marked the end of the state's general assistance welfare program. But that was in fact the last installment of a phase-out that began in 1992—when Democrats still held one legislative chamber.

Of all the messages Illinois Republicans could have delivered to Chicago in their first year of new legislative control, none announced the new order with as much clarity as the 1995 Chicago school reform bill, a wide-ranging plan that gave greater control and responsibility over the schools to none other than Mayor Daley himself. Nearly everyone in the heavily Democratic city had been clamoring for years for more accountability and reform in the school system, yet it took a Republican caucus of suburbanites and small-town conservatives to actually make it happen. "I would say one of the biggest accomplishments that has taken place for the city of Chicago under Republican control is Chicago school reform," says Speaker Lee

City Squabbles

Nowhere is the local struggle between unions and government more apparent than in New York City, where Republican Mayor Rudolph Giuliani has been wrestling with annual multi-million dollar budget gaps in a city historically dominated by organized labor, an institution with close ties to the Democratic Party.

Since 1994, Giuliani has reduced the city's 200,000-plus workforce by some 20,000 positions and has tried to find savings in negotiating union contracts. Last year alone, he grappled with 83 separate contracts that were up for renewal. Union leaders were in no mood to yield to his demands for $160 million in savings.

Among the bargaining groups was the Municipal Labor Committee, a coalition of 14 unions that joined forces to fight collectively for raises and job security. The committee was led by Stanley Hill, executive director of the District Council 37—the New York City component of the American Federation of State and County Municipal Employees—a group of 56 unions representing more than 120,000 city employees and most of the mayor's own clerical workers.

After months of negotiations, the committee agreed to a five-year deal with no raises during the first two years. It did, however, provide for some job protections for workers, "which was a major sticking point," according to Dennis Sullivan, District Council 37's research director. The mayor also agreed to consider alternatives to layoffs such as early retirement incentives.

The disputes between Giuliani and labor over his attempts to gain more control over city operations at times have reached up the Thruway to Albany. In February, Gov. George Pataki—at the urging of Giuliani—vetoed a bill backed by the powerful unions representing New York City police officers and firefighters that would have shifted contract disputes between the city and its officers to the state Public Employment Relations Board (PERB) for arbitration.

The New York City Patrolmen's Benevolent Association, among others, had lobbied strenuously for the measure, which passed both houses of the state Legislature. The playing field for years had favored the city, which traditionally handled contract dispute cases itself, the bill's supporters claimed. By bringing PERB into arbitration, unions hoped to find more sympathetic ears.

Giuliani argued that the city could not afford the estimated $200 million a year in settlements he feared would occur if disputes were controlled by an outside panel. Pataki agreed and vetoed the bill. But the Legislature, including the Republican-controlled Senate, overrode the veto, saying that since other public safety disputes are arbitrated before PERB, it would be unfair to deny the same right to New York City police officers and firefighters.

New York Conference of Mayors and Municipal Officials Executive Director Edward Farrell in February echoed Giuliani's concerns on behalf of other municipalities around the state, saying hearings before PERB have caused tax hikes in localities that cannot afford them. "In times like these when municipal budgets and taxes are going up, the power of local governments to control their own destiny is put in the hands of this outside panel, preventing us from doing our jobs of holding down costs," he complained. The issue of local control was also the subject of Pataki's veto only a week before of a labor-supported measure that would have guaranteed PERB arbitrate disputes between municipalities and their public safety workers. Currently, many public employees facing disciplinary action must defend themselves in front of hearing officers appointed by their employers.

Source: Tom Murnane, "City Squabbles," *Empire State Report* (October 1996): 42.

Daniels. "It was absolutely impossible to get done under Democratic control of the General Assembly."

To describe the school reform plan as a gift to Chicago, however, is to gloss over some huge complexities. It is true that Daley was quietly willing to accept the authority the Republicans wanted to give him. But it is also true that the Democrats in the legislature and their teachers' union allies treated it as something akin to a personal insult. Speaker Daniels and Senate President Philip took great pleasure at steamrolling the angry Chicago legislative delegation and, in particular, the man Daniels had deposed, former Speaker Michael Madigan, a Chicagoan with close ties to the teachers' unions. "There were a lot of vested interests that prevented major reforms over the years," says Timothy Bramlet of the Taxpayers' Federation of Illinois. "Their clout was with the Democratic party. Those restraints were no longer there for GOP leadership."

To the Democrats in Springfield, the school reform bill represented the monumental irony of the new order. Those institutions the Democrats really wanted the Chicago city government to control—airports, stadiums, waterworks—the Republicans were trying to take away from them. The one institution Republicans wanted to reform but didn't care to oversee—the school system—was being dumped in the mayor's lap.

The futile opposition to the Chicago school reform measure from the city's own legislative delegation also underscored one of the more serious problems faced by other urban areas at a time of Republican control: Cities that send a delegation comprised exclusively of minority party legislators run the risk of irrelevance on important issues. "For all practical purposes," says Joe Darden, dean of the School of Urban Affairs at Michigan State University, "unless the Detroit delegation has a coalition with another area, it can pretty much be ignored—and it usually is."

In Illinois, where only three of the 46 Chicago-based House and Senate members are Republicans, the Chicago delegation is not only getting smaller in number but becoming increasingly powerless as the Republican caucus begins to assert itself. "When you have a situation where only one member of the House and two members of the Senate are from the Republican caucus," says William Luking, a private consultant who lobbies for the city, "it's not difficult to understand that certain Chicago agenda and priority items may not be priorities of those caucuses."

Philadelphia has been a little more fortunate under the new system. When the newly Republican-controlled Pennsylvania House debated Governor Ridge's most recent budget proposal, one Philadelphia Republican legislator, John Taylor, was there to preserve medical assistance benefits for 260,000 individuals by winning over 24 other Republicans and combining with Democrats to kill a provision that stood to impact Philadelphia particularly hard.

Of course, it is not a very practical piece of advice simply to tell cities to start electing more Republicans. What they can do is become more effective at reaching out for help from places that do so on a regular basis. Cities and many of the suburbs, says Lynn Montei, executive director of the Du Page Mayors and Managers Conference, might even find more common ground than expected. "So many of our issues are the same," she says. "As time goes on, we find an interdependence which overrides jurisdictional questions of how Chicago is dealt with versus how the rest of the suburbs are dealt with. I think the suburbs identify with the city far more than they ever have because they are encountering more and more of the issues that the city has."

Myer Blank of Chicago's Civic Federation agrees. "It used to be, 'What can we get for the city' or 'What can we get for the board of education,'" he says. "You are starting to see these alliances that weren't traditionally there."

In some instances, it may just be better to allow suburban interests to carry the ball, as was the case with a recent Seattle sports stadium bill passed soon after city voters rejected a ballot proposal in 1995. When it came time to lobby for the new bill, it was suburban King County legisla-tors—not Seattle legislators—who handled the heavy lifting. "If the Seattle Democrats had gone in and lobbied for it, it never would have passed," says political consultant Brett Bader, referring to both the failed ballot vote and the city's reputation for being ideologically out of sync with the rest of the state. "Anybody who really cared about the stadium didn't want the Seattle Democrats to carry it."

Ideally, public policy-making would be based on loftier considerations. But since it is not, cities such as Seattle, New York and Chicago are going to have to get used to both scaled-back expectations and a very different role in the state capital. Who knows, maybe Lee Daniels was right. Maybe it will be good for them.

Saving New York's Cities

by Terry O'Brien

To most of his critics, Buffalo Comptroller Joel Giambra is a municipal Jack Kervorkian—a loose cannon all too willing to aid and abet a mercy killing of his ailing city. To others, Giambra's idea of eliminating his city in order to save it makes sense.

Giambra shocked municipal and county leaders alike last March [1996] when he called for abolishing New York's second largest city and merging it with surrounding Erie County. Like a traveling salesman, he busily has peddled his idea at civic group meetings, radio talk shows and alumni association gatherings.

Giambra's proposal has been dismissed as radical, extremist and politically unworkable. But increasingly, municipal officials in charge of other financially troubled cities are paying attention. "The public is at a point where it is extremely angry that each year [we] are raising taxes or reducing services," Giambra says. The merger is possible, he adds, because residents "are frustrated, and they're not going to take it anymore."

The concept of city-county mergers is not new, but making them happen is a rare achievement. Nationwide, only 19 city-county consolidations have taken place since World War II, according to David Rusk, former mayor of Albuquerque, N.M., and author of *Cities Without Suburbs.*

In fact, only 16 states have statutes allowing such mergers. New York does not, and the concept faces a host of almost insurmountable political, financial and geographical obstacles. Racial and parochial prejudices harbored by some suburban dwellers against their urban neighbors, suburbanites' fears of shouldering greater costs, and the stubborn resistance of local politicians unwilling to give up their offices present major roadblocks.

State lawmakers also may be loathe to offend politically powerful labor unions that represent thousands of municipal workers whose jobs would be jeopardized in any city-county consolidation scheme.

Nevertheless, a bill sponsored by Democratic Assemblyman Jacob Gunther of Monticello and Republican Sen. William Larkin Jr. of New Windsor would clear the way for such mergers. Under the bill, any merger would be subject to voter approval.

Terry O'Brien is an editor and reporter for *The Record* of Troy, New York. This article is reprinted from *Empire State Report* (July 1996): 33–37.

Gunther—whose district crosses two counties and encompasses 19 towns, seven villages and two cities—says he supports the idea of reducing New York's multiple layers of government. The bill had languished in the Assembly since 1994 and was unable to attract a Senate sponsor. This year, however, it passed the Senate and is under consideration in the Assembly.

City-county mergers provide savings by unifying and expanding the tax base, spreading out the cost of providing services, and centralizing planning and zoning authority.

Theoretically, a merger would do away with costly duplications, such as having separate city and county public works departments and purchasing agencies. Spreading the tax base to more affluent suburban areas would make it easier to pay for vital services, including police protection and solid waste disposal. "It must be done," says Ed Hanna, the outspoken mayor of Utica and another merger disciple. "The only salvation for cities today is for meaningful consolidation of departments and services."

Onondaga County Executive Nicholas Pirro has called for merging city and county governments by the year 2000. He notes the county is crammed with a complex labyrinth of 36 general purpose governments, 18 school districts and more than 900 special use districts encompassing such services as water and electricity.

Merging city and county governments has worked in the few instances in which it has been done. In 1970, the merger of Indianapolis with Marion County took place—the first to occur without a popular referendum since New York City became a five-borough entity in 1898. The so-called "Unigov" legislation was expected to improve the delivery of services and transform Indianapolis into a major league community.

Three municipalities, 16 townships and a hospital and airport authority continued to exist separately. The Marion County sheriff's office was left intact. Public education remained dispersed throughout 22 separate school districts. And yet the merger immediately improved Indianapolis's tax base and cemented a blue-chip bond rating. By all accounts, it has brought better delivery of services and lower taxes, Rusk writes.

Nashville—whose situation was more pressing than that of Indianapolis—also merged, and its model has become the basis for New York's merger bill.

In 1960, Nashville's population was dwindling, its downtown was decaying and businesses were on the verge of leaving. Two years later, in a move opposed by Nashville's mayor and entrenched City Council, voters approved the city's merger with surrounding Davidson County. County residents' fears of higher taxes were assuaged by charter provisions that authorized two distinct service districts: an urban services district that provided the "old" city with higher services and higher taxes; and a countywide, general services district. Areas formerly in the county were allowed to petition to be annexed into the urban services district.

With the consolidation, Nashville instantly ballooned in size and population from 73 square miles and 170,000 people to 473 square miles and nearly 400,000 people. Today, Nashville has 488,000 residents and is a thriving center of music, banking and apparel manufacturing in the state.

This is the kind of system Giambra envisions for Buffalo and Erie County. Having dual service districts would alleviate suburbanites' anxieties of assuming greater costs brought on by merging with financially ailing cities, he says.

The idea of city-county unification has caught on in New York, where eroding property tax bases, major state aid cuts and dwindling populations have left desperate municipal officials looking for ways to cut costs.

Schenectady, Rome, Utica and Niagara Falls are buckling under the strain of crippling budget deficits. Over the last two years, fiscal crises in Troy and Newburgh forced the creation of state-led fiscal oversight boards similar to ones that now oversee finances in New York City and Yonkers. City leaders there and throughout the state have been forced to raise taxes while cutting services previously considered politically unassailable.

To deal with its deficits, Troy, a troubled city of 54,000 north of Albany, laid off eight police officers, eliminated its mounted patrol unit and recently voted to raise taxes by 21 percent, all in the face of vociferous local opposition. Despite infusions of additional state aid ushered through the Legislature by Senate Majority Leader Joseph Bruno, who represents the city, Troy still faces about a $2 million structural deficit.

Schenectady hiked property taxes 4 percent and laid off 19 firefighters earlier this year.

"You need a certain amount of courage and a little bit of crisis to do it," says Troy Mayor Mark Pattison of reducing services and increasing taxes. "If everyone's fat and happy, why would you do it?"

Leaders of distressed cities fear that continued tax hikes and service reductions only will exacerbate city population declines. The continuing state recession has eroded property values, which determine tax revenues. Real estate values plummet when businesses move out and higher income residents flee to the suburbs, leaving behind vacant properties and depressed housing demand. Sixty-four percent of the state's cities saw a decline in property values in the last year, according to a recent report by the New York State Conference of Mayors and Municipal Officials (NYCOM).

Sharp cuts in state revenue sharing aid since 1989, when New York began experiencing its own budget troubles, have made the problem worse. Revenue sharing, used extensively to help balance city budgets in the past, has been cut nearly in half over the past seven years. "The cuts in state aid had to be absorbed into the tax base, and the base is not growing" says Edward Farrell, NYCOM's executive director. "This has been going on a while now, and it's starting to reach a head at this point."

Despite tax hikes and service cuts, cities like Troy, Jamestown, Gloversville and Utica have been forced to borrow heavily to cover operating deficits over the past five years. Utica currently faces a $4 million deficit and a $5.7 million cash flow problem, according to Hanna.

Borrowing to pay for day-to-day expenses has wreaked havoc on the credit ratings of some cities. Troy's junk bond status effectively has closed Wall Street markets to the city, forcing officials to allow a state municipal assistance corporation—which can borrow money on Troy's behalf—to take over city finances.

A survey of 25 New York cities by Moody's Investors Service found that most were struggling to keep their budgets balanced, a situation likely to continue for the next several years.

Buffalo reflects much of what is going on in other areas of the state, though some of its problems appear more serious. Between 1950 and 1990, the city lost 43 percent of its population. Between 1990 and 1994, Buffalo lost an average of 297 people per month, according to the Buffalo-based publication *Business First*. The average household income is $18,482, the lowest of cities across the country. The percentage of families living below the poverty level is 22 percent—eighth highest among the nation's 100 largest cities, Giambra says. Taxes have gone up more than 30 percent the last two years, while services have been reduced. The city's credit rating is below average and teetering.

So far, state lawmakers have addressed city financial breakdowns in the same lurching manner that they approach most problems: reacting only when a crisis leaves them no recourse. "Up until now, the policy has been one of benign neglect," says NYCOM's Farrell. "This has been going on a while now."

During the 1996 fiscal year, the Legislature agreed to a one-time acceleration of revenue sharing payments to help bail out cities. Legislative leaders also have proposed boosting Gov. George Pataki's proposed $10 million fund to help distressed cities by another $30 million.

Many leaders have proposed moving slowly with merger-related ideas to help shave costs. But other policy-makers say a more radical approach is needed before the crisis gets out of control. "Three weeks after I arrived [in 1987], we merged the city and town of Canandaigua," says Canandaigua City Manager Bill Bridgio, outgoing president of the Municipal Management Association. While cities and counties can't legally merge in New York, there is no prohibition against cities, towns and villages merging, or school districts merging with each other. The two govern-

ments "were totally redundant operations," Bridgio says. "That type of redundancy exists all over."

Excluding New York City, there are currently 11,147 separate local government entities in New York state, according to the state comptroller's office. They include 62 cities, 932 towns, 557 villages and 707 school districts.

Consolidating services and merging entire units of government have become popular messages among politicians in many of those localities looking to appear fiscally responsible to their constituents.

But in reality, mergers have had limited success in this state. In the last five years, only five villages have dissolved, while three more have been created, Farrell says. In fact, there are other proposals to create even more government entities. The Long Island towns of East Hampton, Riverhead, Shelter Island, Southhampton and Southhold have repeatedly asked Albany for permission to secede from Suffolk County and create a new, independent county government, to be called Peconic County.

School districts in New York remain notoriously fragmented, adding to costs and reducing educational quality. Currently there are 60 K–12 school districts statewide that serve fewer than 500 students each, according to Suzanne Spear, the New York State Education Department's supervisor for district organization. "We have school districts so small, they disappear from the screen," says Rochester Mayor Bill Johnson.

Since 1990, only 14 school districts have merged, Spear says, despite the state's generous financial incentives and tax savings for those that choose to do so. While smaller districts usually are more expensive and, offer fewer educational opportunities, education critics say school administrators have little incentive to encourage mergers because they put their own jobs in jeopardy.

And as with villages and towns, parochial fears that many suburbanites have of being associated with cities kill most merger proposals. Residents of the Wynantskill Union Free School District, a small K–8 district that saw a 29 percent school tax hike in 1995, resoundingly rejected a proposed merger with the neighboring Troy City School District earlier this year. The vote came despite promises that the merger would have eliminated annual, double-digit tax increases in Wynantskill that are expected to occur over the next five years. Many parents openly expressed fears that their children would be bused into city schools, which contain more minorities.

Consolidation of municipal services, a less radical step than the merger of entire movement entities, also have run aground. For instance, Hanna's attempts at consolidating Utica's city services with the county's have been rejected repeatedly by an uncooperative city council. Rensselaer County recently canceled its data processing sharing arrangement with the city of Troy— mainly because the city could no longer afford to pay for data processing personnel—and a contract for the county to do the city's economic development plans was not renewed. A proposal to merge the purchasing departments of Onondaga County and the city of Syracuse also was rejected by the City Council, which was unconvinced that it would save money.

Other localities have had more success. The city of Rochester and surrounding Monroe County are in good financial shape, partly because of a sales tax sharing plan, shared health department and social services functions, and a consolidated emergency 911 telephone system. "But that could change overnight if we experience further reductions in state aid, or the county decides not to renegotiate our sales tax sharing arrangements," Johnson warns.

The city of Elmira, in part because of shared services, also is in better financial shape than many of its urban counterparts.

For every leader who holds out hope for city-county mergers, there are several political leaders who do not believe such mergers ever will take place in New York. "Buffalo isn't going to cease to exist as a geopolitical entity," says John Zagameme, executive director of the New York State Association of Counties (NYSAC).

Like many areas of the state, Erie County's finances are in much better shape than the city of Buffalo's, which provides few incentives for county governments to merge with their poorer sisters. "It's an asymmetrical deal," Zagame says. "There's very little reason for Erie County to do it. Why should [the county] be asked to shoulder the city's costs when the city has not done enough to eliminate its expenditures?"

NYCOM's Farrell says that despite cities' financial woes, the topic has not been a high priority discussion item among his members. He also notes that resistance of suburban dwellers to take on city financial obligations is likely to kill such merger proposals and that the potential savings aren't large enough to justify such a drastic move.

Buffalo Mayor Tony Masiello says the idea of abolishing the city simply is moving too far, too fast. "It's very extreme. We've got some problems and we need to shrink the size of government, but it can't be done tomorrow," he says.

Masiello says consolidations of park systems, purchasing departments and the like are the more realistic way to proceed.

"If you get too drastic or too extreme, it sets you back," he says. "We have 47 police departments in Erie County. We need to consolidate. People say 'fine, but don't take [away] mine.'"

Giambra says the criticism is a natural reaction to any radical change. "To shoot the messenger is not appropriate," he says. "A lot of people are still going through the denial phase and don't recognize the severity of the problem."

"Once I eliminate the fear factor, then I think we have a chance of getting this thing passed," he says.

Labor thinks otherwise. A controversial element of Giambra's plan that carries significant cost-saving features but elicits strong opposition is the elimination of expensive city labor contracts with police and fire unions. Many cities find they are unable to escape old, expensive contracts because unions are unwilling to negotiate new ones that could include concessions not present in current contracts.

Under the Triborough amendment, passed by the state Legislature in the 1970s to protect municipalities against public employee strikes, the provisions and benefits of a contract remain in force when it expires. That gives unions no reason to settle on new bargaining agreements, Giambra concedes. "We're all in the same predicament," he says. "We have no ability to change contracts and very little ability to raise revenue."

If a city is dissolved, those contracts would be voided, and new ones would be negotiated with the resulting county-city entity, Giambra says. City jobs would not be eliminated, he adds, because those services currently provided by the city still would be needed.

Labor officials question the legality of such a move. "The state cannot make laws that have the effect of impairing contracts. This sounds like that's what's possibly happening here," says Nancy Holtman, general counsel to the Civil Service Employees Association (CSEA), the state's largest public employee union, representing 1,100 local government bargaining units.

With so many local obstacles, many people believe state government action is the only way city-county mergers can be implemented. Other solutions available to localities in other parts of the country are available only in theory to New York officials. Unlike in the southern and western regions of the United States, where newer municipalities have expanded tremendously, cities in the northeast are trapped by their own longstanding political boundaries.

Annexation, in which a city absorbs its own suburbs and undeveloped land surrounding its borders, is available to those states in the South and West, but in New York it is an extraordinarily difficult process. It can be initiated only by a petition of property owners, putting any city expansion at the mercy of developers and suburban homeowners. But politicians protecting their districts are not likely to cooperate with the idea. "They don't want to give up their turf, their power, their overloaded payrolls, and they don't think about the taxpayers they're working for," Hanna says.

Many policy-makers agree with Buffalo Mayor Masiello that more modest consolidation moves are the realistic way to proceed. Cities should concentrate on providing public services such as police and fire protection, while counties could take over and coordinate solid waste disposal and social services delivery, NYSAC's Zagame says. He notes that New York City was able to wrest contract concessions from labor unions in the 1970s, when it experienced its own financial crisis. Financially ailing cities in the 1990s can do the same, Zagame says. Inter-city cooperation between bordering communities also could offer practical opportunities for cost savings, Troy Mayor Pattison says.

But proposing such wrenching changes while in office can be political suicide. "The idea hasn't really caught on with anybody, as far as I know," says former Jamestown Mayor Carolyn Seymour, who proposed the merger concept at the end of her term in 1993. "It's actually hard when you're in office to make radical proposals like this."

Such daunting impediments do not discourage Giambra, who says sweeping changes are needed now, before the plight of cities gets worse. If the state legislation is approved, he plans to have a merger referendum ready for Erie County voters as early as 1998. The situation is "getting worse every year, not better," he says. "We cannot sit back and let the status quo continue."

X.   STATE ISSUES

One might think that the goal of state government is to provide the services that citizens need and then raise the money to do so. Actually, the governor and state legislature see just how much money will be available under the current tax structure and then decide the extent of services the state can provide. It comes as no surprise, therefore, that financial issues are at the top of state policy agendas. If additional funds are needed, how should the revenues be raised—taxes, user fees, bonds, lotteries? What kinds of taxes should be imposed—sales, income, inheritance, property? Who will bear the burden of these taxes—the rich, the poor, the consumer, the property holder? These are the most important questions state governors and legislatures address.

The 1980s presented the states with a roller coaster ride in their budgets. In the early 1980s, there was a recession and state revenues dropped precipitously. The fiscal crisis necessitated layoffs, hiring limits, travel restrictions, and delays in expenditures. The budget crunch of the early 1980s greatly lowered expectations of what state government could and would do.[1]

At the same time, the states were waiting to see how the national government would handle the federal deficit, and how that decision would affect state and local finances. Then, in the mid-1980s, a major fear of state leaders came true: the president and Congress decided to solve part of the national deficit crisis by letting the states pay for a considerable part of it. Saving a program that formerly was funded in whole or part with federal funds means increasing state and local taxes. And to many lawmakers, increased taxes can mean defeat at the polls.

During this time, however, the economy recovered and revenues flowed into state treasuries. No matter what the governor proposed and the legislature adopted, there was always a surplus at the end of the fiscal year. State decision makers were confident despite the major changes going on within the federal system.

However, by the end of the 1980s another problem developed in many states: the deterioration of their fiscal health resulting from reduced tax revenues as the nation's economy began slipping into a recession. The states faced a new budget problem: keeping their budgets balanced. The irony here was that the bad news for the states was their low budget surpluses; for the federal government it was the large budget deficit!

What could the states do? As already noted, one option would be to raise taxes. States also could seek new sources of tax revenue. For example, more and more states considered instituting a state lottery, which seemed to be a painless way to raise money. But research on state lotteries indicates that they amount to a "heavy tax"—one that is sharply regressive—because it is levied in part on those who cannot afford it.[2]

In the 1990s, finances dominate the agendas of most state governors and legislatures. After a couple of years of economists arguing whether the country was moving into a recession, it became clear that we had. State leaders observed that an economic slowdown had occurred, which translated into decreasing state tax revenues or a decline of the revenue growth they had experienced in the mid-1980s. This often meant tax increases had to be considered and often adopted if programs were to be maintained at their current levels, let alone starting new initiatives.

There were few states not facing serious budgetary problems. The budget deficits in some cases were enormous; California's for 1992–93 was over $14.2 billion, and even shutting down the state's entire higher education and correctional systems would still have left a large deficit to handle. Governors and legislatures tried to erase these deficits with all types of "revenue enhancements," program and governmental cutbacks, and even reverted to what the federal government had been doing: shifting some responsibilities downward, toward the local governments. However, by fiscal year 1994 the severe instability in most state budgets was subsiding.[3]

But following the 1994 elections, a new set of priorities began to come into focus: cutting taxes and reducing the size of government and its programs. This was most evident at the national level as Congress worked through the Republican "Contract with America." But it was also happening at the state and local levels as elected leaders tried to outdo each other in their calls for cuts. The economy-based money problems that had been evident at the outset of the 1990s were being replaced by politically based money problems in the mid-1990s.

Now, as we move into the late 1990s, the national economy and most state economies are relatively healthy, a situation that translates into a surplus in most state budgets. It is not a large surplus, but it is just big enough to make everyone with an interest in state government look hungrily at how those funds might be directed toward their own needs. Schoolteachers want higher salaries; so do those in higher education and state government employees in non-education positions. There are also environmental issues that need funding…. And the list goes on.

But there is a large, dark cloud hanging over the states and their local governments. When Congress and the president finally agree on the specifics of how the federal government's budget will be balanced—which will obviously include program and funding cuts to state and local governments—what will the fiscal impact be on the states? Before state and local governments can allocate any surplus they may now have in hand, they must be sure that it will not be wiped out in the near future by actions taken at the national level.

After money, what are the issues of greatest concern to the states? Currently, governors and legislatures are focusing much of their attention on crime and corrections. The "solutions" they propose come with large price tags. Health and welfare issues also are high on the agendas of the states, especially as the national government passes legislation such as welfare reform, which places greater responsibility on the states. These issues are at the crux of any pending agreement between the president and Congress and are thus outside of the control of states.

Of course, different regions of the country have different priorities. In the Southwest, water policy is a dominant issue. In the Midwest, farm problems, the declining industrial base, and lack of economic development are major concerns. In the Northeast it is an aging infrastructure that must be rebuilt so the economies can recover. And in California, which is a region unto itself, the state must cope with both in and out migration, a multicultural population, unpredictable weather pattern shifts and earthquakes, and a shifting economic base in addition to a myriad of societal problems.

Waste problems affect each of the states and their local communities, and none appear to be as intractable as disposing of hazardous waste. One example makes the point. Under the prodding of the U.S. Department of Energy, the states have been grouped into a series of regional interstate compacts (legal agreements) to seek processes and sites for the disposal of radioactive waste within each region. But as the time draws near to select the sites for locating this waste, the process appears to be close to collapse due to a lack of trust. In a nutshell, the question that state policy makers are asking is, "Which state will take their turn next and can we be sure that they will do so?" No state wants to be first in a line where no one stands second.

Setting the Agenda

How do particular concerns become priorities on the states' agendas? Although state constitutions provide for the education, health, and safety of citizens, events can trigger new interest in these issues. For example, the collapse of financial institutions such as insurance companies or state-chartered banks can lead to citizen despair and action by state regulators. Campaign promises and court decisions also influence policy making. A gubernatorial candidate who promises to lower utility rates will try to keep this promise once elected. And if a state court finds that some citizens, such as the mentally handicapped, are not receiving the state services to which they are entitled, chances are the governor and state legislators will pay closer attention to this issue.

Provisions of the U.S. Constitution also can force issues onto a state's policy agenda. Since the 1950s, there has been a series of U.S. Supreme Court decisions on "separate but equal" education, reappor-

tionment, and criminal justice based on lawsuits challenging state and local government policies and actions as violations of the plaintiffs' constitutional rights. These decisions have caused state and local government lawmakers considerable anguish as they address and adopt often controversial and expensive new policies, which usually translate into tax increases.

Federal program requirements also can play a role in state policy making and administration. For example, in the early and mid-1980s, the states had to raise the legal drinking age to twenty-one and limit interstate highway speeds to 55 miles per hour or face the loss of federal highway funds. However, federal encroachment on setting speed limits came to a head in a highly publicized and controversial vote to override President Ronald Reagan's veto of a multibillion dollar transportation bill in March 1987. The override allowed those states that so desired to raise the limit to 65 miles per hour on rural interstates.

Innovations and programs in other states can influence a state's agenda, as a new form of activity in one state may lead to similar action elsewhere. This "copycat" method of decision making has proved to be very popular: How did State X handle this? However, as some have noticed, what is "reform in one state may be the exact opposite of reform in another." For example, California made its insurance commissioner an elected official the same time as Louisiana was looking to make that office appointive rather than elective; and Georgia repealed no-fault auto insurance the same time as Pennsylvania added it.[4]

Events not only in another state but in another part of the world occasionally determine the issues that state governments must address. Although the recent decrease in tension between the United

States and the former Soviet Union has raised hopes of a "peace dividend"—a budget windfall from cuts in the defense budget—the states will bear the cost of the dividend. Cuts in the defense budget have meant the closing of military bases in some states, reducing military personnel, and cutting back or cancelling contracts for military hardware and weapons systems and funding for military research. Many states and localities have greatly benefited from the defense budget in years past. Now, as times and concerns change, so too are their economies and fiscal health.

Implementation

Once policy goals and priorities are set by governors and legislators, important decisions must be made concerning who will implement them. This not only means which agency in state government will have the responsibility, but which level of government—state, local, or both.

Implementation decisions are often made with the considerable interest and involvement of the federal government. State and local governments administer some federal programs: food stamps, child nutrition, social services, community action, and senior citizen centers. In other areas federal and state governments *share* administrative and fiscal responsibility: public welfare, Medicaid, interstate and federal highways, hazardous waste, and water supply and sanitation.

The federal system is in a process of change, and since the 1994 elections the process and the nature of these changes have escalated. As already noted, the debates and conflicts in Congress are centering on how to cut back the national government's role in domestic policy. When politicians debate the role of the federal government in domestic policy they are,

for the most part, referring to the extent to which the federal government will work with state and local governments in a wide range of policies. But for state officials and their counterparts at the local level, the outcome of these debates will have a direct impact on their jobs and responsibilities. And by extension, the outcome of these debates will have considerable impact on citizens and on what they can expect from their state and local governments.

The articles in Part X focus on some of the policy concerns states are facing. Alan Ehrenhalt of *Governing* presents analyses of two topics: the regulation and promotion of casinos, gambling, and other "sins"; and how one state is trying to create more low income housing. Peter A. Harkness of *Governing* takes a look at just where state and local governments stand in terms of their capacity to fulfill their roles. Hal Hovey of *Governing* examines money matters at the state and local levels. Penelope Lemov of *Governing* analyzes some states' efforts to remove the sales tax on food, while Scott Mackey of *State Legislatures* looks at the problems of trying to replace the local property tax. Finally, Charles Mahtesian of *Governing* presents the why, who, where, and what aspects of ten major issues currently on the state agendas.

Notes

1. National Governors' Association, *The State of the States, 1985,* 6.

2. Peter Passell, "Duke Economists Critical of State Lotteries," *New York Times News Service,* reported in the *Durham Morning Herald,* May 21, 1989, 11A.

3. "Severe Instability in State Budgets Subsiding," *Governors' Bulletin,* November 8, 1993, 1–3.

4. Hal Hovey, "Ebb and Flow in State Policy," *State Policy Reports* 9:18 (September 1991): 12.

The Dangers of Making Sin Scarce

by Alan Ehrenhalt

Your legislature, after a long and bitter battle, has finally cleared the way for the arrival of casino gambling in your state. But that still leaves the question of how to regulate it—how to decide who can open a casino and start cashing in. Do you A): just offer a license to any card shark who wants one? Or B): place strict controls on the gambling business, limiting the number of licenses and forcing an arduous approval process on anybody seeking entry?

Just about every state chooses Option B. Of all the places that have gone to casinos in the past decade, Mississippi is the only one I know of that has been rash enough to go the other route: throw the gambling business open to all comers and let nature take its course.

For $5,000 in Mississippi, anybody without a criminal record can apply for a permit to set up a casino. There is no limit to the number of permits per customer. The gambling is supposed to take place over water, but that rule is interpreted so loosely that almost anything bigger than a drinking fountain is sufficient to qualify. Two years after gambling became legal in Mississippi, 30 casinos were open for business. As Ellen Perlman wrote in *Governing*

[in 1995], "if you have a spit of land and can clear a background check, you can be a casino king."

Meanwhile, on the other side of the river, Louisiana was doing it the more conventional way. Worried about the impact that a massive gambling invasion might have on the state, the legislature voted to allow just 15 riverboats and one land-based casino, and to create a gambling commission to pore over the credentials of the applicants.

The results of Louisiana's venture into gambling can be described as follows: scandal and bankruptcy. Most of the casino licenses went to people with connections to then-Governor Edwin W. Edwards. A few of them put friends or relatives of Edwards on their payroll. Meanwhile, several of the state's most senior legislators were caught taking payoffs from gambling operators. Parishes are now being given the option of banning casinos from their territory. And, as has been widely reported, the big gambling palace on the New Orleans riverfront

Alan Ehrenhalt is a staff writer for *Governing*. This article is reprinted from *Governing* (September 1996): 7–8.

went bankrupt after less than a year, costing the state millions of dollars in revenue it was counting on.

Louisiana went into the gambling business systematically, and was embarrassed. Mississippi went in recklessly and had exactly the opposite experience. Gambling is bringing the state a huge fiscal dividend. There have been a few bankruptcies, but the vast majority of the casinos remain open and profitable. No gambling company in Mississippi has been found paying off a legislator or hiring the governor's son-in-law, because they don't need to do that. All they need is a check for $5,000.

I'm not arguing in favor of turning every state into Las Vegas. The social and moral risks of gambling ought to trouble every legislature in the country, and critics of casinos make a credible case for keeping them out altogether. I might vote to keep them out myself. The point is this: If you bring gambling to your state, you don't solve any problems by trying to ration it.

It's not hard to see why most states make the Louisiana mistake, even if they don't embarrass themselves in quite as spectacular a way. Gambling never becomes legal anywhere without having to overcome intense opposition. One way the winning side tries to pacify the losers is to insist that it will all be carefully regulated, it won't get out of hand, it won't change the character of life in the state. And so the government creates an artificial scarcity—it makes licenses hard to obtain.

By doing that, it sets up its public officials with a juicy privilege to give away, and exposes them to sleazy operators who know how to tempt them. Even in states with a tradition of reasonably honest politics, this is dangerous. In ... Louisiana, it is asking for trouble, and trouble is what it brought.

Something like this has happened before. In the 1920s, when parimutuel horse racing became the nation's one legalized gambling indulgence—and a major source of state revenue—the psychology was very similar. Betting on horses was a little bit sinful, so it was best not to have too much of it. Betting was permitted only at a restricted number of licensed tracks, and each track was given a limited number of racing days every year.

There was a plausible-sounding economic explanation for this. If all the tracks tried to run at once, and the stronger ones drove the weaker ones out of business, the state [could] lose millions of tax dollars. But ... the economic consequences of the racing date system were dwarfed by the political consequences. The track that got the best summer dates made the most money. The governor and the legislature had the power to award those dates, and the track owners had the money to influence those decisions under the table.

I don't know whether, in the long run, the rationing of horse-racing dates kept marginal tracks in business and thus saved the states valuable revenue. I do know that the whole system brought down two of the more capable and intelligent governors of recent times, Marvin Mandel of Maryland and Otto Kerner of Illinois, both sent to prison for accepting racetrack stock and then using the powers of office to grant the track a lucrative schedule.

This isn't a lesson in how to regulate gambling. It's a lesson in how to regulate anything. Governments should be very careful about creating scarcities where they don't naturally exist. Sometimes it's unavoidable. The American cities of the 1890s needed streetcars, and they couldn't have competing streetcars on the same track. So they granted monopoly power to private traction companies to put in the equipment. Charles Yerkes obtained his streetcar franchise in Chicago by bribing a majority of the aldermen on the city council. It was a mess, but the city got its transit system, and it's not clear how it would have gotten it any other way.

Until just a few years ago, it was assumed that cable television was in a similar category: Local governments had to grant someone a monopoly, or else forests of hideous wires from competing companies would block out the sun on residential streets all over the country. Until technology made cable competition practical, the companies and the governments that licensed them could argue that they weren't creating scarcity, they were just bowing to reality. That made the influence peddling that surrounded cable franchise politics, in the opinion of some, a necessary evil.

But there are plenty of cases in which governments still do what Louisiana did—establish an artificial scarcity of franchises or licenses or permits to do something, and then endure the corruption that the system and the fact of human weakness combine to ensure.

Consider liquor licenses, for example. It's pretty clear that communities are entitled to place some restrictions on who can sell alcohol. A liquor store next to a high school offends most people; a tavern next to a church offends others. But as Hal Hovey of *State Policy Reports*, who has studied the licensing problem, is quick to point out, legitimate community concerns don't come close to explaining the thicket of regulation that surrounds the granting of a liquor license in most of the communities in America.

What does explain them, in Hovey's view, is the unspoken feeling that drinking, like casinos and horse racing, is something less than an honorable activity. It's not prac-

tical to prohibit it, as we learned in the 1920s, but the forces opposed to it can be pacified a bit if the number of taverns and liquor stores is kept to a minimum. The harder it is for people to find a drink (or a slot machine), the argument goes, the less drinking (or gambling) they will do. And the less severe the pangs of moral concern will be.

The only problem with this idea is that it has no basis in the experience of any state or locality that I have ever heard of. People don't drink less in Pennsylvania, where liquor is sold in state stores, than they do in California, where it is available in supermarkets. Those who want it find a way to get it.

Besides, licensing an enterprise and monitoring its performance are two different propositions. Delaware is a place where it is comparatively easy to get a license to sell liquor; it is also a place that has a reputation for keeping a close watch on the establishments it licenses. Mississippi doesn't forget about its casino operators once they pay their $5,000 fee—after they are in business 48 hours, they are required to shut down for the next 48 hours for review by the state Gaming Commission. After that, they are subject to surveillance from cameras mounted on the ceiling of each gambling floor.

Does Mississippi police its gambling operations as intensively as some of the states that take a more restrictive approach? No, probably not. But it does seem to understand a principle that many other states entering the casino era have yet to grasp.

The principle is this: If a particular brand of behavior is sinful, then perhaps it should be illegal. If you decide to legalize it but make it scarce and hand out franchises in a political sweepstakes, you aren't controlling the amount of sin in your state. You are adding to it.

Lucky Winners in the Housing Sweepstakes

by Alan Ehrenhalt

In a hundred leafy suburbs that sprawl out across the prairie from Minneapolis and St. Paul, local leaders are weighing a proposition that sounds suspiciously like the governmental equivalent of a letter from Ed McMahon.

They are being told that they are guaranteed winners of one of three exciting gifts. They are to receive either A: money to help them clean up abandoned waste sites; or B: money to develop their commercial corridors; or C: money to help solve their housing problems. They can choose whichever present they like best.

To collect it, they don't have to subscribe to any magazines or tour vacation homesites. All they have to do is make a promise. They must promise some sort of effort to find places for low-income people to live within their suburban boundaries.

Such are the rewards—and the requirements—of Minnesota's new "Livable Communities Act," a law that may sound like it was written by Publishers Clearinghouse but in fact represents one of the country's most unusual experiments at changing the residential patterns of a metropolitan area.

Minneapolis and St. Paul are far from being the most troubled of America's big cities, but like virtually all of them, they face an array of inner-city social and economic problems that grow worse each year. In the early 1980s, one-third of Minneapolis schoolchildren qualified for subsidized lunches; now more than half of them do. The poorest Minneapolis and St. Paul neighborhoods have crime rates 30 times higher than the average in the suburbs.

The Livable Communities Act, signed into law last year, is designed to attack the area's urban poverty by de-concentrating it: making room for poorer people in affluent places that currently don't contain any. It sets out to entice suburbs into taking on low-income housing commitments that most of them would just as soon avoid.

Whether the new law is a bold experiment or just an interesting one depends on whom you talk to. As envisioned by its original champion, Democratic state Representative Myron Orfield of Minneapolis, the law would have gone considerably beyond enticement. It would have all but bludgeoned the suburbs into creating low-in-

Alan Ehrenhalt is a staff writer for *Governing*. This article is reprinted from *Governing* (July 1996): 7–8.

come housing by withholding sewer and highway money from those that refused to do it.

As ultimately enacted, the Livable Communities Act does nothing remotely like that. If the suburbs make what sounds like a good-faith effort to house some poor people, then they can dip down into the grab bag and pull out some funding for waste cleanup, transit projects or housing itself. If they promise and then renege, nothing all that terrible will happen to them. The idea of sanctions was one that Republican Governor Arne Carlson and most of the state's suburban legislators did not feel comfortable with.

Somebody else who does not like sanctions very much is the law's ultimate administrator, Curtis Johnson, chairman of the Minneapolis-St. Paul Metropolitan Council. Johnson has some very potent weapons in his governmental arsenal. The council controls more than $500 million every year in funding of various kinds for the region's governments; it can even invalidate some local zoning decisions if it has a mind to. But as far as Johnson is concerned, trying to deploy those weapons would amount to a political disaster. "We will not use this program in a vindictive way," he insists. "Forcing people is just not politically possible. If it once was, it isn't now."

So Johnson is spending his time handing out carrots, and, as you might expect, most of the suburbs are finding them pretty tasty. In all, 115 metro-area communities are eligible for the incentive money, and within six months after the law's enactment last year, 97 of them had signed on to the program. That meant they had drafted some general goals for creating low-income housing within their borders over the next 15 years. This summer, they are required to

take one more fairly modest step: They have to provide "action plans" detailing where the housing will go and when it will go up.

None of them are required to start building anything at this stage. Nevertheless, the prizes are already being awarded. This spring, four communities received $2.3 million in demonstration grants, and by the end of the year, the metro council expects to write checks to as many as 20 more local governments. "We want $12 million on the street every year," says Craig Rapp, the council's community development director.

The city of Minnetonka is one of this summer's lucky winners. It is about to get a check from Curtis Johnson for $770,000, which it plans to spend on option B—improvements to its central commercial area. Minnetonka will be sprucing up a park, putting in freshwater ponds, building a community meeting hall and creating lighted walkways for its downtown transit stop.

In return, the town is setting aside 200 "affordable" units in its new Westridge housing development, being built by a private developer. About 100 of those will be apartments for senior citizens; another 100 will be small townhouses made available at a subsidized rate. That will get Minnetonka roughly halfway to the 400 lower-income units it promised the Metropolitan Council it would build between now and the year 2010.

Getting to 400 will not be nearly as easy. Minnetonka was fortunate in that it happened to be creating a big new center-city project just at the time the Livable Communities Act went into effect. Separating out a bloc of units was a relatively simple political accomplishment. But there won't be any more Westridges coming along. To reach its ultimate goal, Minnetonka will have to get into scatter-site housing closer to its spacious homes on big lots, and this is not what anybody would call a slam-dunk. "I'm now beginning to hear opposition," says Mayor Karen Anderson. "There are some initial fears."

They are the same fears that will spring up before too long in many of the communities that have signed up for the program. Minnetonka is typical of the suburbs that Myron Orfield and the affordable housing hard-liners want to change drastically. With a median income of more than $50,000 a year, it is one of the richest communities in the state, and one of the whitest. The last census showed 443 blacks among its nearly 50,000 residents. The city is a textbook example of the low-density development that drives the hard-liners crazy. Many of the new homes built there in the past decade have taken up nearly an acre of land and sold for upwards of $300,000.

Minnetonka, in other words, is a nice, safe place that is doing very well. About the only political constituency it has for low-income housing comes from some of its businesses, which need entry-level workers and find it hard to attract them. Inner-city residents could help solve this problem, but without a car, they have trouble getting to the jobs; transit connections from the suburbs to Minneapolis aren't very good, and between one suburb and another they are almost nonexistent. That is why some of the companies that have chosen to locate in Minnetonka seem to be going along with the new rules. Osmonics, a manufacturer of water-purification equipment with a plant on the outskirts of town, can't fill its blue-collar jobs as fast as it is creating them. Its executives figure that a few hundred low-cost housing units in the center of town couldn't help but be good for their labor problem.

In fact, however, matching job applicants to job openings is only a small part of the agenda that the promoters of the Livable Communities Act originally had in mind. Myron Orfield doesn't just believe that inner-city poor people need transportation to the suburbs. He believes that the only way cities can be saved is by forcibly breaking up the ghetto and scattering the people throughout the Minnetonkas that exist in every metropolitan area in the United States.

At the moment, Orfield is more upset with the progress of the Livable Communities Act than most of the conservative Republicans who fought its passage. "Other than developers," he complains, "there's nobody that doesn't think this is a total sham. They're not even trying to push the envelope." As far as he's concerned, Johnson and the Metro Council are simply handing out goodies upon request to rich suburban governments that won't ever get around to the toughest housing decisions.

In making those arguments, Orfield is lining up alongside a phalanx of current social critics who argue that the inner city simply lacks the resources to renew itself from within and that the only real way to help the residents of the ghetto is to get them out. Nicholas Lemann made the same argument in *The Promised Land,* his 1992 book about the housing projects of Chicago's South Side, and David Rusk, the former mayor of Albuquerque, makes it in countless speeches all over the country, with a whole battery of statistics to prove his point.

They are strong arguments. One can only say in rebuttal that it is a lot easier to make them as an urbanologist than as a suburban mayor, balancing the demands of diversity against the political requirements of the job, or a metro council chairman, seeking to knit together the fragile strands of regional cooperation in the face of powerful centrifugal forces working against it.

The truth is that as long as the crime rate in inner-city Minneapolis is 30 times as high as the crime rate in Minnetonka, there are going to be immense political barriers in the way of any demographic redistribution of the sort that Lemann, Rusk and Orfield want to carry out. Sermonizing about suburban complacency isn't going to change that, or get new housing built.

"We can run around issuing orders, sounding righteous," Curtis Johnson says, "and all we'll do is create a revolution." That idea may not be palatable to everyone, but it is true. It's hard to see how the results of such a revolution would be helpful either to Minneapolis or to Minnetonka.

Government by the Numbers: A Snapshot of Capacity

by Peter A. Harkness

As state and local leaders look forward to 1997 and beyond, a few things are clear: A healthy economy is offering up steady revenues and suppressing demand for social welfare spending; the gradual movement of authority and responsibility out of Washington is continuing; and pressure to cut costs, integrate services and make government more effective with fewer resources is increasing.

What is not so clear is how states and localities will respond. Will they have sufficient resources, even in the event of an economic slowdown? Do they have the management capacity and the political will to redesign national programs for providing social services, enforcing pollution laws, ensuring that everyone receives adequate health care and the like? Will cutting administrative costs make enough of a difference? Will some states simply pass the buck to their local governments? Will there be some kind of "race to the bottom," as devolution's detractors have warned?

No one knows the answers to those questions, at least not yet. But to get an idea of what states, cities and counties might do in the future, it makes sense to take a look at what they have been doing, and how they compare to one another....

Revenue

Collectively, state and local revenue and spending totals are impressive—now closing in on $1.4 trillion. Much of the money is concentrated in what we call the GOVERNING 100, the 50 states, 25 largest cities and 25 largest counties in terms of revenue. All but nine of them had revenues in excess of $1 billion in FY 1994, and it's a safe bet at least two of those do by now.

In all, there are more than 85,000 governments in the nation: 50 states, 3,043 counties, more than 19,000 municipalities and almost 17,000 towns and townships, with the rest being school districts and special districts. But if you add up the total revenue of the GOVERNING 100, it comes to more than $800 billion, or almost 60 percent of the total for all state and local governments.

By any standard, these governments are large enterprises. In fact, an overlay of

Peter A. Harkness is editor and publisher of *Governing*. This article is reprinted from *Governing Sourcebook 1997* (January 1997): 6, 8, 12–14.

the GOVERNING 100 against the Fortune 500 corporations reveals that the governments of 46 states, six cities, three counties and two school districts are "larger" in terms of revenues than the 500th company on *Fortune*'s list—Dow Corning.

Comparisons are interesting, but they must be used with care.

The state of California, with 31 million people, takes in $90 billion a year. Michigan collects $27 billion. But the two state governments are just about the same size in terms of revenue per capita.

New York City, the third largest government in America, serves 7 million residents and collects almost $40 billion in revenue, more per capita than any other governments in the GOVERNING 100, except for Alaska and the District of Columbia. Los Angeles County, larger than all but 19 states, takes in more than $11 billion and employs 83,000 people, almost the same as the state of Indiana.

The relative sizes of government work forces can be surprising. New York State, for instance, employs 147 people per 10,000 residents, but New Mexico weighs in with 265 workers on revenue per capita that is about the same. Hawaii employs 444 people per 10,000 residents (more than any other state government) and spends almost $700 more per resident than New York. But in Hawaii, the state does much more than most, including paying for all education and most health and welfare costs.

Arguably the largest government in the country for the size of its population is that of Washington, D.C., with more than $8,000 in revenue per citizen (trailing only Alaska) and 746 employees for every 10,000 residents, far more than anyplace else. Although the numbers undoubtedly reflect bureaucratic inefficiencies—the

city is now being overseen by a federal control board—strict comparisons with other cities are impossible since Washington has to perform the functions of three levels of government—state, city and county.

And that is a central point to keep in mind when comparing state to state or city to city: different jurisdictions have different sets of responsibilities. So while California and Michigan may be about the same in per-capita revenue, a comparison of the two states along with their local governments shows a different picture, with California ranking ninth in the nation in combined total revenue per capita and Michigan ranking 19th.

To get a true reading of how states compare in revenue or spending, it's more meaningful to group them with their local governments and then determine revenue from combined state and local sources as a portion of personal income within the state.

Those adjustments turn up some surprises. Massachusetts, for instance, often is thought of as a liberal, relatively big-government state (jokingly dubbed "Taxachusetts"), and predictably it comes in 12th in the country in per-capita revenue. But when total state and local collections are measured as a percentage of personal income, it slips all the way down to 42nd place.

Mississippi is a state with a reputation for chronically being near the bottom in many categories, and sure enough, it ranks 47th in per-capita revenue. But when judged against its residents' ability to pay, the state comes in a surprising 11th. Mississippi may be the most extreme example, but it reflects a trend among many Southeastern states that take in quite a large amount of tax money given their citizens' ability to pay. These states aren't alone,

State and Local Governments
Ranked by FY 1994 General Revenue

1.	California	36.	New Mexico	69.	Detroit, Mich.
2.	New York	37.	West Virginia	70.	Sacramento Cty.,
3.	New York City,	38.	Alaska		Calif.
	N.Y.	39.	Hawaii	71.	Prince George's Cty.,
4.	Texas	40.	Utah		Md.
5.	Pennsylvania	41.	Washington, D.C.	72.	Harris Cty., Texas
6.	Florida	42.	Los Angeles, Calif.	73.	Suffolk Cty., N.Y.
7.	Ohio	43.	Nebraska	74.	Riverside Cty., Calif.
8.	Michigan	44.	Maine	75.	Westchester Cty.,
9.	Illinois	45.	Dade Cty., Fla.		N.Y.
10.	New Jersey	46.	Nevada	76.	Houston, Texas
11.	Massachusetts	47.	Chicago, Ill.	77.	Alameda Cty., Calif.
12.	North Carolina	48.	Rhode Island	78.	Baltimore Cty., Md.
13.	Washington	49.	Philadelphia, Pa.	79.	Maricopa Cty., Ariz.
14.	Georgia	50.	San Francisco, Calif.	80.	Denver, Colo.
15.	Virginia	51.	Idaho	81.	Clark Cty., Nev.
16.	Indiana	52.	Delaware	82.	Erie Cty., N.Y.
17.	Wisconsin	53.	New Hampshire	83.	San Diego, Calif.
18.	Minnesota	54.	Montana	84.	Dallas, Texas
19.	Maryland	55.	Orange Cty., Calif.	85.	Hillsborough Cty.,
20.	Louisiana	56.	San Diego Cty.,		Fla.
21.	Los Angeles Cty.,		Calif.	86.	Cuyahoga Cty., Ohio
	Calif.	57.	Nassau Cty., N.Y.	87.	Hennepin Cty.,
22.	Missouri	58.	North Dakota		Minn.
23.	Connecticut	59.	Wyoming	88.	Phoenix, Ariz.
24.	Tennessee	60.	Montgomery Cty.,	89.	Nashville, Tenn.
25.	Kentucky		Md.	90.	Wayne Cty., Mich.
26.	Alabama	61.	Fairfax Cty., Va.	91.	Indianapolis, Ind.
27.	Arizona	62.	Baltimore, Md.	92.	Memphis, Tenn.
28.	South Carolina	63.	Santa Clara Cty.,	93.	Honolulu, Hawaii
29.	Oregon		Calif.	94.	Seattle, Wash.
30.	Colorado	64.	Cook Cty., Ill.	95.	Jacksonville, Fla.
31.	Iowa	65.	Boston, Mass.	96.	Virginia Beach, Va.
32.	Oklahoma	66.	Vermont	97.	San Jose, Calif.
33.	Mississippi	67.	South Dakota	98.	Minneapolis, Minn.
34.	Kansas	68.	San Bernardino Cty.,	99.	Anchorage, Alaska
35.	Arkansas		Calif.	100.	New Orleans, La.

Source: "The Governing 100," *Governing Sourcebook 1997* (January 1997): 16.

though. New Mexico, for instance, a comparatively poor state with a high percentage of residents on welfare, ranks third overall in revenue as a percentage of income even though it's in the middle of the pack in per-capita collections.

To some extent, the riddle can be explained by federal funding. Mississippi and New Mexico both receive a disproportionate amount of money from Washington. Mississippi ranks third in the country, behind only West Virginia and Louisiana, in federal funds received as a percentage of total revenue. In fact, the top 10 places in that category are dominated by small states, with Wyoming, Arkansas, North Dakota, Montana, South Dakota, Vermont and Maine filling out the list. At a time when federal funding will likely be cut back, those states have a lot to lose compared with states such as Florida, Nebraska, Colorado, Maryland and Nevada, which don't depend much on federal funding either per capita or as a percentage of total revenue.

A relatively high-tax state such as New York is more predictable, ranking second in per-capita revenue, fourth in revenue as a portion of personal income, and third in per-capita revenue supplied by the federal government. Surprisingly, conservative Wyoming is almost the same—third in per-capita revenue and second as a portion of income, though clearly a big chunk of it comes from Washington.

In some states, the balance in public funding is very close. Ohio, for instance, a state that often is used by market surveys as a microcosm of the country, has the same rank both for per-capita revenue and for revenue as a portion of personal income—placing 15th in each. Indiana comes close to balance, as do Georgia, Texas and Wisconsin.

Some states rank low in both. Missouri and Virginia, for example, are close to the bottom of the list by both measures. And Virginia ranks dead last in the share per capita of revenue supplied by federal funding. (Both Virginia and Maryland rank low in dependence on direct federal funding, but both economies are heavily reliant on the federal payroll.)

Spending

Spending patterns among state and local governments closely track revenues. States spend 61 percent of the combined state-and-local total, and on average states and localities spend an amount equivalent to 23.6 percent of their residents' personal income (including federal funds).

Setting aside top spenders such as Alaska and Wyoming—low-population states that rely heavily on revenues from oil and mineral extraction—the range in spending levels is striking.

New York upholds its big-budget reputation, finishing second in per-capita spending and third in spending as a percentage of personal income. Compared with Missouri, which finished second to last (just above Arkansas) in per-capita spending and last in spending as a portion of income, the actual dollar difference is considerable. A New Yorker receives services carrying a $7,116 annual price tag, while the total price of services received in the "Show Me" state is less than half that, at $3,311.

Other comparatively high-tax states come in about where one would expect them to be. Connecticut, California, Minnesota, New Jersey and Massachusetts all finish in the top 10 in per-capita spending, although they diverge significantly when ranked by spending as a portion of personal income, with Connecticut and New Jersey dropping all the way to the bottom 10 in the rankings.

The totals spent by states and localities across the country for different activities offer some clues as to priorities. Elementary and secondary education (at $240 billion) remains the largest and most expensive task undertaken by state and local governments, followed by welfare ($167 billion), infrastructure ($136 billion), health care ($95 billion) and then higher education ($88 billion). Health care, which has been the fastest-growing part of state budgets for some time, eclipsed higher education in spending only a few years ago. Now it's thought that corrections has replaced health care as the fastest-growing line item in most state budgets.

Some observations on spending patterns by function:

• Education: Aside from some small states, such as Alaska, Vermont, Wyoming, Delaware and North Dakota, where funding (for both K–12 and higher ed) is spread over a relatively small population, the heaviest-spending states are all in the upper Midwest: Iowa, Michigan, Minnesota and Wisconsin. Some larger states, such as New York and New Jersey, spend a lot per capita, but not as a percentage of personal income. The laggards: Florida, Georgia, Massachusetts, Missouri, Nevada and Tennessee.

• Welfare: New York is hands-down the spending leader, ranking first in welfare spending per capita and as a portion of income. New York's aggregate number also is stunning—$22 billion a year—even more than the number for California, which finishes in the middle of the pack. Other big-spenders include Maine, Minnesota, New Hampshire, Rhode Island and West Virginia.

• Law Enforcement: Some of the larger states turn out to be the leaders in this category, with New York spending $7 billion (second per capita), California almost $11 billion (fourth per capita), Florida more than $4 billion (ranking fifth) and New Jersey more than $2 billion (ranking sixth).

• Environment: The "green" states— those placing in the top 10 in spending on the environment both per capita and as a percentage of personal income—are mostly ones you might expect: Alaska, Delaware, Hawaii, Oregon, Washington, Wisconsin and Wyoming. Those states ranking in the bottom 10 in both categories: Alabama, Colorado, Georgia, Indiana, Kansas, Missouri and Tennessee.

Capacity

In general, both state and local spending and employment have been climbing steadily upward for some time, reflecting increased responsibilities as well as population growth. The trend is a function of more kids in the public schools and universities, more trash and waste water, more roads, more people on Medicaid, and far more prisoners.

States in particular have improved their fiscal and management capacity in the past two decades. The recovery from the 1981–82 recession gave them an enormous economic boost just when they needed it. Since they have to balance their operating budgets, most states were forced to raise tax rates as the full effects of that recession, the worst since the Great Depression, cut into revenues. As the recovery took hold, those revenues boomed just as federal funds were being withdrawn by the Reagan administration. State governments in many cases filled the vacuum in aid to localities left by federal withdrawal.

For decades, state and local agencies have been administering federal programs in addition to their own, including welfare, Medicaid, job training, education, and highway construction and maintenance.

The risk in the new devolutionary scheme is on the resource side. If Congress cuts its contribution for shared programs substantially, as seems inevitable, and then the economy falters—thereby lowering state revenues and increasing demand for services—governors could be in a real fix. And that scenario seems very predictable. The current robust growth in state revenues comes at what most likely is the top of a business cycle. At some point, the indicators will start turning down.

While state and local governments appear to have done a better-than-average job of taking advantage of the economic recovery of 1993–96 to build their reserves, on average they have not done enough to avoid major fiscal problems likely to trigger tax increases and spending cutbacks when the next recession occurs.

Most at risk are the states that have not been building strong reserves and have balanced their budgets with optimistic assumptions. Most of these are concentrated in the Northeast and Mid-Atlantic, particularly states such as New York and New Jersey that have cut taxes deeply and have further automatic cuts poised to take effect in the future.

Performance

Of course, tracking revenues and expenditures isn't the same as measuring performance. Because a government spends a lot on something doesn't necessarily mean that it is effectively filling a need or addressing a problem. In fact, it may be just blowing money.

There isn't any national report card on state and local governments; such measurements are very tough to perform. But this doesn't prevent a broad assessment of how things are going, reflecting both public perception and objective indicators of progress and problems.

Confidence in government is low. Countless surveys show that Americans don't trust the motives of their public officials and think of government employees as overpaid and under-worked.

The perception that everything isn't going all that well is hard to avoid.

Public schools, for instance, don't seem to be improving. Even when adjusted for inflation, massive increases in spending per pupil don't seem to have improved basic skills such as the ability to read newspapers, follow instructions, make simple calculations or have some basic understanding of how our economy and government work. Many classrooms lack the fundamental order and discipline necessary for learning to take place. By most indicators, other industrial nations are doing a better job with schooling than we are.

Higher education has done better, but there are serious doubts expressed in state legislatures around the country over how well public universities and colleges are administered, whether their curricula have become unfocused, and whether their graduates have received enough of value for life in the real world.

Social services for children and families have not produced the desired results. An increasing percentage of the nation's children are growing up poor or being reported abused or neglected. Juvenile crime is increasing. Drug abuse is on the rise again.

The fear of crime continues to increase even though the nation is incarcerating a larger portion of its population than any other industrialized nation. Experts seem convinced that a recent drop in the crime rate is attributable only to demographics, and that a whole new generation of extremely violent criminals is on the verge of creating a more horrifying crime wave.

The Future

How will all of this play out in the future?

In the long term, the biggest risk to state and local governments is that fiscal realities will force the feds to concentrate their spending on three expensive activities: defense and foreign policy, interest on the debt, and entitlements for retirement and health care.

This means very little money for anything new, and reduced amounts for programs already authorized. And if a political solution isn't found to defuse the entitlement bomb, the scenario could be worse, unless of course, there are massive tax increases, which isn't likely.

While state and local governments might be able to pass along the impact of many federal cuts to program beneficiaries, voters may demand action on problems such as care for the truly helpless, food for the hungry and education for all kids even if they are physically or mentally disabled.

As the devolution trend continues, the hope is that it will achieve a better balance between the three levels of government—that our federal system will be less competitive and more cooperative, less ambiguous and more sharply defined. Voters rarely differentiate the services of one level from those of another; they want government services to be seamless.

Perhaps that's where we are headed.

Money In, Money Out: State and Local Revenue and Spending

by Hal Hovey

... State and local practices are rife with situations where technical distinctions between local and state tax collections are meaningless in terms of what government costs the taxpayer or which level of government controls the money. For example, for the convenience of taxpayers and to minimize administrative costs, many states collect all fees for vehicle registrations, drivers' licenses and gasoline taxes, but they rebate a fixed proportion to local governments.

The popular belief that large differences among states in per-capita taxes and spending can be explained by differences in the cost of living is simply not true. Genuine cost differences due to location exist only for Alaska and Hawaii. Elsewhere, goods such as lumber, appliances, food, clothing, school supplies, paper, computers and highway patrol cars cost about the same. Entry-level wages for unskilled work are quite similar throughout the United States, while highly skilled workers sell their services in the national market. Even the cost of building a new house on an available and developed lot is about the same nationwide. Big differences in market prices can be caused by scarcity—workers in a tight labor market, downtown office space in New York, beach-front property—but these differences are local, not statewide.

The most noticeable differences among states in household and business costs are the result of government decisions to impose certain taxes or to regulate utility rates. There are also big differences in government costs imposed by state or local governments themselves—their wage scales, employee benefits and practices in staffing, such as average class sizes in elementary and secondary schools.

There are logical reasons why some states spend more per capita than others. Most compelling are demographic factors: Some states have greater need to spend more per capita because a larger percentage of their population is of school and university age or a larger percentage of their population is poor, potential recipients of welfare grants and free health care through Medicaid. And yet some states with these factors—Arkansas, Mississippi and Utah are examples—do not spend

Hal Hovey is president of State Policy Research Inc. This article is reprinted from *Governing Sourcebook 1997* (January 1997): 26–29.

Hidden Costs

Some government costs are hidden because they don't count in either budget data or Census Bureau reports. For example, governments often give themselves free or reduced-rate services in their regulation of utility rates. The line between fees, taxes and gifts is often hard to draw.

Governments often require developers to pay the costs of streets in new subdivisions. If the cost is covered by an up-front developer payment to government, it's a fee. If the cost is covered by a special assessment on the property, it's a tax. If the cost is covered by making the developer build the streets to government specification and then turn over ownership to local government, it's a gift and not considered income to government as either a fee or a tax.

There are no satisfactory data to measure such involuntary levies, nor tax-like levies of entities such as condominium associations and downtown business district associations.

Source: Hal Hovey, "Money In, Money Out: State and Local Revenue and Spending," *Governing Sourcebook 1997* (January 1997): 26.

---

more than other states, mostly because they have lower per-capita incomes and cannot afford to spend more.

In similar fashion, the single most powerful reason that some states spend more per capita than others is that their residents have more to spend—their assets and income are greater. So their residents demand and can more easily pay for better-maintained streets for their more-expensive cars, better police protection to complement their higher-cost home security measures, and better schools for their children.

But some puzzling differences remain even after differing needs and income levels are taken into account. Why, for example, is government in New York so expensive and government in Texas so cheap? The answer lies in the decisions of state and local officials about how much to pay government workers, how large school classes should be, how large welfare payments should be and how easy it should be to qualify for Medicaid benefits.

The Tastiest Tax Cut

by Penelope Lemov

It was the legislative equivalent of a blitzkrieg. On the opening day of Georgia's 1996 legislative session, Tom Buck, chairman of the House Ways and Means Committee, handed his committee a bill to eliminate the state's sales tax on food. Four days later, Governor Zell Miller was blotting dry his signature on the measure, which had passed near-unanimous muster with both houses of the General Assembly.

A $500 million tax break had been signed, sealed and delivered in 72 hours.

If there's one revenue cut that appeals to both Democrats and Republicans, it's the sales tax on food: Democrats—at least the bleeding-heart wing of the party—consider food levies about as regressive a penalty on the poor as a tax can get; Republicans—especially the read-my-lips contingent—like any break that puts money in the hands of the people rather than the government.

In ratcheting its 4 percent sales tax on groceries down to zero, Georgia will bring the total number of states that exempt food from their sales tax base to 27. Another recent addition to that list is Louisiana, which also opted to begin phasing out its sales tax on food this year. But it doesn't include North Carolina. After a politically charged debate this year on an exemption, legislators settled instead on shaving 1 percent off the 4 percent state sales tax rate that applies to food.

When the changes are phased in, the total number of states that still levy a food tax will stand at 18. Twenty-five years ago, the numbers were reversed: 29 states taxed food purchases; 16 exempted them. And the current trend may accelerate in the next few years. A few states, notably Alabama, Arkansas and Missouri, are likely to consider the issue of rate cuts or exemptions for groceries in 1997.

Welfare reform may also provide the impetus for some of the food-taxing states to think about an exemption option. That's because the food stamp program has been included in welfare reform, and one of the rules of food stamps is that states must exempt food stamp purchases from sales taxes. As welfare reform reduces the level of food stamps available to any one family, food stamp recipients will find

Penelope Lemov is a staff writer for *Governing*. This article is reprinted from *Governing* (November 1996): 29–30.

States and Food Taxes, 1996

Have food tax (20)		Do not have food tax (30)		
AL	NM	AK[4]	ME	NY
AR	NC[3]	AZ	MD	ND
GA[1]	OK	CA	MA	OH
HI	SC	CO	MI	OR[4]
ID	SD	CT	MN	PA
IL[2]	TN	DE[4]	MT[4]	RI
KS	UT	FL	NE	TX
LA[1]	VA	IN	NV	VT
MS	WV	IA	NH[4]	WA
MO	WY	KY	NJ	WI

[1] Voted to phase out in 1998.
[2] Subject to 1 percent tax.
[3] Reduced from 4 percent to 3 percent in 1996.
[4] No sales tax of any kind.

Source: National Conference of State Legislatures.

themselves paying more money (the tax on groceries formerly purchased with food stamps) for their daily bread.

That raises the question—in the minds of tax theorists, academicians and state policy makers—of whether food-tax breaks are as good public policy as they are popular politics, and whether the exemptions might eventually come back to bite the hands that, as devolution is played out, may have to feed a lot of people.

In the here and now, the driving force behind the most recent food-tax recisions has been the fullness of state revenue plates. Money is pouring in. The intake on income and sales taxes was so healthy this year that no state ended fiscal 1996 with a deficit. In fact, state general fund balances stood at 5.8 percent of general fund spending—the fullest state coffers have been since 1980. "States are in fabulous fiscal shape," says John Mikesell, a professor at Indiana University who studies sales tax-

es. "For the moment, they're in a position where they believe they can give away money."

Certainly, that was the case in Georgia, a state that has enjoyed growth in revenue and surpluses over the past few years. Growth won't pay for all of the $500 million revenue hole (in a $11.3 billion budget) that the exemption will create when it is fully phased in in October 1998. The budget committee will, Buck admits, have to redirect funds and cut back on some appropriations to make up for revenue losses.

But such losses weren't big enough to be foremost in Buck's or anyone else's mind when the measure was passed. Rather, the affordability of a little old-fashioned politics was the primary motive. "We wanted to show taxpayers we were fiscally conservative and not liberal," he says. "We wanted to do something to get money back to taxpayers."

The governor, who had dabbled with the idea of cutting the food tax ever since he was a state senator back in the 1960s, offers a higher-road justification for a bill he'd been pushing for several years. "I have never believed that a sales tax on groceries was fair or right," Miller says.

The issue of regressivity has, in fact, been the overriding rationale for states to change their position on taxing food. Since low-income families spend a greater share of their income on groceries than do high-income families—as much as 28 percent for those in the lowest quintile of families versus less than 5 percent for those in the highest quintile—the sales tax on food clearly falls harder on the poor than on the rich.

No one disagrees with that. Or that struggling families would benefit from not having to pay such a tax. But there are those—and some are advocates for the poor—who take note of a peculiarity of food-tax exemptions: They're of much greater value to the rich than to the poor. That means, some argue, that the solution to tax fairness lies not in doing away with the food tax but in seeking other means of letting the poor avoid the tax. While it may seem counterintuitive, many tax experts and advocates for the poor say the positives of a food tax outweigh the negatives.

One of the problems with a food-tax exemption is that it is inefficient. It costs a state that has a sales tax a lot of money—about 20 to 25 percent of total sales tax revenue—to provide the tax relief. But the bulk of the tax savings goes to affluent households that may spend a smaller proportion of their income on store-bought food but buy more groceries and a lot more expensive cuts of meats and gourmet edibles at the supermarket.

According to the 1994 Bureau of Labor Statistics' Consumer Expenditure Survey, for instance, families in the lowest quintile bought an average of $1,833 worth of food to prepare at home while families in the highest quintile shelled out $3,851. When those numbers are multiplied by a sales tax rate of 5 percent, the tax saving for the poor is $91.65 versus $192.55 for the rich.

"The food-tax exemption reduces regressivity for the poor by giving a whole lot of money to the not terribly poor," Mikesell argues. "I enjoy tax relief, but I don't deserve welfare."

It is possible, tax experts such as Mikesell point out, to cure the regressivity problem without giving the whole store of food-tax money away by granting poorer households income tax credits or other forms of targeted exemptions to offset the sales tax they pay for food. Eight states have

targeted credits: Half of them allow poor families to take a credit against the income tax, while the other four administer the credit independently of the income tax.

In some states, such as New Mexico, the sales tax may be refunded if it exceeds income tax liability. Others, such as Georgia, have a tax credit that is so small—$5 for a family earning between $15,000 and $20,000—that it is hardly a solution at all.

Hawaii takes a different approach. With its huge base of affluent tourists, many of whom rent vacation condos and villas and spend a good deal of money on groceries, Hawaii gives all resident income-tax payers a tax credit for the sales tax—$27 per exemption. Since out-of-state tourists do not pay income tax in Hawaii, they do not get a credit on the food tax. So Hawaii gives its residents tax relief without foregoing the bonanza that a food tax represents.

And that bonanza is another reason that a food-tax exemption is not necessarily sound fiscal policy. By eliminating food from the sales tax base, a state does away with the lion's share of goods that are part of taxable commerce. "People complain, 'Oh my goodness, we're not taxing services,'" Mikesell points out. "Good heavens, the purchase of food in grocery stores is larger than household spending on services. The states are missing a pot of gold."

In so doing, states that exempt food from the sales tax shrink the sales tax base, and that has implications for the sales tax rates they set. The ineluctable tenet of sales tax rates is this: The broader the tax base, the lower the tax rates and the smaller the increases in rates over time. In other words, when food is included in the tax base, the state can raise the revenue it needs with a lower overall tax rate than it would have to set if food was not included.

Food also stabilizes the base and the revenue produced by that base. In a recession, for instance, people tend to put off purchases of such taxable items as cars, appliances, computers, even clothing. But everyone has to eat. "By including food purchases in the tax base," Mikesell points out, "state governments are more assured that their revenue base can finance a floor of governmental services in difficult economic times."

North Carolina, which considered a full food-tax exemption but ended up with a more modest proposal, appears to have split the difference between the two sides of the argument: The state reduced the sales tax rate for food purchases from 4 percent to 3 percent—thus providing some relief from regressivity—but did not eliminate groceries from the base altogether.

The reason for doing so, however, had more to do with revenue and potential budget squeezes than with policy solutions. Elimination of the sales tax would have cost the state more than $300 million a year; a one-cent break only costs about $85 mil-lion—the equivalent of a $130-a-year tax credit for 650,000 families, according to Dan Gerlach of the North Carolina Budget and Tax Center. Governor James B. Hunt Jr. was reluctant to ask for a total elimination since the revenue loss would have translated into program cuts and an inability to fund such costly priorities as higher teacher salaries and a cleanup plan for the state's polluted rivers.

Besides, once eliminated, a tax is tough to put back in place. By comparison, it's much easier to raise the rate when necessary—such as when a recession rolls around or when budgets are otherwise pressed. And that brings up the issue of welfare reform once again.

No one knows as yet how welfare reform will ultimately affect state budgets, particularly during an economic downturn. Nor can anyone tell whether, once federal aid ceases to have the elasticity of an entitlement, states will regret no longer having revenue from the fancy foods that affluent citizens buy available to help the poor.

Ways to Skin the Property Tax Cat

by Scott Mackey

Michigan's dramatic property tax reduction in 1994 sparked predictions that other states—particularly those with high property taxes—would follow suit with major reforms of their own. After all, Michigan lawmakers proved that you could roll back property taxes, raise state sales and cigarette taxes to replace the revenue, and still survive at the polls.

Proposals emerged in a half dozen states, including the high property tax states of Vermont and Wisconsin, to repeal the property tax as a school funding source. Some of these proposals were on the fast track. Yet when the dust settled, no states adopted a Michigan-style "overnight" property tax fix.

This is not to say, however, that states failed in their efforts to relieve the property tax burden. Quite the opposite—a dozen or so states have provided substantial relief to property taxpayers in the last two years. It's just that their incremental tax relief strategies failed to generate the media attention showered upon Michigan....

Taking Small Steps

Iowa is a perfect example of how ... small steps can produce big results. In the 1994 session, the Legislature bought some time by adopting a property tax freeze on county governments. This temporary measure was followed in 1995 by a phased repeal of property taxes on manufacturing machinery and equipment. New business manufacturing machinery and equipment were fully exempt, while property taxes on existing machinery were to be phased out over eight years. State funds are slated to replace the lost revenue, at a cost of $200 million annually when the exemptions are fully phased in. Also in 1995, the state assumed half of county mental health program costs. Transferring these costs to the [state] will reduce county property taxes by $78 million in FY 1997 and $95 million in FY 1998. Finally, in the 1996 session, the Iowa Legislature provided an $85 million property tax cut for homeowners by increasing school aid and boosting state funding for the homestead credit program.

Scott Mackey is a property tax expert for the National Conference of State Legislatures. This article is reprinted from *State Legislatures* (September 1996): 28–30.

209

Wisconsin is another state that has significantly reduced the property tax burden by taking small steps. In 1994, growing taxpayer frustration with rising property taxes led the Legislature to adopt a freeze on local school property taxes. Strong state revenue growth allowed the state to pump additional money into the school aid formula, preventing hardship for most schools. The Legislature came back in the 1995 session, continued the tax freeze and pledged to increase the state share of school spending from 45 percent to 66 percent by the end of fiscal year 1997.

So far, Wisconsin is on track toward keeping its promise. State spending for K–12 education was increased by 12 percent in 1995, 10 percent in 1996 and by a whopping 32 percent more in 1997. Overall K–12 spending has increased from $2.2 billion in 1994 to $3.5 billion in 1997. Property taxes on the median valued home were reduced by 11.5 percent, or $245, according to a recent analysis by the Legislative Fiscal Bureau. This was accomplished by putting all new revenue growth into school aid, tapping budget surpluses and making cuts in other areas of state spending. Wisconsin's phased approach, combined with a healthy economy, allowed the state to provide property tax relief without increasing taxes, a key goal of legislative leaders.

Indiana also provided substantial property tax relief as a result of measures passed in the 1995 and 1996 legislative sessions. In 1995, the General Assembly approved a measure to phase out the steep automobile property tax beginning in January 1996. As originally passed, the bill would have cut the auto property tax by 50 percent when fully implemented in the year 2001. In the 1996 session, with revenues exceeding expectations, the legislature accelerated the auto property tax cut

and doubled the state-funded property tax homestead exemption. Taxpayers will pay $650 million less property taxes over the next four years.

The Illinois General Assembly has also adopted an incremental approach. Back in 1991, taxpayers in suburban Chicago counties—the so called "collar counties"—were complaining loudly about escalating property values and the resulting increases in property tax. However, this was the height of the recession, and the state had no money to provide tax relief. Instead, the General Assembly imposed "tax caps" on the collar counties that prevented local government revenues from increasing by more than 5 percent. The caps were extended to Cook County (Chicago) in 1995 and to the rest of the state in 1996.

Examples Abound

Other examples of incremental property tax relief abound. Kansas adopted a phased reduction in automobile property taxes in 1995. Utah expanded its homestead exemption program in both the 1995 and 1996 sessions, providing more than $100 million in property tax relief. Idaho provided a $40 million, 6 percent property tax cut by assuming more school costs. Maine and Ohio increased eligibility for their property tax rebate programs. The Arizona Legislature passed property tax relief legislation appropriating $199 million for FY 1997. Of this amount, approximately $151 million replaces reductions in the state general fund, primarily due to elimination of a 47-cent state property tax rate. The balance, $48 million, will provide property tax relief at the local level.

Connecticut is phasing out the property tax on automobiles. Ohio expanded its homestead credit program. New Jersey provided indirect property tax relief: It allowed homeowners and renters to deduct property taxes paid (or their equivalent amount in rent) on the state income tax. Kentucky and Georgia both repealed property taxes on intangible assets—holdings like stocks and bonds—although Supreme Court decisions forced these repeals.

In the 1996 session, the Georgia General Assembly referred to the voters a proposed constitutional amendment that would allow local voters to decide whether to adopt a local option sales tax for education. The tax would replace a portion of the property taxes that currently fund schools. Many localities will have both the constitutional amendment and the proposed local sales tax on the ballot in November. If both measures pass, this would mark a major shift in how schools are financed in Georgia.

South Carolina probably came closest to a Michigan-style reform in 1995, when the General Assembly exempted the first $100,000 in value of a primary residence from any school property taxes. In its first year, the homestead exemption's $195 million cost was funded primarily with surpluses and other "one time" funds. However, the legislature found money in FY 1997 to fully fund the program's $213 million cost from ongoing revenues, without new taxes.

Contrast these successes with those of states that tried to adopt dramatic property tax reform bills. Vermont failed for the third consecutive year to adopt a sweeping property tax reduction. Measures adopted by the House would have substituted a local school income and a statewide property tax for school property taxes on primary residences. This plan ultimately failed in the 1995 and 1996 sessions, along with more modest Senate proposals to institute a new homestead exemption for a portion of school taxes.

In Colorado, the House passed a proposed constitutional amendment that would have repealed school property taxes and directed the legislature to find replacement revenues. The measure died in the Senate in 1996. And in Idaho, a bill to repeal all school operating property taxes cleared both houses of the Legislature, but was vetoed by the governor in 1994.

What lessons can be drawn from recent state property tax experiences? First, judging from the high priority given to it in the last few years, property tax relief is still good politics. Taxpayers dislike the tax and want their burden reduced. Second, as with many issues before legislative bodies, sweeping reforms often fail where incremental change can succeed. Third, states that are flush with cash have a much easier time cutting the property tax burden than states that must raise taxes or cut spending to replace property tax revenue.

The success of state efforts to relieve the property tax burden should probably be tempered with a note of caution. It remains to be seen whether these property tax relief efforts can be sustained during the next economic downturn. Property taxes have historically been the most stable of major state and local taxes, while sales and income tax collections are susceptible to economic cycles. States' best intentions in reducing property taxes sometimes unravel—along with state revenue collections—during recessions.

Ten Legislative Issues to Watch in 1997

by Charles Mahtesian

Same-Sex Marriage

WHY IS THIS AN ISSUE? Sometime in the near future, the Hawaii Supreme Court is expected to uphold a circuit court ruling that the state cannot refuse to give marriage licenses to same-sex couples. [It did in April 1997.] Legislators in other states want to be ready with countermoves.

WHO ARE THE MAIN PLAYERS? Gay-rights activists and the liberal left are opposed by social conservatives and the religious right.

WHERE WILL IT BE DEBATED? Sixteen states have already passed laws against recognizing gay marriage. Arkansas, California and Texas will be among those attempting to this year.

WHAT CAN WE EXPECT? So far, Republican-controlled legislatures have registered the most success in enacting these measures. States with politically active gay populations or large Democratic majorities are more likely to reject the bills outright—or at least bury them in committee.

Managed Care

WHY IS THIS AN ISSUE? Driven by constituent horror stories about "drive-through" childbirth and surgeries, legislators are under pressure to impose limits on the managed care industry.

WHO ARE THE MAIN PLAYERS? Doctors and consumer groups are lined up against insurers and major employers that are seeking to control health care costs.

WHERE WILL IT BE DEBATED? A majority of states will visit some aspect of the managed care issue. In Illinois, the debate will center on a patient "bill of rights." In Delaware, two different state agencies will report recommendations to the General Assembly.

WHAT CAN WE EXPECT? Public sentiment—and legislative momentum—seems to favor more disclosure and bans on so-called physician "gag clauses."

Public Schools

WHY IS THIS AN ISSUE? Discontent with the state of public education is as widespread as ever. Many education reformers are attracted to the elements of flexibility offered by charter schools and vouchers.

Charles Mahtesian is a staff writer for *Governing*. This article is adapted from *Governing* (February 1997): 22–23.

WHO ARE THE MAIN PLAYERS? The Catholic and Christian schools' lobby wholeheartedly embraces vouchers; teachers' unions and school boards go ballistic over the idea. Support for charter schools is more broad-based, though teachers are still somewhat hostile.

WHERE WILL IT BE DEBATED? Connecticut, Florida and Oregon are states to follow on the voucher issue, while charter schools will get another hearing in Ohio and Pennsylvania.

WHAT CAN WE EXPECT? 1996 was a terrible year for voucher proponents; prospects for this year aren't much better. Charter schools are a better bet, particularly in states such as Washington where election turnover was kind to the charter movement.

School Finance

WHY IS THIS AN ISSUE? A politically feasible solution to the spending gap between the richest and poorest school districts remains elusive. In some statehouses, the issue is equity. In others, it is adequacy. The clamor for property tax relief complicates matters.

WHO ARE THE MAIN PLAYERS? This perennial battle typically pits property tax-rich suburban districts against less wealthy urban or rural areas.

WHERE WILL IT BE DEBATED? Long-running struggles continue in Kansas, New Jersey and Texas. Nebraska is worth watching, but keep an eye on Wyoming, where a court directive recently ordered the state to equalize funding.

WHAT CAN WE EXPECT? Promises of sweeping changes to outmoded public education financing schemes usually go unfulfilled. More states are likely to end up with incremental, short-term solutions than with a Michigan-style property-and-sales-tax swap.

Higher Education

WHY IS THIS AN ISSUE? The same accountability demands placed on other state agencies in the 1990s are now being visited upon the ivory tower.

WHO ARE THE MAIN PLAYERS? Budget-conscious legislators from both parties are putting state university administrators on the hot seat.

WHERE WILL IT BE DEBATED? Faculty tenure will be debated in Colorado and a few other states. University-system governance will be at issue in Maine, Minnesota, Tennessee and Washington, among others.

WHAT CAN WE EXPECT? Higher education professionals are becoming increasingly adept in defense of their institutions. Nevertheless, legislators will scrutinize faculty practices and demand less duplication of services within the university systems.

Tax Relief

WHY IS THIS AN ISSUE? Revenue surpluses in many states and the enduring popularity of tax cuts will place tax relief high on the legislative agenda.

WHO ARE THE MAIN PLAYERS? Depends on who the beneficiaries are. Economic development officials tout targeted business tax cuts. Taxpayer groups favor returning personal income tax dollars to individuals. The left would like to see the sales-tax burden lessened.

WHERE WILL IT BE DEBATED? In Maryland, the contentious debate over [the governor's] increased spending and 10 percent, phased-in income-tax-cut package [makes it] the most interesting [one]....

WHAT CAN WE EXPECT? Tax-cut mania is not running as high as it has been over the past two years. Nevertheless, look for one-time reductions and an emphasis on delivering relief to individuals.

Environmental Audits

WHY IS THIS AN ISSUE? The ascendance of business-friendly Republican majorities is increasing interest in this self-policing approach [aiming] to protect companies that report their own environmental violations.

WHO ARE THE MAIN PLAYERS? Chemical companies, poultry processors, mining interests and other industries line up behind the measure. The federal Environmental Protection Agency leads a coalition of environmentalists and trial lawyers against it.

WHERE WILL IT BE DEBATED? The American Legislative Exchange Council reports that 19 states will take up this issue in 1997.

WHAT CAN WE EXPECT? Increased public attention to environmental issues and Democratic gains in the 1996 elections cloud prospects for passage in many states.

Campaign Reform

WHY IS THIS AN ISSUE? The troubling and manipulative role of money and special interests in elections was never clearer than in the 1996 presidential campaign.

WHO ARE THE MAIN PLAYERS? Common Cause and good-government groups versus state parties, legislative leaders and the most influential lobbies.

WHERE WILL IT BE DEBATED? In several states—most notably Maryland—excessive exploitation of loopholes is spurring reform interest. Claims of wide-scale ballot fraud and abuse in Texas and Louisiana may lead to changes in those capitols.

WHAT CAN WE EXPECT? In a non-election year, prospects ... are not promising. The intensity of media coverage will play a role in determining the scope of reform.

Welfare for Immigrants

WHY IS THIS AN ISSUE? July 1, 1997, the deadline for filing state plans under the 1996 federal welfare reform law, is fast approaching. Since the new federal statute gives states the right to deny benefits to non-citizens, that provision is likely to be a point of contention.

WHO ARE THE MAIN PLAYERS? Social service advocacy groups and Hispanic interests are battling to preserve benefits for legal immigrants. Conservative policy makers are not eager to expand eligibility.

WHERE WILL IT BE DEBATED? The messiest fights will occur in [the] states with the largest caseloads. But an influx of immigrants into such non-traditional destinations as Maine and Minnesota means a broad group of states will be addressing the situation.

WHAT CAN WE EXPECT? California has moved swiftly toward curbing benefits to both legal and illegal immigrants. Other states appear more cautious.

Electric Power

WHY IS THIS AN ISSUE? Deregulation promises to do for the electric power industry what it did for the long distance phone business. Legislators will have to determine how best to sort it out.

WHO ARE THE MAIN PLAYERS? Manufacturers and other large industrial users insist they need cheaper power to remain competitive. Consumer groups worry that small customers are in for a price shock; labor fears work-force reduction will be a consequence.

WHERE WILL IT BE DEBATED? Most legislatures will look closely at the substance of recently passed laws in California, New Hampshire and Pennsylvania. Vermont and Michigan are states worth watching for 1997 action.

WHAT CAN WE EXPECT? Many states are not planning to wait until Congress weighs in.

INDEX

Index